The Presidency of
CALVIN
COOLIDGE

AMERICAN PRESIDENCY SERIES

Donald R. McCoy, Founding Editor
Clifford S. Griffin and Homer E. Socolofsky, General Editors

The Presidency of

CALVIN
COOLIDGE

Robert H. Ferrell

UNIVERSITY PRESS OF KANSAS

Published by the University Press of Kansas (Lawrence,
Kansas 66049), which was organized by the Kansas
Board of Regents and is operated and funded by Emporia
State University, Fort Hays State University,
Kansas State University, Pittsburg State University, the University
of Kansas, and Wichita State University

Library of Congress Cataloging-in-Publication Data

Ferrell, Robert H.
The presidency of Calvin Coolidge / Robert H. Ferrell.
p.   cm. — (American presidency series)
Includes bibliographical references and index.
ISBN 0-7006-0892-3 (cloth : alk. paper)
1. United States—Politics and government—1923–1929.
2. Coolidge, Calvin, 1872–1933.   I. Title.   II. Series.
E791.F47   1998
973.91′5′092—dc21   97-51128

British Library Cataloguing in Publication Data is available.

Printed in the United States of America

10 9 8 7 6 5 4 3 2 1

The paper used in this publication meets the minimum requirements of
the American National Standard for Permanence of Paper for Printed
Library Materials Z39.48-1984.

To Donald R. McCoy (1928–1997) and
Clifford S. Griffin (1929–1997)

CONTENTS

Photo insert follows page 144.

FOREWORD

The aim of the American Presidency Series is to present historians and the general reading public with interesting, scholarly assessments of the various presidential administrations. These interpretive surveys are intended to cover the broad ground between biographies, specialized monographs, and journalistic accounts. As such, each is a comprehensive work that draws on original sources and pertinent secondary literature yet leaves room for the author's own analysis and interpretation.

Volumes in the series present the data essential to understanding the administration under consideration. Particularly, each book treats the then-current problems facing the United States and its people and how the president and his associates felt about, thought about, and worked to cope with these problems. Attention is given to how the office developed and operated during the president's tenure. Equally important is consideration of the vital relationships among the president, his staff, the executive officers, Congress, foreign representatives, the judiciary, state officials, the public, political parties, the press, and influential private citizens. The series is also concerned with how this unique American institution—the presidency—was viewed by the presidents, and with what results.

All this is set, insofar as possible, in the context not only of contemporary politics but also of economics, international relations, law, morals, public administration, religion, and thought. Such a broad approach is necessary to understanding, for a presidential administration is more than the elected and appointed officers composing it, since its work so often reflects the major problems, anxieties, and glories of the nation. In short, the authors in this series strive to recount and evaluate the record of each administration and to identify its distinctiveness and relationships to the past, its own time, and the future.

ACKNOWLEDGMENTS

My heartfelt thanks to the editors of the American Presidency Series: the late Donald R. McCoy, the late Clifford S. Griffin, and Homer E. Socolofsky. And to Fred M. Woodward, director, and Melinda Wirkus, senior production editor, of the University Press of Kansas. Thanks also to Timothy Walch, director of the Herbert Hoover Library; Dwight M. Miller, senior archivist; Dale C. Mayer, archivist; J. Patrick Wildenberg, reference archivist; and Cindy Worrell, archives technician. Similarly to Cyndy Bittinger, director, Calvin Coolidge Memorial Foundation; James Grant, editor of *Grant's* and fellow historian; Ellis W. Hawley, professor of history emeritus, University of Iowa; Milton F. Heller, Jr., son-in-law of the late Vice Admiral Joel T. Boone; Lu Knox, curator of the Coolidge Room, Forbes Library, Northampton; John Lukacs, historian; D. F. Shaughnessy, historian; Jerry L. Wallace, Regional Archives System, National Archives; Lawrence E. Wikander, curator emeritus of the Coolidge Room at Forbes. Betty Bradbury did the word processing. Again, so many thanks to Lila and Carolyn.

1

★ ★ ★ ★ ★

A NEW ENGLAND PRESIDENT

John Calvin Coolidge was born on 4 July 1872, in Plymouth Notch, Vermont, a community of three houses, a store, a school, and a church. The Notch stood a mile up a steep gorge from another village, Plymouth Union. Nearby localities went by the names of Kingdom, Frog City, Five Corners, Pinney Hollow, Tyson, and Ninevah.

Tourists now throng to his birthplace in summer (the presidential shrine closes in winter, for the weather is inclement) and can sense what life was like over a century ago when Coolidge was a youth. Not much has changed, save for the now well-paved but still narrow road and the number of tombstones in the cemetery south of the houses—notably, more stones for the Coolidge family. A man who remembered Plymouth Notch from Coolidge's time said that the greatest changes have been in everyday sounds; no longer does one hear the ax ring out in the woods, producing the winter's supply of fuel, nor the squeal of the runners of sleighs nor the jingle of bells on horses in winter, nor the bells of cows in the fields, nor the hooting of lovesick bears. Those sounds are gone, replaced by automobile and occasionally airplane sounds.

The president was the fifth generation of Coolidges in the Notch. The first Coolidge, another John, had come about 1780, shortly before the end of the Revolution. When the president was growing up, he certainly would have noticed that the farms and villages were diminishing, for people were leaving. Between 1870 and 1880, 115 people left the township of Plymouth. The railway boom of the 1840s had come and gone, but the lines never reached Plymouth Union, not to mention the Notch. The nearest rail town, twelve miles away, was Ludlow. Wool was the principal crop of farmers, and dairying would come in the 1890s; meanwhile, farming was largely for subsistence. But that was all right with young Coolidge and his father, John (later known as Colonel John, having been named in 1900 to the staff of Governor William W. Stickney).

Together with farm children in the neighborhood, Coolidge attended the one-room stone school just up the road from where he lived, enduring a succession of teachers good, indifferent, and bad. Reading and recitations were accomplished mostly in winter, because the children had to work during the farm season. Little has survived to testify about Coolidge's scholarship during those early years. He seems to have been a fairly well-behaved pupil, although one incident tells a different story. The teacher asked two of the boys to go out in the woods and cut a new switch (used to punish unruly pupils). The boys cut circles into the switch so that it would break at the slightest touch. During geography class, Coolidge purposely displayed an arrogant attitude. The confrontation went something as follows:

Teacher: "What is the capital of Spain?"
Calvin: "Lisbon."
Teacher: "Wrong. Try again. What is the capital of Spain?"
Calvin: "Lisbon."
Teacher: "I told you that was wrong. Lisbon is not the capital of Spain."
Calvin: "I say Lisbon is the capital of Spain."
Teacher: "I say it is not and I guess I know because I have the book in
    front of me."
Calvin: "I say it is and I guess I know because I studied my lesson."

The teacher strode to the corner, seized the switch by its butt end, and aimed a savage blow at Calvin. He ducked just in time, and the switch came down on the desk with a crash and broke into pieces, leaving the teacher holding a small fragment.[1]

Not long after this event, Coolidge left the school in the Notch. It was an ungraded school, and he had gone as far as he could, having reached the age of thirteen. He and his father decided that he would spend his high school years in Ludlow at Black River Academy, known as BRA. That winter, in bitter-cold temperatures of thirty below, the youth and his father made the journey over the hills to Ludlow, to the house where arrangements had been made for Calvin's room and board. They were accompanied by a calf that the elder Coolidge was taking to the railroad depot to sell. The last advice of John Coolidge was some Yankee wisdom: "Well, Cal, here you are in school in Ludlow. . . . Study hard and maybe you'll get to Boston some day, but remember that the calf will go there first."[2]

Coolidge entered BRA in 1886 and graduated in 1890, in a class of nine scholars enrolled in the classical curriculum. The school's total enrollment was perhaps one hundred. For forty years, a former church had housed the academy in its three downstairs rooms. When it burned, the students moved to rooms above a bakery, then to a place next to the lot where the school's new building was being erected. The towered stone structure of Victorian proportions was finished in 1888 and still stands; it is now a museum.

Coolidge decided at the outset to take the classical curriculum at BRA, which meant preparation for college. Presumably he talked this over with his father, but nothing survives of the discussion. A principal at BRA, John Pickard, divined that Coolidge might actually be college material and encouraged him in that direction. The principal left after a year, but it was long enough to influence the youth, who obtained the assent of his father. Graduation from BRA took place in the spring of 1890 in a ceremony that, according to custom, involved several speeches. Each member of the class enrolled in the classical curriculum gave an oration, and Coolidge's topic was "Oratory in History." In his autobiography he mentioned that "I dealt briefly with the effect of the spoken word in determining human action."[3] Some time after graduation he took the train to Massachusetts and sat for the entrance examination to Amherst College. He contracted a bad cold during the journey and could not complete the examination. Early in 1891 he went back to BRA for more preparation and, on the advice of the new principal, George Sherman, went for the spring term to St. Johnsbury Academy, eighty miles north of Plymouth. He graduated with the St. Johnsbury class and was accepted automatically into Amherst "on certificate"; BRA was not so accredited.

The decision to attend Amherst College was not marked by excess ambition; rather, it was a stolid and sometimes almost imperceptible movement toward whatever it was the youth desired, propelled more by happenstance than anything else. The faculty members at Amherst who had rejected Coolidge based on his half-finished examination would have been correct in believing that the young man from the hill country was no promising lad; at best, he would probably graduate without distinction, disappear back into the hills, and take over the general store from his father, which seems to have been what John Coolidge had in mind for his son. Nothing thus far predicted future accomplishments. Coolidge had been encouraged by two principals at BRA, and without their interventions, he would have gone back to Plymouth Notch to spend the rest of his life.

When he entered Amherst, he still was unpromising. The thin, wispy youth with the long nose, straight mouth, and reddish hair was arriving at a sophisticated educational institution. Amherst had seen great men pass through its doors, and the faculty contained teachers of erudition. The college was ensconced in a town of formidable houses and apparently formidable residents. Coolidge arrived without fanfare. The only thing anyone remembered about his initial presence was a display of humor during the first days at his boarding house, where he and his fellow boarders were served hash one evening. Dwight W. Morrow, a future Morgan partner, ambassador to Mexico, and senator from New Jersey, often told the story of how Coolidge had looked at the hash and said, "Bring me the cat."

During Coolidge's first two years, he was hardly noticed. He worked at his studies, but his grades were as nondescript as his presence. This lack of achievement might have been attributable to a belief that ambition was of no use, since he might not live long enough to fulfill it. Death tended to come early in the Coolidge family, but one cannot really know how this affected Calvin, for all that survives is unrevealing correspondence between him and his father, and their letters are prosaic to a fault. When he was twelve, his mother died as a result of a carriage accident caused by a runaway horse. She had been seriously wounded, and the wound never fully healed. A pretty woman with fragile features who looked much like her presidential son, the former Victoria Josephine Moor had been named after Queen Victoria and Napoleon's Empress Josephine. A few years later, Coolidge's younger sister Abigail, who followed him to BRA, came down with what was probably appendicitis. The physician in attendance never made a clear diagnosis, and within a week she died. Her brother sought to explain to his father that they should think of her "as we would of a happy day counting it a pleasure to have had it and not a sorrow because it could not last forever."[4]

Whatever the reason for his slow progress, after a while, something happened. The courses not merely caught Coolidge's attention but enthused him. He became a serious student.

A large part of this turnaround seems to have been caused by two faculty members. One was Anson D. Morse, a tall, slight man with a wispy beard who taught history. The professor's Vermont origins doubtless were a recommendation, but Morse was no provincial; he was a leader in his discipline. In Coolidge's first year, Morse published an essay on the American party system in the *Annals of the American Academy*, and two years later, another such article appeared in the *Annual Report* of the American Historical Association. Morse was a writer and must have been a fine lecturer, and in his analysis of the history and purpose of political parties, he put them at the center of republican government. At the beginning of his *Annals* article, he pointed out that parties were once thought to have no rights in politics and that their exclusion led them to excesses under European governments that rested on force. In such circumstances, a party acted for both good and ill. "Treated as an outlaw it behaved as an outlaw. Conventional morality it set at defiance. It grew up in the atmosphere of irresponsibility." Perhaps for this reason, the fathers of the Constitution ignored parties and committed a grave error, as evidenced by the electoral college. But with the development of parties, magnificent changes resulted. The colonies had received the institution of the party, and the nation had developed the institution until "today the American party system presents a perfection of organization not elsewhere to be found." Party, he wrote, was by far the most important agency through which "the crude first thoughts and blind first feelings of the people are transformed into the rational thinking and feeling which is public opinion."[5] Morse's tutelage was heady doctrine for a youngster who would develop into a party man. It would be interesting to see what notes Coolidge took and how carefully he listened to this explanation of political party.

Then there was the strange, almost mystical Charles E. Garman, who taught philosophy, psychology, and ethics. His teaching enthralled Coolidge, who described him as "one of the most remarkable men with whom I ever came in contact."[6] Garman's influence was lifelong. Grace Coolidge said that her husband kept a Bible on the table next to their bed, together with a memorial volume of Garman's letters and lectures. Coolidge's autobiography testifies at length to Garman's influence.

What it was about Garman that attracted students is not easy to say. Garman published almost nothing, and his students, although enormously taken by him, were remarkably uncertain about what he did to influence them. Some of his effect on a generation of Amherst students, from 1880 until his death in 1907, was due to his campus presence. Pale, slender, and clean-shaven with dark, deep-set eyes, he was an unforgettable figure. He had acquired a malady of the throat that required protection against the elements, and even in summer he wrapped his throat to protect it and wore two overcoats to avoid chills. He kept the temperature of Room 10 of Walker Hall at the level of a greenhouse. He prepared students for his classes by handing out printed pamphlets produced by a servant who operated a hand press in the basement of his house, and he insisted on their return, as their covers told borrowers: "This pamphlet though printed is not published; it is in every respect private property. It has been only loaned to the students in the psychology division on two conditions. First, that it be carefully preserved and promptly returned when called in; Second, that the student to whom it is loaned does not in any case let it come into the hands of any person not a member of the psychology division. The taking of this pamphlet is considered an agreement on the part of the student to conform to the above conditions."[7] During Coolidge's time, Garman was out of favor with the president of Amherst, Rev. Merrill E. Gates, an autocrat who turned the students against his administrative measures. Gates insinuated that Garman was not fully a Christian, but the professor and his students asserted his innocence.

But there was clearly something beyond Garman's appearance and the pamphlets and the row with Gates; otherwise, he would not have received an offer to teach at the University of Michigan, which he turned down. Nor would William James have written of the "extraordinary" effects of his teaching, "not only on the intellect, but on the character."[8] What he possessed was a vast reading knowledge of his trinity of disciplines, which gave him power in the classroom. The pamphlets set out the sides to questions but offered no conclusions. Perhaps with exaggeration, Coolidge wrote to his father that the reading for Garman's course required "thirty-five hours each week and then one does not get all that is in it."[9] Garman was no classroom lecturer, but an organizer of classroom debates, which took on strenuous proportions. Everything was according to logic: process not product, carry all questions back to fundamental principles, weigh the evidence, and repeatedly, "Gentlemen, define your terms." He enrolled most of the senior class in the fall term of 1894 when Coolidge was in attendance and had his sixty students debate all the issues of the time: evolution, the basis of the mind, the psychology of people acting together, the existence of God. In regard to the last, he might ask whether God existed objectively or was a creature of human imagination; was there human imagination, or merely a set of chemical responses in the brain? Coolidge and his Amherst friends found in Garman a key to understanding themselves. The teacher never forced himself on students but demanded conclusions. "Truly he drew men out," the youth from Vermont would write. The experience stood apart from instruction in all other classes.

The effect on Coolidge is difficult to know precisely, but it is possible that the logical content of his later speeches derived from this Amherst teacher. Garman's ethical goal was service, and Coolidge may have become a lawyer and gone into politics because of it. The spare prose that marked the president's speeches and writings may have come from an appreciation of Garman's style. Garman wrote well; after receiving a long private letter from Garman, G. Stanley Hall, a psychologist and president of Clark University, asked the professor's permission to publish the letter in the *American Journal of Psychology*.[10]

During his junior and senior years, Coolidge became adept at public speaking and gained considerable importance on campus. It might have had some connection with Garman. During a campus frolic, Coolidge and members of his class, dressed formally and wearing bowler hats, ran across a football-sized field, with the last seven runners having to buy oysters and beer for the others and make speeches. In a much remembered talk at the Plug

Hat Dinner, Coolidge counseled the winners that the last shall be first. In another speech, having been chosen Grove Orator, he again showed an ability to make points. Because these were college occasions, he had the presence of mind to adorn his aphorisms with wit, with the drollery that was so well known in Vermont hill country. He began the Grove Oration by remarking that "the mantle of truth falls upon the Grove Orator on condition he wear it wrong side out. For the Grove Oration is intended to give a glimpse of the only true side of college life—the inside. And how can this be displayed but by turning things wrong side out?" He turned words in ways that brought shouts of laughter: "Wherever we go, whatever we are, scientific or classical, degreed or disagreed, we are going to be Amherst men."

During his college years, he did not always make his mark with words. One summer he went back to Plymouth and gave a Fourth of July oration in which he filled the air with post–Civil War banalities. On another occasion, writing in the Amherst *Literary Monthly,* he offered an account of a maiden "just blossoming into womanhood" who promised herself to an unworthy wretch who robbed a government stagecoach, killing the driver. After admonishing the villain by remarking rather plaintively, "I plead for you before a Higher Tribunal," the maiden plunged into a dark pool of water and drowned.[11] Fortunately, these effusions had no successors. He never spoke or wrote that way again.

Upon graduation in 1895, he informed his father of his vocation. By this time, the young man was no longer consulting but informing. He said that he would read law in a law office in Northampton, a small city of twenty-three thousand that was half a dozen miles from Amherst. Geographically, it was convenient. To his father in Plymouth Notch, it may have seemed a small step and therefore easier to accept. For Coolidge, it was a fateful move, for Northampton would become his political base and his home. Years later, after leaving the presidency of the United States, he would return to Northampton.

The law student associated himself with the firm of Hammond and Field. Both John C. Hammond and Henry P. Field were prominent lawyers (Field later became a judge). Hammond was from the Amherst class of 1865, and Field from the class of 1880, which doubtless assisted Coolidge's application to study with them. Beyond that were their solid personalities; both were men of principle and character. They were outgoing and well suited to watch over a fledgling lawyer. In Field, Coolidge found a mentor who would watch the younger man's career and give him all the local assistance he could provide.

In the law office, Coolidge spent his days preparing writs, deeds, wills, and other dull documents. He took the work seriously. As he described his studies in his autobiography, "That I was now engaged in the serious enterprise of life I so fully realized that I went to the barbershop and divested myself of the college fashion of long hair." Evenings he read speeches of Daniel Webster and Rufus Choate, models of his era. He dipped into English literary masters, essays of Macaulay, writings of Carlyle. He read Milton and Shakespeare, leavened with poems by Kipling and popular American poetasters Eugene Field and James Whitcomb Riley. He translated orations of Cicero on the value and consolation of literature. His first Christmas as a law student, he received notice of award of a gold medal worth $150 by the Sons of the American Revolution for the best essay in a nationwide competition on "The Principles Fought for in the American Revolution." He had written it during his senior year. Sensitive to the fact that he was reading law—the old-fashioned way to gain admission to the bar—rather than studying it in a law school, he wrote to his father, "I think my gold medal is evidence that I can discuss questions with some success. While my attainments in law have been as rapid as could be expected I am not sure that I have not lost much in discipline from the lack of direction and precision which a classroom gives."[12]

When the young man of twenty-five finished reading law and passed the bar, he wrote to his father that he would be staying in Northampton, where the cost of living was no greater than that in a small town. He believed that the possibilities would be better there.

Not long thereafter, he sought and won his first public office.

What took Coolidge to the presidency of the United States were four opportunities, three of which were matters of happenstance. In the beginning, he occupied local offices, and then the first opportunity arrived: Contrary to custom, he decided to take a third term in the Massachusetts state senate. What he saw as a bare possibility in the next legislative session, the chance to become leader of the state's Republicans, became reality after the election. Then over the next years came the three pieces of fate: the telegram he sent to the president of the American Federation of Labor, Samuel Gompers, at the end of the Boston police strike in 1919; his nomination for the vice presidency in 1920; and the death of President Warren G. Harding in 1923.

The choice of political party was not difficult, for in Plymouth Notch, Coolidge had grown up with Republicanism, and his father had spent three terms in the Vermont house of representatives and one term in the Vermont senate. In 1880, the eight-year-old future president sought to borrow a penny from his father (this became a well-known story), who told him that he could not advance it until after the presidential election, for if James A. Garfield were not elected, the Democrats would plunge the country into hard times. In 1896, Coolidge distributed ballots for his mentor

Judge Field, who was running for mayor of Northampton. When a Democrat published an account in the city newspaper advocating the William Jennings Bryan doctrine of free silver, Coolidge responded with a point-by-point defense of the gold standard. As for public office, Coolidge explained in his *Autobiography* that at first he thought the experience would make him a better lawyer. Only when he was elected mayor of Northampton did ambition for office come, and even then it was a mixture of purposes: the mayoralty would advance him in his profession of the law, would please his father, and would enable him "to be of some public service." As higher offices came, the last purpose appears to have dominated.

Coolidge the politician moved slowly. He began on the first rung in 1898 when he was elected to the Northampton common council. He served for a one-year term. The next year he ran for the office of city solicitor, which he won and held until 1902. For a while he was out of office. He ran for the school board in 1905 and lost—what would be his only loss in twenty races. This he ascribed to the entrance of another Republican in the primary, which divided the vote. It is possible, however, that in 1905 his mind was not on the electoral contest, although he would never have admitted it. That year he married a pretty young teacher at the Clarke School for the Deaf, Grace Goodhue, and not long before the election, the couple took a wedding trip to Montreal, one of the two times Coolidge traveled outside the United States. In 1906, he ran for the state legislature and took two one-year terms, in 1907 and 1908.

It is of interest how his closest friend during those years, a young teacher of history at Smith College, Alfred P. Dennis, described the fledgling politician. In an account written many years later, Dennis admitted that Coolidge was a "stick." He did not possess an outgoing personality, but he possessed the ability to concentrate. Dennis illustrated his point: One beautiful June evening the two friends took a trolley to a nearby amusement park, "bowling along in the open car across green meadows, by the shining river, and then up, up the heights to Mountain Park on the crest of the hills." There the band played, peanut roasters hissed, young ladies giggled and screamed on the roller coasters. After a while, Coolidge spoke his first words: "I guess we have had about enough excitement without taking in any shows." On the return ride, Dennis beheld the "dim outlines of the river, the green hills, the grassy meadows bathed in moonlight." As he was dreaming, he heard the voice of his companion: "I have been kind of counting up the amount of labor and material such as crossties, rails, poles, copper wire, to say nothing of rolling equipment, that have gone into this line."[13]

Coolidge employed the most primitive of electoral tactics, which seemed to work. Night after night he walked from house to house, went up to the door and rang the bell, and was invited in. Then he stated in his dry, nasal voice that he was running and said, "I want your vote. I need it. I shall appreciate it."[14] He backed out and made for the next house. The tactic was an old one, but what was new was the taciturnity of the exercise, the statement of the point without flourish, the aridity. People were taken aback.

When concentrating on political business, Coolidge allowed no distractions. After his election to the legislature, he took the train to Boston every Monday morning, punctually. Once there, he undertook no diversions for the rest of the week. He spent his nights in a decaying hostelry known as the Adams House, which would also be his address when he was in the state senate in 1912–15, lieutenant governor in 1916–18, and governor in 1919–20. As his fortunes advanced, he took a second room with a bath. Years later, a friendly biographer visited the place, listed as "suite" number 60, and found it awful. It was on the third floor in the center of the building, abutting an inner courtyard about the size of an air shaft. Light came through half a window cut off by an interior chimney. Cheerful as a cell, its sole attraction was the price, one dollar a night. "A traveling man," the biographer wrote, "would take it as a last resort."[15]

In his two years in the legislature, Coolidge showed a feeling for progressivism, which was in vogue in local, state, and national politics. The word stood for bringing government into the service of the people; it arose out of feeling that government had served the interests primarily of owners of capital, as opposed to people with small incomes who were wage earners or lived on salaries. Progressivism expressed the concerns of people who observed the flight from the farm to the growing towns and cities, where the closeness of life required rules, which meant intervention by government. Coolidge naturally turned to progressive legislation, for he had come from the people. He had not enjoyed an easy life and, beginning with Plymouth Notch, had always lived modestly. Part of the manner in which he lived was necessary, he felt, because he desired to live within his income. Part was a matter of background, for he had grown up under the tutelage of his father, who believed in modesty. He instinctively voted for measures that would protect working people against the rapacity of exploiters. He saw unfairness in laws, or a lack of laws that stood for fairness. On the national level, he came out for direct election of United States senators, which would remove them from the control of state legislatures, where interests dominated choices. He favored women's suffrage, which would bring local issues into politics. On the state level, he supported a six-day workweek for laborers, a limit on hours of work for women and children, pensions to families of firemen and for schoolteachers, half fare on streetcars for schoolchildren, lower railroad fares for workingmen, and the equipment of factories with surgical instruments. This last showed the dangers to limb, if not to life, in the factories of the time.

Something happened to Coolidge's brush with progressivism, however, for his enthusiasm diminished, but not altogether because he lost belief in it. Perhaps he was incapable of supporting President Theodore Roosevelt, who gave the impression that everything needed changing. More likely it was a discernment that reform had gone as far as possible, that a conservative feeling was abroad. He was no revolutionary. He did not believe in excess and never espoused grand plans. And perhaps as Coolidge rose politically, his concern became administrative, which led him to believe that administering laws already on the books was more important than making new laws.

Leaving the legislature, Coolidge made certain of his base in Hampshire County, primarily the city of Northampton, by serving as mayor in 1910–11, during which time he decreased the city debt by $90,000 and raised the pay of teachers and other employees. Then he branched out, running for the state senate, which meant running in two adjoining counties as well as his base. He timed this move to coincide with Hampshire County's turn to take the senate seat. In his first two years in this office, 1912 and 1913, he observed the organization of things, how majorities were arranged, and achieved a prominence he had failed to reach in the lower house. In the senate there were forty members, and he became chairman of the committee on agriculture. He proposed a solution to the milk business and the dairymen's difficulties by the appointment of a special commission. When that proposal was rejected, he opposed each of the substitute bills and managed to have them all defeated. In 1912, after a textile strike at the Lawrence Duck Mill, a legislative committee under Coolidge's chairmanship pressed the manufacturers and managed a settlement agreeable to both sides, including a wage increase. Then he became chairman of the joint committee on railroads, and every measure he sponsored was accepted. It may have been at this time that the political boss of the western part of the state, W. Murray Crane, told a business acquaintance who was going to Northampton to visit his daughter at Smith College, "Find out all you can about a young man named Coolidge there. You will save trouble in looking him up now! He is one of the coming men of this country."[16] The remark seems apocryphal. Crane was U.S. senator from 1904 to 1913 and a power thereafter, and he helped Coolidge politically. It was said that if Coolidge owed anything to anyone, it was to Crane. But during Coolidge's state senate years and for a while after, it was too early to tell what the Northampton politician might accomplish.

As Coolidge was rising, he made alliances with people of his own kind from western Massachusetts. He admired Crane, an intelligent, principled paper manufacturer who thought like Coolidge, tending toward conservatism. Coolidge saw much of Crane's "Boston man," a textile manufacturer named William M. Butler, a former member of the state legislature. Butler was even more conservative than Crane. Because of their western origins, the three stood apart from Boston conservative Republicans, wealthy people who lived in the Back Bay and whose spokesman was U.S. Senator Henry Cabot Lodge.

Coolidge's first big opportunity came when the president of the state senate lost a bid for reelection in 1913, largely because of his opposition to women's suffrage and his antagonists' determination to make an example of him. Coolidge became senate president. He reportedly arranged his elevation by taking an 8:00 A.M. train to Boston on the day after the election, where he secreted himself with Crane and solicited enough votes by long-distance telephone to ensure his election. Another story—less likely, for Coolidge was not one to leave anything important to chance—is that after the election a group of Coolidge supporters in Boston made the arrangement. The post was assuredly to his advantage. When Roosevelt had sought the White House in 1912 through the Bull Moose party, it had divided Massachusetts Republicans, normally the state's majority party. As a result, the Democrats controlled the governorship and lieutenant governorship for several years. With the state's two principal offices in the hands of the opposition, Coolidge as senate president became the state's ranking Republican officeholder. He could not influence national issues, for they were the province of Crane's successor and Lodge, but he stood first among officeholders at the state level.

It was about this time that Coolidge encountered Boston dry-goods owner Frank W. Stearns, who proved to be of much assistance. Unimpressive, Stearns stood five feet six inches tall (well below Coolidge's five feet nine), he was overweight, and had a round face and a small mustache. At the outset he did not like Coolidge. He later described his first encounter to the White House assistant physician, Lt. Comdr. Joel T. Boone.[17] Stearns had walked into an office equipped with only a desk and a single chair. Coolidge sat behind the desk, and Stearns had to stand. He was asking a legislative favor involving the sewage system of Amherst. As conversation developed, Coolidge became interested; he went over to a closet, took a key from his pocket, unlocked the closet door, took out a chair, shut the door, placed the chair near his desk, and with a nod indicated that Stearns should sit down. After the conference, Stearns stood up, and Coolidge took the chair, put it back in the closet, and locked the door. The whole episode was disquieting. But in due course, Coolidge sent Stearns a note enclosing a piece of legislation he had introduced into the legislature, with notification that it had passed. Stearns changed his mind. Here was a politician who could get things done.[18]

Like Coolidge, Stearns was an Amherst man (class of 1878), and in 1915 he arranged a dinner meeting of graduates who believed that Harvard had taken too many state offices and that it was Amherst's turn. The obvious person to advance was Coolidge, and Stearns took the lead in doing so. Stearns was no kingmaker, however, nor even an adviser, which suited Coolidge, who liked his own counsel. Years later, in 1926, with Coolidge in the White House, the president made this quite evident. That year the first two volumes of *The Intimate Papers of Colonel House* appeared, and Coolidge called Stearns's attention to the book. There was not going to be any Colonel House in his administration, he said. Stearns asked meekly, "Did I ever try to advise you?"[19]

With such help, and with his own considerable ambition, Coolidge moved upward in state politics. Each new office was a rung on the ladder. It was during this time that Grace Coolidge came to Boston on the train to attend a meeting at the Copley Plaza at which her increasingly distinguished husband spoke, and she heard him recite the lines from Josiah G. Holland's "Gradatim":

> Heaven is not reached at a single bound;
> We build the ladder by which we rise
> From the lowly earth to the vaulted skies,
> And we mount to its summit round by round.[20]

The senate presidency made possible the lieutenant governorship and then the governorship, with the help of Stearns and, of course, Crane. Also helpful was the gradual return of state and national politics to its two-party arrangement, for Roosevelt brought his followers back to Republicanism in 1916. As lieutenant governor, Coolidge did not have a great deal to do. He was ex officio a member of the governor's council, and he approved gubernatorial appointments, checked on expenses for state contracts, watched other details of administration, and visited institutions throughout the commonwealth. As governor for two years, Coolidge had much more responsibility and could take pleasure in the legislative results. Measures were passed for the benefit of soldiers returning from Europe after the war, including bonuses of $100. The first bill Coolidge signed was for the Yankee Division, an appropriation of $10,000 for its reception in Boston. Veterans were given preference in public appointments. He presided over a new budget system, arranged by constitutional amendment the previous year. In the 1919 legislative session, he vetoed the Salary Grab Bill, which increased the compensation of legislators from $1,000 to $1,500; both houses of the legislature passed the bill over his veto, but he received credit for attempting to stop it. The next year he vetoed a bill for the sale of beer and light wines, in contravention of the Eighteenth Amendment; he informed legislative "wets" that "there can be no constitutional instruction to do an unconstitutional act." Crowning his accomplishments as governor was consolidation of the commonwealth's 118 separate government departments into 18, a courageous thing to do, for many people lost lucrative posts.

But the Massachusetts politician would have gone no further than the governorship had it not been for the three pieces of fortune that began with the Boston police strike. Fundamental to what happened was the city's failure to pay the police a living wage during and after the war, when the cost of living escalated and anyone on a fixed income was in trouble. The condition of the station houses deteriorated. It would have behooved city authorities to look into the policemen's lot, but they did not, and when matters were in danger of going too far, they procrastinated.

In the more immediate miscalculations that led to the strike, one must agree with Coolidge biographer Donald R. McCoy, who pointed out errors in the behavior of all the principals.[21] The policemen maintained a local organization to negotiate with the city, and in August 1919, it asked for and received an affiliation with the AFL. Commissioner Edwin U. Curtis thereupon made a signal error by dismissing the men who had arranged the AFL affiliation. Curtis, Mayor Andrew J. Peters, and Governor Coolidge all forbade the police to strike. When the police went out on Tuesday night, 9 September, no one expected a mass exodus of the force—1,100 of 1,500 men. Curtis was totally unprepared for this exigency, and so was Coolidge, who had pledged to back Curtis but had taken the commissioner at his word that matters were under control. Looting and violence began the morning after the walkout, 10 September. Peters took control of the police with assistance of National Guardsmen resident in the city. Advised by a group of public citizens he had appointed, he proposed a compromise that would have made Curtis take back the strike leaders. Coolidge, however, had supported Curtis in advance, and his word was now in question. The next day, 11 September, Coolidge called out the remainder of the state guard and overruled Peters, returning authority over the police to Curtis. Property damage was modest, amounting to $34,000. With Curtis back in control, all striking policemen lost their jobs, a sad result. Although it was not much consolation, Governor Coolidge promised them every assistance in obtaining employment elsewhere.

When Samuel Gompers asked for reinstatement of the strikers, Coolidge did not expect to become the hero of the occasion. It is not clear why he chose to send a resounding telegram to the AFL president, stating, "There is no right to strike against the public safety by anybody, anywhere, any time." In retrospect, it seemed a brilliant stroke, but at the time, it appeared to be a foolish piece of behavior. Labor was strong in Massachusetts. Coolidge was making a moral point, but it could easily be said that he was protecting his ill-chosen position of supporting the hapless Curtis. It is entirely possible that he decided to put a gloss on a bad occasion. He feared the worst. In a letter to his stepmother that has not survived, he wrote that he expected to lose the fall election. John Coolidge had married a local schoolteacher, Carrie A. Brown, in 1891, and her stepson often wrote to her about his prospects, personal and political. Years later, a member of his presidential cabinet wrote that the governor of Vermont, Percival W. Clement, had talked on the telephone with Coolidge after Gompers asked for reinstatement and Coolidge had said, "I have just committed political suicide."[22] Instead, he became a national figure, a hero to the mass of private citizens who, alienated by postwar strikes, felt that labor was becoming contemptuous of the public interest. Coolidge was reelected over a lackluster Democrat, Richard H. Long, by a massive majority: 317,774 votes to his opponent's 192,673.

Nomination for the vice presidency was in fair part a result of his prominence after the police strike. The indefatigable Stearns had collected Coolidge speeches and public statements in a volume that was in galley proofs when the strike broke out. The book was to be entitled *Bay State Orations.* Stearns added Coolidge's statements on the strike, and in a stroke of wisdom, the editor at Houghton Mifflin retitled the book *Have Faith in Massachusetts,* from a speech Coolidge had made upon his election as leader of the senate. The book came out in time to help sweep the governor into his second term. A few months later, Stearns sent free copies to delegates to the national convention in Chicago, in preparation for anything that might happen.[23] At the convention, a small presidential boom for the governor collapsed. The Senate clique that engineered Harding's nomination was set to nominate another senator for the vice presidency, Irvine L. Lenroot of Wisconsin, when the delegates rebelled and nominated Coolidge.

Coolidge's nomination was a complicated event, and luck played a part. Despite his confidence afterward—he remarked that if Wallace McCamant of the Oregon delegation had not nominated him, someone else would have—he could not have been certain.[24] The Massachusetts delegation made no effort to nominate him. After Coolidge's failure to get support for first place on the ticket, they received word from Murray Crane, "Don't put the governor up. He's been beaten once, and he doesn't want a second defeat." Crane must have talked with Coolidge. It was not at all clear what was going to happen. After the nomination of Harding, another of the also-rans for first place on the ticket, Sen. Hiram Johnson of California, refused the second-place nomination. At that juncture, with no one in sight, the Harding people did not know who should run with their man. Perhaps Harding was letting the convention have its head, because anyone he named could have had the ticket's second place. The Senate group resorted to its own membership, and Lenroot made a retrospective error by refusing the nomination, not realizing that he was going to be nominated anyway and that if he had sought Harding's designation he could have had the place. Meanwhile, Senator Lodge, who would have been Johnson's running mate if Johnson had been chosen as the presidential nominee, released the Oregon delegation, which had been pledged to Johnson in the state's primaries. This opened the way for that delegation to designate McCamant to propose Coolidge. The former member of the Oregon Supreme Court possessed a foghorn voice, and he stood on a chair and gained recognition from a complaisant chairman. In a noisy hall, with many of the delegates bored by the proceedings and walking out after a long day, he uttered the words that created a president:

> When the Oregon delegation came here instructed by the people of our state to present to this convention as its candidate for the office of vice president a distinguished son of Massachusetts [Lodge], he requested that we refrain from mentioning his name. But there is another son of Massachusetts who has been much in the public eye during the past year, a man who is sterling in his Americanism and stands for all that the Republican party holds dear; and on behalf of the Oregon delegation I name for the exalted office of vice president Governor Calvin Coolidge, of Massachusetts.

Hearing little of what McCamant said, other than the name of Coolidge, the delegates remaining in the hall went wild and rushed Coolidge through, 674.5 against Lenroot's 146.5.

In November 1924, with Coolidge president in his own right, John L. Rand, associate justice of the Oregon Supreme Court, wrote that he had suggested Coolidge's name because of his handling of the police strike. Otherwise, Coolidge would not have been nominated. McCamant had come into the equation only because another Oregon delegate did not want to make the nomination. The president responded that he knew this, that McCamant had not claimed too much credit, but after all, it was McCamant who did the deed.[25]

When Coolidge was nominated at Chicago in 1920, he was at his customary Boston residence. He had never been west of the Alleghenies and had only once visited Washington. Since the time of William McKinley, all the presidents—including the next president, Harding—had been men of not merely national but also international acquaintance, if not experience. Harding had visited Europe twice. Coolidge was a provincial.

During the campaign, he traveled out of New England, but not far. Senator Harding invited him to Washington, and the two conferred over a breakfast of waffles and chipped beef, a Harding favorite. The vice-presidential candidate went on a speaking tour, making an address at a fair in

Minneapolis. There he received little attention, and many in the audience left the hall. He also spoke in Kentucky and Tennessee; Harding's managers may have sent Coolidge where he could do no harm. Most of the country's attention centered on the enlarged front porch in Marion, Ohio, to which Coolidge himself went after the election, on one of the pilgrimages that for a short while made the little city in central Ohio famous.

Whatever he did in the campaign did not matter, for the outcome was never in doubt. Harding and Coolidge were elected by a landslide: 16 million votes for Harding and Coolidge; 9 million for their Democratic opponents, Governor James M. Cox of Ohio and his vice-presidential running mate, young Franklin D. Roosevelt. The Democrats lost by such a margin because of the country's tiredness with the Wilson administration, the Democratic president's inability to carry out his peace program through the Treaty of Versailles and the League of Nations. Wilson had suffered a stroke in 1919 that left him incompetent to conduct his presidential duties, and everything collapsed in his administration, awaiting the choice of his successor.

At last the time came to leave Northampton and take up residence in Washington. Before leaving, Coolidge went around his city, bidding friends good-bye. Among others, he shook hands with shoemaker James Lucey, an early supporter. Lucey looked up and there was his friend standing in the doorway. The vice president elect's words were, "Well, I've come to say good-by," which he did with a shake of hands and then was gone, down the street to shake more hands.[26]

One must ask whether the newly elected vice president sensed what lay in store, whether he knew that Harding, who looked the picture of health, was already an ill man with a systolic pressure of 180. Years later, two physicians said that they told friends at the time that Harding would not last out his term. Coolidge, as described by Barrett Wendell, a Back Bay Brahmin and professor of literature at Harvard, was no fool. "A small, hatched-face, colorless man," Wendell opined, "with a tight-shut, thin-lipped mouth, very chary of words, but with a gleam of understanding in his pretty keen eye."[27] If Coolidge had any inkling of the future, he was careful not to record anything. An early biography, published in 1924, offered a hint of foreknowledge. A few weeks before Harding's death, a Boston friend called on the vice president at his suite in the New Willard Hotel. "Governor," the friend said, "I've heard bad reports of Mr. Harding's condition. You'll be president before the year is up." Grace Coolidge was playing solitaire on the back of the piano and said, "How can you say such an awful thing!" Characteristically, Coolidge said nothing.[28]

In Washington, the Coolidges settled in for whatever would happen. They took up residence at the Willard in the four rooms occupied by their predecessors during the Wilson administration, Vice President and Mrs.

17

Thomas R. Marshall. The Marshalls hailed from North Manchester, Indiana, and hotel residents looked on the new vice president and his wife as no more conspicuous. One evening, a fire in the hotel brought all the guests down to the lobby, many of them in less than full dress. Once the fire was under control, Coolidge started upstairs. The fire marshal halted him. "Who are you?" asked that functionary.

"I'm the vice president," Coolidge replied.

"All right—go ahead," said the marshal.

Coolidge went a step or two and was halted a second time. "What are you vice president of?" the marshal asked suspiciously.

"I'm the vice president of the United States."

"Come right down," said the marshal. "I thought you were the vice president of the hotel."[29]

Coolidge's anonymity was symbolized by the addition of a middle initial on a complimentary pass issued by the National Baseball League, which designated him Calvin G. Coolidge. The American League gave him a pass for Calvin C. Coolidge.

Socially, the Coolidges cut no figures. They did much dining out, partly because they were asked and partly because Florence Harding was not in good health, suffering a kidney ailment, and she and her husband usually were unavailable for dinners and other social events. Mrs. Harding apparently did not think much of the Coolidges, socially speaking. In 1923, the wife of former senator John B. Henderson of Missouri sought to donate her Washington house, a turreted mansion known as Henderson Castle, as a residence for the nation's vice presidents. Mrs. Harding opposed the offer. According to Nicholas Murray Butler, president of Columbia University and something of a gossip, who was visiting the White House at the time, Mrs. Harding almost shouted: "Not a bit of it, not a bit of it. I am going to have that bill defeated. Do you think I am going to have those Coolidges living in a house like that? An hotel apartment is plenty good enough for them."[30]

Politically, the vice president did not make much of an impression. This may have been because he made no effort to be a maker of policies. He presided over the Senate in an impartial, disinterested manner. Stearns told the well-known Washington reporter Mark Sullivan that in a conversation about Harding's policies, Coolidge had said: "My conception of my position is that I am vice-president. I am a member of the administration. So long as I am in that position it is my duty to uphold the policies and actions of the administration one hundred percent up to the point where I cannot conscientiously agree with them. When I cannot conscientiously agree with them it is then my duty to keep silent."[31]

The vice president was available for speeches, but judging from the assignments listed in his autobiography, his talents were not in demand.

"I was honored by the President," he wrote, "by his request to make the dedicatory address at the unveiling of a bust of him in the McKinley Memorial at Niles, Ohio." The affair made so little impression on Coolidge that he forgot that it took place at Canton, Ohio. He remembered one other speech, an address at the dedication of a Grant statue in Washington.[32]

Harding died on 2 August 1923; and Coolidge was sworn in by his father late that night in the farmhouse at Plymouth Notch, by the light of a kerosene lamp. Afterwards, life became much more hectic. The two and a half years in the vice presidency—the least busy years in his adult life—were almost forgotten. The twenty years of politics in Massachusetts might have seemed the work of a century before. When he was vice president and visiting the Notch, he was seen carrying his mail from the post office across the road to his father's house, and he carried it in one hand. Within days, the mail increased to four thousand letters a day.

After going back to Washington for Harding's funeral and to Marion for the obsequies there, Coolidge became frantically busy. There was little rest, save summer vacations in Swampscott in 1925, the Adirondacks in 1926, the Black Hills of South Dakota in 1927, and a fishing camp in Wisconsin the next year—the last of his presidency. Even vacations were replete with diplomatic pouches, telegraphic correspondence and mail, and the reception of important people. There also were the frequent press conferences that marked the Coolidge presidency; Coolidge was the first president to meet regularly with reporters.

In Washington, his routine rarely varied. He would rise at 6:30 and, after shaving with an old-fashioned steel razor, take a walk with his bodyguard, Col. Edmund W. Starling. He and Mrs. Coolidge would breakfast together in their rooms, having fruit and half a cup of coffee, accompanied by homemade cereal comprising two parts unground wheat and one part rye. To this was added a roll and a strip of bacon, which "went mostly to our dogs." At 12:30 each day, the president shook hands with an average of four hundred callers. One of his predecessors, William Howard Taft, described this ceremony as "pump-handle work." Coolidge, Taft knew, disliked shaking hands and did it with ill-concealed disdain.[33] The president sometimes spoke to callers, saying "Mawnin'." After this chore, he would go out to the grounds and pose with groups of officials or visitors. After a nap that could last as long as two hours, he would sign commissions and orders and, if possible, work on correspondence; even after winnowing by assistants, there were stacks upon stacks of it. He would sit at his desk, feet in a drawer, smoking a big cigar, and pen his sentiments on the letters in a word or two or, if necessary, a phrase, after which his secretaries would translate the sentiments into something that said the same thing in a decent number of words. Typical of Coolidge's annotations was his response to

President John Grier Hibben of Princeton, who on 15 January 1924 wrote to invite the president to receive an honorary degree. At the top of the letter Coolidge wrote, "Sorry." Secretary of State Charles Evans Hughes once sent a letter relating that a group of women wished to call and present a memorial seeking the end of international war. Across the top of Hughes's letter the president scrawled expansively, "Let 'em call."[34]

Part of the presidential routine were the social breakfasts for which Coolidge became noted. They were his idea of goodwill projects, and the individuals upon whom he conferred that goodwill were mostly members of Congress. The breakfasts were well catered and included a great deal of food, in particular hotcakes and Vermont maple syrup. But although no one seems to have informed Coolidge, the famed White House breakfasts failed to generate much appreciation from the individuals invited. The guests always questioned why the president had summoned them, and on this score, Coolidge never gave an inkling; perhaps he felt it unnecessary to explain the meaning of goodwill. Since the guests were busy people, they began to look upon their attendance, which was difficult to refuse, as a chore. The White House head usher, Irwin H. (Ike) Hoover (who did not much admire Coolidge because the president had refused to raise Hoover's salary), remembered some of the excuses. Sen. Key Pittman of Nevada had his wife telephone to say that a wheel had come off his automobile down the road. Sen. Frederick Hale of Maine contended that his man forgot to wake him. Senator Johnson, who may have had his own reasons for not coming to a Coolidge breakfast, said that his barn had burned down. This was true; he lived on a country estate. One congressman had been out all night, and no one could find him.[35]

All the while, Coolidge could rest assured that his family life was as supportive as possible. Here he was vastly assisted by his choice of Grace Goodhue as his wife. Of all the first ladies, Grace Coolidge may well have been the most attractive. Alfred Dennis remembered her when she came to Northampton to teach at the Clarke School. He described her as a creature of "spirit, fire, and dew, given to blithe spontaneous laughter, with eager birdlike movements, as natural and unaffected as sunlight or the sea, a soul that renders the common air sweet." He thought her "the most charming girl in town."[36] She had been of enormous assistance to Coolidge as he climbed the political ladder. Her White House appearances, her receptions, her thoughtfulness in sending flowers to ill individuals, her simple welcomes to groups of visitors on the lawn in back of the mansion, all were memorable. When standing in line at formal presidential receptions, she had a word for everyone and melted the ice that otherwise might have gathered around the handshaking. She made up for her husband's social inadequacies.

The Coolidges' sons were sources of great satisfaction to the president and his wife. John Coolidge had the looks and much of the personality of the president's father, who was laconic, sensitive, commonsensical. John attended Mercersburg Academy in Pennsylvania with his younger brother, Calvin, Jr., and then Amherst College. After graduation, he took a position with the New York, New Haven, and Hartford Railroad; married Florence Trumbull, the daughter of the governor of Connecticut; and virtually disappeared from public view, which was what his father and mother desired him to do. His brother died tragically after playing tennis on the south lawn of the White House and developing a blister on his toe that became infected. The death of Calvin, Jr., who greatly resembled his father, was the greatest tragedy of the president's life. Coolidge wrote to his ailing father on 9 December 1925, "It is getting to be almost Christmas time again. I always think of mother and Abbie and grandmother and now of Calvin. Perhaps you will see them all before I do, but in a little while we shall all be together for Christmas."[37]

Contrary to what might have been expected of this New England presidential family, Coolidge and his wife were extraordinarily hospitable in inviting guests to the White House. They had more guests than were invited during any of their predecessors' administrations. Apart from relatives, close friends, and members of the administration, there were 102 house guests during Coolidge's five years and seven months as the nation's chief executive. One of the president's biographers, Claude M. Fuess, discovered that in four years Taft had had thirty-two house guests, in eight years Wilson had had twelve, and Harding had had five.[38]

And what of the New England president as a personality? What traits did he display to the American people from 1923 until 1929? Coolidge's personal qualities often have been drawn, and most of the portraits are fairly accurate, although the colors have been heightened for what is considered the benefit of the whole. There undoubtedly was a dark side to the president. He could be utterly rude, as when a member of the Washington diplomatic corps and his wife mistook the time of a dinner for 9:00 instead of 8:00 and arrived at 8:40. Coolidge waited a short time, took the other guests in to dinner, and let the latecomers wait in one of the drawing rooms until dinner was over. He could also be rude to his family. When he was moving up in Massachusetts politics, he was in Northampton only one day a week and was often tired and testy, putting the entire family on edge. He was particularly difficult with the boys, criticizing them for small things. In the White House, he often showed little regard for his wife's sensitivities. He would invite guests aboard the presidential yacht *Mayflower* without informing her of the guest list. Secretive to a fault, he would not tell her where he was planning their summer vacations, nor the times of departure and return. He kept political information of all kinds from her and became angry if he thought that she was taking any part in politics. One day, two women from one of the largest and most populous states in the country came by appointment to confer with Mrs. Coolidge, and she saw them in the Red Room. When she joined the president for lunch, she told him of the call. He inquired what their purpose was, and she said that it was a political interest. He snapped, "Did you tell them you didn't know anything about politics?" His wife carefully replied that the women had found that out in one or two minutes. Perhaps most remarkable was that the president gave his wife no advance notice of his decision not to run again for the presidency, which he announced during a press conference in the Black Hills in 1927. Grace Coolidge learned of it from a senator who had been present at the press conference and returned with the president for lunch.[39]

He could show temper on trivial occasions; this may have been his worst trait. He was irritable when writing a speech, for he put effort into his speeches and never passed them off. His wife found it wise not to bother him when he was trying to form in his mind an important speech, and she told Dr. Boone that at such times "I let him alone as much as possible," and that afterward his nervous system seemed to level off. She attributed his temper to the fact that he had been raised by his grandmother and did not learn to control his disposition as he should have. She herself, she told Boone, tried to be his safety valve. If he came home from the office amiable and affable, she was apprehensive that he might have exploded that day and been offensive to some caller, but if he came home irritable and nervous and blew up, she was consoled, because she knew that he had not acted that way in the presence of visitors or the office staff.[40]

What can one say about the way Coolidge treated his wife? There seems to be no answer, other than that he was forcing himself to be polite to the many people he had to see every day, most of whom wanted something, and he let himself go when in the presence of his family, knowing that for all his meanness, he possessed his wife's undying love and did not need to worry that he would go too far.

How could such a lovely woman have married such a stick and, at times, a good deal worse than that? Grace Coolidge told much to her friends. There were two occasions when she might have divorced him, had she lived in an era when divorce was taken lightly. She confided to Stearns's wife that just after the marriage in 1905, she was unsure that she could continue. Twenty years later, Dr. Boone saw her vacationing in the Adirondacks during the first anniversary of the death of Calvin, Jr. She was ignored by her husband, who refused to allow their son John to come to visit. But there was clearly more to the marriage than came out in conversation or met the eye. It could have been her sense of a gentle, caring personality behind the actions of the child of Plymouth Notch, the youth of BRA, the long-haired Amherst student, the scholar in the outer office of Hammond and Field, the orator who recited Holland's "Gradatim" at the Copley Plaza. Late in 1932, Coolidge's successor, President Herbert Hoover, begged him to make a speech at Madison Square Garden in New York in support of Hoover's campaign for a second term. The former president and his wife were at the Notch, and Coolidge was working on what would prove to be his last public address. His wife was at her desk writing a letter. She heard a quiet tiptoeing into the room, and then a pause. "I see feet standing just under my right elbow," she wrote to her correspondent,"—a voice, 'Mommy, do you know what day this is?' 'Yes.' 'What day is it?' 'Our wedding anniversary, twenty-seventh.' 'Why didn't you tell me?' 'I thought you had enough on your mind.' 'Well, I wanted to know about it.' Then, a little kiss down under my ear somewhere and retreating footsteps, closed doors in the sitting-room and a low murmur of dictation."[41]

In a sort of middle range of qualities, neither unattractive nor attractive, was his quietness. This was no pose to encourage descriptions of "Silent Cal." Boone was aboard the *Mayflower* one day and saw the president sitting at one end of a davenport with his father, Colonel Coolidge, at the other, and quite a space between them. They were looking at the scenery along the river as the ship slowly passed by, not saying a word, communing, the physician thought, in silence, according to a lifetime habit. As Boone stood there, the president said in his nasal Vermont twang, without looking toward his father but straight out over the water, "How is the sheep business?"

His father, looking straight ahead, without turning toward the son, said, "Good."

After quite a long pause, the president inquired, "What are they bringing the pound?"

Another sizable silence, and his father replied with the price.[42]

Coolidge once said of his speech writing, but it also applied to his personality, "I always knew that there was some water in my well, but that I had to pump to get it. It is not a gushing fountain."[43]

Last among Coolidge's traits, and it overshadowed the others in determining the course of his presidency, was his sense of public service. That was the reason he had remained in politics. He liked the law when he began its study in 1895, and for years it attracted him, but politics drew him because it was subsumed in the word "service." Coolidge's critics could not understand this part of the president's makeup. Hiram Johnson sensed a quality in Coolidge that was narrowly personal. Johnson wrote to his sons that "I really believe there never was a man in high position so politically minded. I do not think there is any principle or policy of government that for one instant will sway him when he believes his personal political fortunes may be influenced." Johnson was not being rhetorical. "This isn't a nice estimate to have of the President of the United States," he wrote, "but I firmly believe it to be a just estimate." Yet he misjudged the president. Coolidge believed that public service was the end of all proper political action. "I am going to try to do what seems best for the country, and get what satisfaction I can out of that," he wrote to Stearns shortly after he became president. "Most everything else will take care of itself." As McCoy has written, Coolidge's reason for being in politics was that the citizen had an obligation to serve. It was his duty to God and society. Politics held society together, and the task of the politician was to seek the people's will.[44]

2

★ ★ ★ ★ ★

STATE OF THE UNION

When Coolidge became president of the United States, not quite five years had passed since the end of World War I. Most Americans felt that the war had ended on Armistice Day, 11 November 1918, but such was not the case in terms of the war's effect on the government, not to mention the economy, society, and U.S. citizens' attitude toward the world and their part in it. The war's influence lasted for years; although it was immeasurable in any exact sense, its importance was clearly discernible in all aspects of American life.

In government, which was Coolidge's concern, his predecessors Wilson and Harding had seen to it that the size of the governmental mechanism had diminished—if not to what it had been before U.S. entrance into the war, then to something approximate. There could be no question that what the New England president inherited was the small government of prewar times. Because Coolidge had grown up with small government and always believed in cutting the cloth of expenditure to suit the materials provided by taxpayers, he was happy with what he found and hoped that it would remain that way; indeed, during his presidency, it did. As for the influence of the war on the U.S. economy, society, and foreign relations, those were issues that were less under his control. The economy and society he took as he found them. He gave foreign relations little thought and, for the most part, let them go whichever way circumstances pointed, which meant that as chief executive of the government of the United States, he did not need to do very much.

It is necessary in this chapter to look at the state of the Union in two general ways: first at the organization of government under President Coolidge, and second at the way in which Coolidge's fellow citizens were spending their lives, a quick *tour d'horizon* of the society of his time. The economy of the United States—its industry, labor, and agriculture—and the portions of American society that government touched (only a few in Coolidge's day), and the country's foreign relations are examined in later chapters.

In the federal government of 1923, receipts were $3.8 billion and expenditures $3.1 billion. President Coolidge devoted the balance to reduction of the national debt. In March 1917, the debt had been $1.3 billion; in 1919, it stood at $26.6 billion, and it was down to $22.3 billion in Coolidge's first year. It was worrisome because of its incessantly accumulating interest. In 1929, the debt was down to $16.9 billion. That year, receipts of the national government were $3.8 billion and expenditures were $3.1 billion, the same as in 1923.[1]

The principal expenditure in the post-1918 budget, apart from interest and principal on the debt, was for the army and navy. In Coolidge's time, there was no separate air force; the army and navy each maintained an air service. The cost of the army in 1923 was $397 million; of the navy, $333 million. In the national budget, nearly one dollar of every four was going to the military. After the war, these expenditures seemed high, and Coolidge believed that they were not altogether necessary, although like most of his fellow citizens, he believed in national defense; the war had brought home the lesson of unpreparedness. But it was perplexing to see the cost of preparedness in the 1920s. The new president was especially concerned about the navy, whose admirals were always thinking about constructing more ships. A battleship could cost $30 million, a cruiser $10 million. The president hoped to reduce the size of the navy through international negotiation, a hope that proved impossible in his time. Military expenditures when he left office were slightly higher than when he entered: $425 million for the army, $364 million for the navy.

The lack of an air force concerned the administration, and in due time, Coolidge did something about it. Col. William (Billy) Mitchell sought to demonstrate in 1921 that planes could sink warships. His fliers passed over a former German battle cruiser off the Virginia Capes and sank it. He infuriated the officers of the U.S. Navy, who pooh-poohed what they described as his exhibitionism, for the ship was dead in the water, could take no evasive measures, and was old and did not possess much in the way of watertight bulkheads. Having achieved unpopularity with his sister service, Mitchell defied the leaders of his own service, the U.S. Army, by making claims about the country's lack of air defenses. In 1925, the army brought him before a court-martial and forced his resignation. Coolidge undertook damage control by appointing a board to look into the colonel's claims, and the board secured $76 million for aviation development, quieting the controversy.

The strength of the army in 1923 stood at 113,243, the navy 94,094. In 1929, the figures were 119,118 and 97,117. The navy's Marine Corps had a strength of 19,674 in 1923 and 18,796 in 1929. In 1915, army strength had been 91,757, navy 54,559, and marines 10,312.

The number of other federal employees was not large: 436,900 in 1923 and 479,559 at the end of Coolidge's presidency. This compared with 395,429 in 1915. The increase could be attributed not to the war but to the rise in population. In 1915, the population was 100 million. The country's population in 1923 was 111 million; in 1929, it was 121 million. Employees during the Coolidge administration were concentrated in the post office department. Actually, half of all federal employees worked there: 268,000 in 1923 and 295,000 in 1929. The next largest category of employees worked for the military: 94,000 in 1923 and 103,000 in 1929. Almost all government employees were in the executive branch, apportioned among the cabinet departments. The legislative branch contained 9,000 employees in 1923 and 10,000 in 1929; the judicial branch had 1,800 and 1,500 for the respective years.

As had been the case since the Theodore Roosevelt administration, President Coolidge conducted the nation's business from two offices. One was a private office on the second floor of the White House. The other was in the executive offices in the building Roosevelt had constructed in 1902 to the rear and west of the mansion. (After construction in 1942 of another office building to the east of the White House, this would be known as the West Wing.) The executive offices were convenient to the mansion, connected by an arcade.

Coolidge's office staff was small. As had the presidents before him, he maintained a single presidential secretary. At first his secretary was a former Virginia congressman, C. Bascom Slemp; he departed in 1925 and was replaced by a former congressman from Indiana, Everett Sanders. The latter had an assistant, Edward T. (Ted) Clark (Amherst class of 1900). In addition to the secretaries, there were typists and a stenographer. These individuals were important to the president's administrative procedure—annotation of his mail. For a few letters, the president employed his stenographer, Erwin C. Geisser. When the president held his twice-weekly press conferences, on Tuesdays and Fridays, Geisser took down verbatim Coolidge's answers to the written-out questions he chose to address.

A special help to the president was the Bureau of the Budget, created by the Budget and Accounting Act of 1921. Until that time, the executive branch of the government had no way to sort out the budget proposals of cabinet departments and independent agencies or calculate the effect of congressional bills. Each year the budget was an approximation, and many an improper appropriation was slipped into Congress by interested parties in the executive branch or through the efforts of congressmen. The huge national debt incurred because of the war had brought about the need for economy. Harding's first budget director had been Brig. Gen. Charles G. Dawes, a Chicago banker and President McKinley's comptroller of the currency, an aggressive and experienced administrator. Dawes became Coolidge's vice president in 1925, and his replacement as budget director was Brig. Gen. Herbert M. Lord, equally efficient if less aggressive.

Coolidge held weekly cabinet meetings in which he listened to problems and the solutions suggested by cabinet members. At the outset, he kept Harding's entire cabinet. He announced that he would carry on his predecessor's policies, and to be sure, he needed time before arranging any replacements. Fortunately, he knew the abilities of Harding's cabinet; unlike previous vice presidents, he had sat in the cabinet. He had not said much, perhaps maintaining his reputation as the "little fellow," as Harding once described him.[2] Assistant Secretary of the Navy Theodore Roosevelt, Jr., had sat in frequently for his department chief, Secretary of the Navy Edwin N. Denby, and when Coolidge became president, Roosevelt was bewildered as to the former vice president's points of view, if he had any. He need not have worried, for the little fellow—now the big fellow—had everything under control. A few months later, the time came to expel Harding's attorney general, Harry M. Daugherty, who had been Harding's campaign manager in 1920. Coolidge knew exactly what sort of individual he was dealing with. He liked Daugherty, but the attorney general was politically inconvenient and at one point had spoken disrespectfully to the new president. Similarly, he let Denby go because of political inconvenience. The ambitious younger Roosevelt went of his own accord, ill advisedly attempting to displace Governor Alfred E. Smith in New York's gubernatorial election of 1924; he then entered a political wilderness from which he never emerged.

The cabinet changed in succeeding years, and Coolidge's appointments usually made sense, sometimes privately rather than publicly. Elder statesman Elihu Root—secretary of war in McKinley's cabinet, secretary of state under Theodore Roosevelt, then a senator from New York—once described Coolidge as not possessing an international hair in his head. Thus it was fortunate that the president was assisted in the Department of State by two such able individuals as Charles Evans Hughes and Frank B. Kellogg. Although the two men were quite different, with Hughes possessing by far the larger reputation, both were highly competent.

Hughes had been governor of New York, was associate justice of the Supreme Court in 1916 when he became the Republican presidential nominee, and had been head of one of the most prestigious New York City law firms. He was levelheaded and instinctively a leader. During his tenure at the State Department, he held its apparatus in his hand, his control radiating out to seven hundred people in Washington and a larger number in the field. If he had a single flaw as secretary, it was his tendency to assume responsibility for more tasks than he should have.[3] He would have liked to stay on for a second term beginning in 1925, but he submitted his resignation in a pro forma way, and Coolidge accepted it in a similar manner. It is possible that in 1921–23, when Coolidge was vice president, Hughes may not have given him attention, although as with so many of Coolidge's decisions, there is no way to be certain of the reason for this one. Hughes did have a coldness about him. He was tall, erect, impressive, sharp of eye, and firm of jaw, the latter covered with a pointed white beard. Coolidge's secretary of commerce, Herbert Hoover, not noted for his warmth, said that Hughes was "the most self-contained man I ever knew. . . . He simply had no instinct for personal friendship that I could ever discover."[4]

Kellogg was an old Rooseveltian and in the early years of the century had made a reputation as a lawyer in St. Paul. He and Theodore Roosevelt were about the same age and had the same temperament. Kellogg once went into the presidential office and told Roosevelt that he had with him the railroad builder James J. Hill, who constructed the Great Northern. He asked if he should bring him in. "Sure," was the laughing reply, "bring him along. I'd like to see the old gorilla."[5] Under Roosevelt's successor, President Taft, Kellogg prosecuted the Standard Oil Company and in 1911 obtained a decision under the Sherman Act and became known nationally as "the trust buster." Elected to the Senate in 1916, he served one term, was defeated, and became ambassador to London by appointment of President Coolidge, with whom he had been friendly. Coolidge brought him back as secretary of state in 1925, and according to Sen. Reed Smoot of Utah, the president's choice produced "great disappointment" from "nearly all Senators." They had expected the prestigious post to go to a better known individual, but they agreed to Kellogg's appointment because of senatorial courtesy.[6] The sixty-nine-year-old Kellogg was small of stature, stocky, blind in one eye, and possessed of wavy white hair—not nearly as physically impressive as Hughes. But he was as levelheaded in all matters save sponsorship of the Kellogg-Briand Pact in 1928, which undertook to outlaw war, and a pronouncement the previous year that implied that the Mexican government was full of Communists.

When Hughes left the administration and Kellogg replaced him, the man from Minnesota nominally became the first secretary of the cabinet, sitting at the right of the president in accord with time-honored custom. But in the popular mind and perhaps in Coolidge's, the leading cabinet member became the secretary of the treasury, the small, frail, white-haired Andrew W. Mellon. He had come in with Harding and would go out during the Hoover administration. In the Coolidge years, as earlier, he was very prominent. He was the third richest man in the United States, after John D. Rockefeller and Henry Ford. In the 1920s, the size of the national debt required attention from the treasury department, and his successive proposals for reform of the nation's system of taxation, most of which Congress eventually passed, kept him in the public eye.

The individual who carried out the president's laissez-faire policies toward industry was Secretary Hoover, almost as large a figure as the secretaries of state and the secretary of the treasury, and equally competent. Arthur M. Schlesinger, Jr., characterized the qualities that placed Hoover in the center of economic policy during the 1920s. "Contained, wary, enormously capable and efficient, with round face, hazel eyes, straight mouse-colored hair, and broad shoulders, he transmuted all adventure into business, as a [Richard Harding] Davis hero would transmute all business into adventure."[7] He had lived abroad for twenty years working as an engineer, traveling to the ends of the earth and employing his professional competence, as he would have put it. His public service during the war as the head of Belgian relief, and afterward as food administrator for his own country, changed his life, bringing out the Quaker side of his background. In administering the Department of Commerce, he infused his administrative duties with evangelistic fervor for the economic well-being of his country and, almost as important, that of the people of the world.

Hoover's nemesis in the Harding and Coolidge cabinets was Secretary of Agriculture Henry C. Wallace, a farm journalist who had edited the nationally known *Wallaces' Farmer* in Des Moines and spoke for farmers throughout the Midwest and the South. Wallace had been born into a farm family, and his father, also named Henry, had founded the journal. His son was Henry A. Wallace, who took over the journal when his father joined the Harding cabinet and eventually became secretary of agriculture under Franklin Roosevelt. Hoover and Wallace barely suffered each other for a year during Coolidge's presidency. Wallace considered Hoover bloodless, stuffy, and opinionated, as well as an empire builder.[8] Hoover thought that Wallace possessed no vision. The secretary of agriculture took ill in the summer of 1924 and died. He was succeeded by a Hoover protégé, the president of Kansas State Agricultural College, William M. Jardine, a rigid free-enterprise advocate who, unlike his predecessor, refused to back federal legislation supporting higher farm prices.

When Attorney General Daugherty left the cabinet in 1924, dismissed nominally because of his refusal to furnish Department of Justice documents pertaining to the conduct of his department, the president chose a former dean of Columbia University Law School, Harlan F. Stone (Amherst class of 1894). The next year he appointed Stone to the Supreme Court and sought to replace him in the cabinet with the able but conservative Charles B. Warren of Michigan, a rich man whom senators believed was a tool of the nation's sugar interests. This led to an extraordinary event five days after Vice President Dawes was inaugurated as the new presiding officer of the Senate. To this day it is unclear whether Dawes's undiplomatic address upon his inauguration, in which he harangued the senators for wasting time under Senate Rule 22, which allowed unlimited debate, resulted in the defeat of Coolidge's nominee Warren. The Senate divided 40–40. Such divisions in Congress are usually contrived for some good purpose; they seldom happen by chance. Prior to the vote, Senate leaders of both parties had assured Dawes that no vote on the nomination would take place that day, as six senators were scheduled to speak. Dawes left the chair and adjourned to his rooms in the New Willard, for the purpose of taking a nap. Five of the senators scheduled to speak then relinquished their time. Dawes's secretary frantically telephoned him, and the vice president dressed, raced through the lobby, commandeered a taxicab, and rushed up Capitol Hill. Just before he arrived in the Senate chamber, Sen. Lee S. Overman of North Carolina, the only Democrat who had voted for Warren, changed his vote, making the vote 39–41. The motion to confirm was defeated. For the first time since Henry Stanbery had been rejected for attorney general in 1868, the Senate rejected a presidential cabinet nominee. After submitting Warren's name again and losing the vote, Coolidge considered a recess appointment, gave up the idea, and nominated an old friend and country lawyer from Ludlow, John G. Sargent, who was promptly confirmed.

For months, Dawes was a laughingstock in Washington and not altogether a favorite of President Coolidge. Some wag put up a sign at the Willard, "Dawes Slept Here." A few days later, the vice president was taking a friend around the Capitol and stopped in at the Supreme Court. It was a dull court session, with Justice Oliver Wendell Holmes, Jr., pulling at his mustache to keep awake and Chief Justice Taft yawning. When the chief justice saw Dawes, he sent down a note: "Come up here. This is a good place to sleep."[9]

The other cabinet members of the Coolidge administration were of less importance. Secretary of Labor James J. Davis had an early connection with laboring men in the tin-plate industry and had founded the Loyal Order of Moose. He would continue as secretary in the Hoover administration. The secretaries of the navy, Denby and Curtis D. Wilbur, and the secretaries of war, Boston banker John W. Weeks, who died in 1925, and his successor Dwight F. Davis, were of little importance, although Davis obtained some notice as contributor of the Davis Cup in tennis competitions. The secretaries of the interior—until 1928, the physician Hubert Work; then a lawyer and former chairman of the Republican national committee, Roy O. West—similarly remained out of the limelight.

And what of American society during the Coolidge years? Much has been made of life during the Roaring Twenties or the Golden Twenties; the appellation varied with the telling. People who remembered the era often thought of it as a happy time between the world war that preceded it and the Great Depression and world war that followed. It was a period when young men and women could grow up looking forward to the future, without the worry and confusion of the generations that preceded and followed. Were the 1920s, then, as roaring or as golden as memory made them? Was the state of the Union, socially speaking, that attractive?

Economically, it was a good time. The unemployment rate was very low, albeit with the usual ups and downs. The price level was remarkably steady, in comparison to the inflation during the war, the hyperinflation afterward, and the tumble of prices during the recession—a virtual depression—of 1920–21. The economy rose reassuringly during America's happy time. It was in no sense the spirited rise that came after World War II, when the economy boomed. During the Coolidge era, production went up only 12 percent. Nonetheless, it was a notable, steady rise, and Coolidge's countrymen felt good about it.

One special reason that made the 1920s so memorable was the automobile, which became a common sight during that period, with millions of cars on the road all over the country. In 1921, automobile registrations reached 9.3 million; in 1929, they were 26.7 million. During the decade, state and local governments busied themselves with improving roads sufficiently to allow automobile travel. Road building during the Coolidge years became a preoccupation of government, and the federal government encouraged road construction by a system of matching grants.

Another measure of society during Coolidge's presidency was the number of telephones across the country. The telephone had long since ceased to be a novelty. Alexander Graham Bell had first exhibited it at the Philadelphia Centennial Exhibition in 1876. But for many years, the installation of telephones proved to be a slow process. As late as 1923, there was only a single telephone in Plymouth Notch, at the general store. The Coolidge years saw a marked increase in installations. In 1923, there were 15.3 million telephones in the United States. By 1929, there were 19.9 million.

Radio appeared on the scene in 1920 with the establishment of KDKA in Pittsburgh. By 1923, 556 stations were operating. By 1929, the figure was

606. From 1923 to 1929, the number of families with radio receivers, as they were known, increased from 400,000 to 10 million. The *Readers' Guide to Periodical Literature* for 1919–21 listed two columns of articles on radicals and radicalism, indicating the "Red scare" that followed the world war. In the volume for those years, there was less than a quarter of a column of articles about radio. The *Guide* for 1922–24 had half a column on radicals and radicalism and nineteen columns on radio.[10]

As stations multiplied, organizational changes became necessary. In the beginning, many of the stations were private operations, belonging to educational institutions and churches. As late as 1925, commercial broadcasting companies owned less than 4 percent of stations. In this period, Secretary of Commerce Hoover ventured a remark that he must have had second thoughts about later. "I have never believed," he said, "that it was possible to advertise through broadcasting without ruining the industry."[11] Changes followed one after another with increasing commercialization and the organization of networks—the National Broadcasting Company in 1926, the Columbia Broadcasting System in 1927. Meanwhile, the obvious legal weakness of the Department of Commerce's attempts to regulate wavelengths for stations led to defiance by the owners of a Chicago station and by the Los Angeles evangelist Aimee Semple McPherson. The evangelist's station did not seize any special wavelength but drifted over the lengths, interfering with competitors. When Hoover objected, he received a telegram: "Please order your minions of Satan to leave my station alone. You cannot expect the Almighty to abide by your wave length nonsense. When I offer my prayers to Him I must fit into His wave reception."[12] The secretary asked Congress for what became the Radio Act of 1927, creating the Federal Radio Commission and giving it regulatory responsibility, with Hoover as administrator. Among other provisions, it provided equal opportunity for political candidates.

If one chose to go out for entertainment in the 1920s, the thing to do was go to the movies. That great source of entertainment had been around since the turn of the century, but the principal change during the Coolidge years was the coming of sound, or "talkies." In 1923, inventor Lee De Forest displayed the first sound movies in a theater in New York—shorts of vaudeville acts. In 1924, he made a six-minute film of Governor Smith of New York, who was seeking the Democratic nomination for president but did not receive it until four years later. He made a film of Coolidge speaking on the economy, but it was impossible to show in theaters because of the lack of equipment. In 1927 came Warner Brothers Vitaphone. Its only problem was the need to coordinate a sound track with the picture—the sound was on a disc and had to be played separately, and if the disc got ahead of or behind the picture, the audience would be unhappy. Next year a system appeared that worked, Fox Movietone, with the sound track on the film. It became the standard for talking pictures.

Another novelty in movie production was the star system. The great stars could ensure automatic attendance. The star system brought fantastic salaries to the stars, along with special engagements or arrangements for advertising. Box-office receipts easily supported the system's cost.

Largely because of the talkies, and partly because of the star system, the end of the 1920s saw a massive rise in theater attendance. In 1922, 40 million tickets were sold each week. Seven years later, attendance had climbed to 100 million. There were 23,000 movie theaters. A researcher calculated that with four performances daily at every theater, by 1929, Chicago had enough seats for half the city's population to attend the movies each day.[13]

The movies had their attraction, but people discovered in the 1920s that anything could sell if properly advertised. Florists of the nation discovered that the correct words could double their sales. Major P. F. O'Keefe received a gold medal from a florists' society for inventing the slogan "Say it with flowers"; O'Keefe doubled the flower business between 1921 and 1924. Use of the word "halitosis," seldom heard until an advertising genius employed it, easily overcame the complaint of the American Medical Association that Listerine only covered one smell with another. Someone created a phrase for the American Tobacco Company that candy makers hated: "Reach for a Lucky instead of a sweet." Tobacco ads were especially ingenious. At the beginning of the decade, women asked men to blow some of the smoke their way. At the end, women were shown with cigarette in hand.

Methods employed by advertising executives were subtle. Advertisers spoke not about price but about something being cheaper in the long run. They related the need to keep up with the Joneses. Whatever the item being sold, it would help the buyer be a success. Goods were sold as novelties. There was the indirect approach, in which no blatant message would appear in the ad; for example, a new car stood against a backdrop of luxury or next to a pretty girl, with the name of the automobile printed in the corner. There was an appeal to beauty; stress was not on goods but on appearance. The aesthetic appeal went over well, because women did much of the buying. There was also an appreciation of the value of euphemism—"secondhand" became "used" or "rebuilt," "installment plan" became "deferred-payment plan," the real estate agent became a Realtor, the undertaker a mortician in charge of a funeral home.[14]

Advertising was costly, and apostles believed that it had to be. In 1927, a New York banker estimated that $1.5 billion went into advertising that year. He broke the figure down, counting old-line costs as well as novelties, but the amounts were startling: $800 million to newspapers, $200 million to magazines, $200 million for outdoor displays, $300 million in mail campaigns. Next year, 1928, an estimated $1,782 million went into advertising.[15] The figure was so exact it was unbelievable. For every dollar spent that year for education in the United States, from primary school to university, seventy cents was being spent to educate consumers about what they might buy.

The 1920s was an era of fads. In 1923, the French philosopher Emile Coué charmed Americans by teaching them to say, "Day by day in every way I am getting better and better." Coué Institutes lasted for a short while. In sports, the desire to see Jack Dempsey fight Georges Carpentier approached the proportions of a fad, for 75,000 people paid $1.5 million to see Dempsey flatten Carpentier in the fourth round. Murder cases such as the Hall-Mills trial, in which a minister and his choir leader were found dead in DeRussey's Lane in New Jersey, startled newspaper readers. In 1923, the great news from abroad was discovery of the nearly untouched tomb of Tutankhamen; for a while, it produced a fad of Egyptian-styled clothing.

Beyond fads was real-life heroism, such as Charles A. Lindbergh's 1927 flight from New York to Paris in a single-engine plane. Equally attractive was his modesty, his smile, the pleasure he took in the receptions held across the country. After his return aboard a U.S. Navy cruiser, he was put up by President and Mrs. Coolidge at the temporary White House on Dupont Circle; the mansion on Pennsylvania Avenue was being refurbished. The U.S. Army proudly awarded him the reserve rank of colonel. He went to New York, where the head of the city's reception committee took him through Manhattan at the noon hour (when one could always raise a crowd), bringing down a rain of ticker tape, office memoranda, and torn-up telephone books—eighteen hundred tons of it. "Lindy" flew to Mexico City, where he met the daughter of Ambassador Morrow and, to the delight of his admirers, married her after a storybook courtship.

In the realm of real-life trials, there was the Sacco-Vanzetti affair, which lasted most of the decade—beginning in 1920 and ending with the executions of Nicola Sacco and Bartolomeo Vanzetti in 1927. The men were accused of murdering a paymaster and a guard in South Braintree, Massachusetts. The case elicited countless commentaries from political leaders and journalists, clergymen and philosophers, law professors from Harvard University and elsewhere, producing a great variety of opinions about immigrants and anarchism. Years afterward, in the 1960s, ballistic tests on Sacco's gun showed that it was the weapon that killed the guard, and there were disquieting revelations about the possible complicity of Vanzetti.

In education, the big change was an increase in the high school population: by 1927, half of all youths of high school age were enrolled. The previous century had made primary education universal. In a single decade, high school enrollment moved in that direction. There was improvement in the enrollment of rural youths, but only a third as many country youngsters went on to high school as did city youngsters. College and university enrollment in the 1920s nearly doubled, from 598,000 in 1920 to 1,101,000 in 1930. Yet higher education reached only about one in eight high school graduates.

In theater and poetry, the 1920s did not shine. There were notable exceptions in poetry, however, such as T. S. Eliot's *The Wasteland* (1922) and the poems of Edna St. Vincent Millay. The novel was represented in the books of Sinclair Lewis, *Main Street* (1920) and *Babbit* (1922)—not so much novels as caricatures of life in American towns and cities. They were so cleverly done that they were difficult to dispute. In *Arrowsmith* (1925) he brought back idealism, but in *Elmer Gantry* (1927) he took it away. The 1920s were also the time of Willa Cather's classic *Death Comes for the Archbishop* (1927), and Thornton Wilder's *The Bridge of San Luis Rey* (1927), depicting the places and values of another century and people. Popular novels of the decade were the fictionalized morality tales of Harold Bell Wright, the western tales of Zane Grey, the Tarzan series of Edgar Rice Burroughs, the saccharine stories of Gene Stratton Porter.

In criticism it was the era of Henry L. Mencken, who could amuse readers by describing his journey through dry Pennsylvania seeking a saloon but whose humor paled when he described the political failures of the American people. He was an aristocrat who saw in American politics almost no redeeming features. Sometimes with humor, most of the time with tedious attempts at it, he pointed out the shortcomings of twentieth-century presidents. Theodore Roosevelt was interesting but a boob. Wilson offered his countrymen weekly appendices to the Revelation of St. John the Divine. Harding was "a third-rate political wheel-horse, with the face of a moving-picture actor, the intelligence of a respectable agricultural implement dealer, and the imagination of a lodge joiner."[16] In 1924, Mencken pronounced Coolidge a prospect worse than Harding.

Architecturally, the 1920s saw continued construction of skyscrapers. The dedication to height had its beginnings in the 1890s in New York and Chicago. The Woolworth Building with its sixty stories had gone up in 1913, and during the 1920s it remained the tallest building in New York. By 1928, several higher buildings were under construction. A statistician noted that sixteen hundred buildings in New York City were taller than ten stories. The architecture of the skyscraper was changing, however. In the design competition for the *Chicago Tribune* building in 1922, there was much interest in the second prize awarded to the Finnish architect Eliel Saarinen for a design of vertical mass, without horizontal lines and cornices and curlicues.

Art of the decade belonged to the impressionists, the cubists, and the futurists, with the United States a follower rather than a leader. All these styles had doubtful futures and did not wear well.

In music the 1920s witnessed a flourishing of city symphony orchestras. Opera, too, was staged not merely in New York but in cities across the country. In composition it was the era of such native composers as George Gershwin, who possessed a background in popular music and moved to the concert hall with *Rhapsody in Blue* (1923), *Concerto in F* (1925), and *An American in Paris* (1928). Aaron Copland drew on jazz elements in *Music for the Theater* (1925). The work of Charles Ives, written mostly between the 1890s and 1921, was delayed in recognition until the 1920s. His was the musical language of the 1920s and later, full of quotation of American tunes, patriotic, sentimental, humorous. The period also was a time for blues singers and jazz combos, with W. C. Handy's *St. Louis Blues* (1914) a favorite. The 1920s marked the advent of such jazz soloists as Louis Armstrong, who set new standards of improvisation on the cornet and trumpet.

For the majority of Americans, the decade marked the first time when women, having received the right to vote in 1920, could hold up their heads as equals of men. It was no longer possible to say that "men are God's trees, women are His flowers." The intellectual assertion of equality was often a willingness to talk in the new words of sex (inferiority complex, sadism, masochism, Oedipus complex), to use the words of Sigmund Freud and Carl Jung. Freud had lectured to American psychologists in 1909, but his ideas became important after the war. As for the other assertions of equality by the new woman, the decade's social essayist and assistant editor of *Harper's*, Frederick Lewis Allen, believed that their origin was 100 percent American: Prohibition; the automobile; the confession and sex magazines such as Bernarr McFadden's *True-Story*, with 2 million circulation in 1926; the movies. Youth, Allen wrote, was the pattern, but not youthful innocence. For the new woman, dress was important, which changed from the use of yards of cottons or woolens to cover almost everything to short skirts, long waists, straight silhouettes, topped with bob haircuts and cloche hats. The low point in skirts was perhaps 1919, but happily they were knee-length by 1927. Lipstick was an adornment, when only a few years earlier it would have been more than daring. It was at this time that beauty became an industry, with the appearance of beauty shops that advertised their operators as beauticians.

Despite all the novelty of the decade, the verities had their continuing attraction. In the 1920s, there was a large increase in church membership. The Catholic Church showed remarkable vitality, evident in the Eucharistic Congress of 1926 near Chicago that attracted a million pilgrims from around the world. Membership in the Protestant denominations increased by one-fifth, to include fully half the country's population. In an action much noticed, Coolidge joined the First Congregational Church of Washington on the Sunday after he became president; he had been attending services, and when he became president he took communion and was received into membership.

The 1920s was a markedly religious decade. Every prominent Protestant denomination, an observer declared in 1928, "stands today at the highest point of its history in respect to adherents."[17] Arguments arose for and against fundamentalism, epitomized by the Scopes trial of 1925 in Tennessee, during which William Jennings Bryan defended the Bible against the gibes of agnostic Chicago lawyer Clarence Darrow. The case concerned whether a high school teacher of biology, John T. Scopes, had the right to teach evolution. Scopes and Darrow lost, and commentators lost their judgment watching this virtual circus. "Bible Institutes" of orthodoxy were established to challenge what seemed to be the excesses of liberalism in theological seminaries. But during the decade, neither fundamentalism nor modernism was the issue in religion. Theology did not attract the average church member, who simply thought that she or he ought to go to church on Sundays and believe in the future as well as the moment. If many people read the biography of Jesus, *The Man Nobody Knows,* by Bruce Barton (the head of a New York advertising agency who knew an ideal product), one must doubt that they grasped its message that Jesus was a seller of the Gospel. To them, it was one more devotional book that might help them live out their lives in a proper way.

3

★ ★ ★ ★ ★

I THOUGHT I COULD SWING IT

Coolidge's first reaction to the news that he was president was, "I thought I could swing it." That is what he told artist Charles Hopkinson some years later when Hopkinson was painting his portrait.[1]

There were other reactions from people who had never thought of him as a national figure. Coolidge's elevation nonplussed observers. During his two and a half years under Harding, the vice president had become so inconspicuous he seemed to have painted himself into a corner. A man in charge of booking public figures for speeches around the country told public-relations specialist Edward L. Bernays that he had the vice president on his list and could offer his services cheap. Bernays considered the offer and decided on another speaker.[2] At the outset of Coolidge's presidency, he did not appear to be anything more than Harding's temporary successor, holding the office until the next election. His position within the party was uncertain. The situation was best described by Chief Justice Taft, who wrote that Harding's death turned politics into "a complete jungle," the party "all broken up," no one able to guess what would happen.[3]

It was necessary to convince the unbelievers. In this regard, the new president's first test was to deal with the initial session of the Sixty-eighth Congress, which met from December 1923 until June 1924. He had to control the same proud, sensitive, contentious individuals his predecessor had encountered, notably in the Senate. Harding had sought to get along with Congress, found it impossible, and was beginning to assert himself, marshal public opinion against his opponents, when he died. Coolidge knew little about the legislative branch of the federal government, even though he presided over the Senate. The experience did not make him privy to the Senate's inner workings. Only a few senators had made any effort to make his acquaintance; the rest ignored him, for he seemed to know nothing about national politics. The way in which he had arrived on the national scene did not impress his congressional critics. Mark Sullivan, in December 1923, heard a joke about how Coolidge "got his first base on balls, stole around second (police strike) to 3rd (V.P.) on an error and reached home because the catcher fell dead."[4]

The president's second requirement in proving himself was to show that he could obtain his party's nomination and win the election in 1924. Almost from his first day in the presidential office, Coolidge undertook to do so. He employed his Massachusetts canniness to get rid of several presidential hopefuls within his own party, and before these worthies realized what was going on, they found themselves out of the running. At that juncture, his good fortune reappeared. In a raucous convention at Madison Square Garden in New York that lasted for weeks, two strong Democratic presidential candidates battled each other to a standstill. After 103 ballots, the delegates nominated John W. Davis, a Wall Street lawyer and no party figure. The nominee proved to be an abysmal campaigner, losing votes every time he made a speech. And what the two would-be Democratic presidential nominees and Davis did not do to the Democratic party, Sen. Robert M. La Follette of Wisconsin accomplished. A nominal Republican who was secure in his home state, where every six years his constituents reelected him, he decided that 1924 was his year for the presidency. He was suffering from heart trouble and may have sensed his last chance. He chose to make an independent run, reviving the name of Theodore Roosevelt's Progressive party of 1912. He hurt the Democrats far more than the Republicans, picking up the votes of Wilsonians who would not take Davis. He played into Coolidge's hands.

The first task was to face up to Congress, and the president must have wondered whether he could. When he went before a joint session in the House chamber on 8 December 1923 to deliver his state of the Union message, he did not know that Congress was not going to give him anything; for the next four months, the House and Senate did not act on a single executive proposal.

The scene for Coolidge's initial address to Congress was especially dramatic because of the physical contrast between the president and his predecessor. Harding had been the very picture of a president, tall and dignified, if a little paunchy. He had spent years on the speech circuit and knew how to cut a figure. He was an accomplished orator, possessing an ability to make his audience believe that he was speaking to each individual in the hall. Coolidge, in contrast, had never been an engaging speaker. As one of his Massachusetts friends described him, "His words are trenchant, exact, meaningful, and the delivery of them cold."[5] When he was lieutenant governor and Samuel W. McCall governor, it was said that McCall could fill any auditorium and Coolidge could empty it. One of Coolidge's early biographers, Horace Green, watched him on the day of his maiden speech to Congress and thought that he looked slimmer, younger than he had seen him. His poise and dignity were evident. But the biographer, sitting directly above him in the gallery, saw how his thin hands trembled when turning the manuscript, especially at the beginning. The new president gave the impression of a child "using grave words."[6]

At the beginning of his administration, the New England president decided that because of the circumstances—his replacing an elected chief executive—he should support Harding's legislative program, and in his address, he came out for it. Symbolized by Harding's word "normalcy," the program favored an end to the calls for regeneration and renewal that had characterized President Wilson's first years and then the ardent, idealistic, driving purposes of the war years, followed by the great hope for world peace through the League of Nations. Harding had believed, and Coolidge agreed absolutely, that it was time to return to the time-honored purposes of the Republic, to let opinion catch up with legislation. Like Harding, he said nothing about joining the League of Nations. He favored membership in the league's associated institution, the World Court, as had his predecessor. He opposed the recognition of Russia, for the Bolshevik regime needed to act in a civilized manner. He opposed the cancellation of war debts owed because of credit extended to the nation's associates during the recent war: "I do not favor the cancellation of this debt, but I see no objection to adjusting it in accordance with the principles adopted for the British debt." By that he meant a reduction not of the principal but of the interest rate, which meant a reduction of the total owed.

On domestic issues, he took conservative positions. The drastic drop in the income of American farmers caused by the collapse of world markets after the war did not move him to support legislative measures to dump American grain and other farm products abroad. "No complicated scheme of relief, no plan for government fixing of prices, no resort to the public treasury will be of any value. Simple and direct methods put into operation by the farmer himself are the only real sources for restoration." He was careful to praise veterans of the war as he moved to the touchy subject of a soldiers' bonus, known as adjusted compensation, to make up for low military pay compared with civilian wages during the war. The measure before Congress was in the form of paid-up insurance and would allow veterans to borrow up to 25 percent of its value. "No more important duty falls on the government of the United States than the adequate care of its veterans," he intoned. Then, with typical Coolidge frankness, almost jarring in its expression, he came to the point: "But I do not favor the granting of a bonus."

As for the fiscal program championed by Secretary Mellon, he was completely supportive. For this reason alone he did not want a soldiers' bonus. He advocated reduction of taxes. "Of all services which the Congress can render to the country, I have no hesitation in declaring this one to be paramount. To neglect it, to postpone it, to obstruct it by unsound proposals, is to become unworthy of public confidence and untrue to public trust. The country wants this measure to have the right of way over all others." Lower taxes would bring higher national income and produce more revenue for the treasury, and Mellon could use it to reduce the national debt and thereby the cost of government, which included interest on the debt.

In his state of the Union speech, the president asked for one special tax measure that neither he nor his successors would ever receive: abolition of tax-exempt securities. He and Mellon believed them to be tax shelters, unfair to taxpayers.

A popular proposal of the time, taken partly in hand by the Harding administration, was overhauling the immigration laws, ending the influx that had quickened in the 1880s and by the start of the war in Europe had reached huge proportions. Coolidge endorsed the continuing restriction of immigration embodied in the bill then before Congress.[7]

But it was one thing to propose and another to dispose. Unfortunately for Coolidge, he rose to the presidency at the height of congressional pretensions. The Senate had determined to have its way in all things, but it had little coherence. It was nominally a Republican body but was in fact divided between Republicans of the East, an essentially conservative group, and those of the West, who were conservative on everything but the problems of farmers; on those issues they were not merely radical but were consumed by their constituents' desire for any change that would increase farm income. Similarly, the Democratic senators divided into factions: the southern standpatters who defended the lost cause, which was denial of civil rights to black Americans, and the northern senators who represented large cities with immigrant populations and desired laws protecting city dwellers against rural interests. By and large, the members of the House of Representatives were divided into the same groups, but they were less disciplined than the senators because their elections came every two years.

With Congress fractionalized, Coolidge could only propose legislation and hope that it did not get lost in the swirl of interests. Understandably, he did not get far. He managed to obtain a turndown of a heavily supported agricultural bill. It was not much of a victory, however, only guaranteeing that the agricultural bloc in Congress would put its program up again the next year. He prevented a $68 million raise in post office salaries. Congress nonetheless passed the bill for the bonus to veterans, Coolidge vetoed it, and the House and Senate overrode. It was not kind of Congress, particularly members of Coolidge's own party, to bring up such bills during an election year and, in the case of the bonus bill, defy him.

Congress also undertook three investigations that, although not designed to humiliate the president, gave evidence of doing so. Just a few weeks after he took office, two Senate committees opened hearings on the Veterans' Bureau and on the leasing of naval oil reserves at Teapot Dome in Wyoming and Elk Hills in California to private operators. These investigations were joined early the next year by a third into the conduct of Harding's, now Coolidge's, attorney general, Daugherty. The presumption of the senators was that Daugherty had failed to move quickly enough against the malfeasance of the director of the Veterans' Bureau, Col. Charles R. Forbes, and against the leasing of the oil reserves. These three investigations, all of which involved hearings, looked into what were described as the Harding scandals. They also were congressional object lessons for Harding's successor, showing who was in charge of the federal government.

The Veterans' Bureau scandal was an almost classic affair, involving an administrator who had seemed capable but proved to be the opposite. Forbes had purchased sites for veterans' hospitals at absurdly high prices, involved himself in the construction of the hospitals, and held a clearance sale of hospital supplies housed in a huge depot in Perryville, Maryland. Several individuals told Harding of Forbes's almost obvious malfeasance. According to one story, later verified, Harding summoned Forbes to the White House, seized him by the throat, and shook him like a rat. Unfortunately, Harding had nothing on him at the time; Forbes had continued to sell supplies from the depot, despite a presidential prohibition, but there was no proof that Forbes personally had taken money. Harding dismissed him from the bureau. The proof of Forbes's venality came later when the hearings opened, three months after Harding's death. At that time, the agent for one of the hospital construction companies, Elias H. Mortimer—who was not angry with Forbes for taking money but for paying attentions of an unspecified nature to Mortimer's pretty young wife—told everything he knew about the wayward colonel, which was enough to cost Forbes $10,000 and a prison term.

As testimony developed over management of the Veterans' Bureau, members of the Senate sought to inflate the scandal. To the American public, the newspaper stories, which involved veterans of the recent war, seemed shameful, and the senatorial allegations took the headlines away from the truth and toward what the senators said was the truth. Democrats led by Sens. J. Thomas Heflin of Alabama and Thaddeus Caraway of Arkansas explained how the Republicans had allowed the bureau to get into trouble. The La Follette Republicans agreed with the Democrats and told reporters to expect anything, because "predatory interests" had controlled the Harding administration.

The Senate investigation into the leasing of naval oil reserves at Teapot Dome and Elk Hills to wealthy oilmen Harry F. Sinclair and Edward L. Doheny commenced the day after the opening of the hearings on Forbes, and at the outset, it appeared to be of lesser importance. Things did not heat up until mid-January 1924. Then it became the talk of the nation, the principal point of discussion of American politics. It required Coolidge's careful attention because it raised questions about his party's stewardship and because of its extraordinarily inconvenient timing, just before the Republican national convention in Cleveland, scheduled for mid-June.

Teapot Dome, as the hullabaloo became known, had its quiet beginnings early in the Harding administration when Secretary of the Interior Albert B. Fall arranged with Secretary of the Navy Denby to have the oil reserves transferred to his own department. Harding signed the transfer without much thought, believing that he was simplifying a jurisdictional problem. The next year, Fall arranged for leasing, which seemed sensible because of the widespread belief that private drillers at the edges of the reserves were siphoning off oil and reducing the underlying pools. Secretary Fall announced in January 1923 that he was resigning from the cabinet in March to look after his personal affairs on his ranch at Three Rivers in New Mexico.

Meanwhile, the conservationists of the nation, who had been so prominent during the Theodore Roosevelt administration and had taken great interest in the creation of national parks and the preservation of unexploited portions of the country, were aroused and enlisted Senator La Follette. The Wisconsin senator favored conservation, and he also favored what seemed to be a political opportunity; he had interpreted the Harding administration's loss of congressional seats in the 1922 election as a sign of weakness, and he espied a campaign issue that might assist him in a run for the presidency. Sen. Thomas J. Walsh of Montana, a Democrat, took over leadership of the resultant investigation. Being from a mining state, he was no conservationist. He wanted to hold down any political consequences from the conservationists' claims, in the hope that they would not hurt the Democratic party. Most of the progressives were Democrats, and they might decide to endorse a La Follette candidacy.

At the time of Harding's death in August 1923, there was not the slightest sign that anything would come of Teapot Dome, nor was there when the hearings began in October. When Coolidge gave his state of the Union address in December, there was only a small cloud on the horizon, indiscernible even to the president, who ordinarily could see political clouds smaller than a man's hand. Perhaps he had been encouraged by Chief Justice Taft, who believed that it was just another Ballinger-Pinchot affair (in which President Taft's secretary of the interior, Richard A. Ballinger, was accused by the chief forester of the Department of Agriculture, Gifford Pinchot, of not conserving the country's natural resources). Coolidge agreed and told Taft that "the Republican senators are a lot of damned cowards," meaning that they were not supporting him against the conservationist malcontents and the La Follette progressives.[8]

Fall had seemed an effective administrator when he was in the cabinet. A sign of the esteem in which he was held was the letter that Secretary of Commerce Hoover sent him upon his resignation, which related that the department "never had so constructive and legal a headship as you gave it."[9] But when Fall's sudden affluence became visible through the notable improvements he made on his Three Rivers ranch, Senator Walsh inquired as to the source of Fall's wealth, and the former secretary made his fatal pronouncement that he had borrowed $100,000 from the owner of the *Washington Post*, Edward B. McLean. One assertion led to another, and by mid-January 1924, Teapot Dome was on the front pages every day. McLean could not come to Washington to testify because he was in Florida caring for his sinus trouble. Walsh went to Palm Beach and on 12 January confronted McLean, who said that he had not lent Fall the money. Fall was staying with McLean at the time but refused to give testimony to Walsh, saying that he had borrowed money from McLean but had given it back and then borrowed elsewhere. Furthermore, he would not discuss his private business with Walsh, who was there to talk with McLean, and in any event, Walsh was only one member of the committee. Doheny, the lessee of Elk Hills, then testified before the committee on 24 January that he had lent the money to Fall and that his son had carried the cash to Fall in November 1921 "in a little black bag." In the next days, the committee heard testimony that Sinclair, the lessee of Teapot Dome, had provided Fall with liberty bonds.

Damage control was needed, and Coolidge supplied it as best he could. He issued a "midnight" statement on 28 January. Understanding of his developing crisis had overwhelmed him while aboard the *Mayflower*, forcing him to turn the ship back to Washington and hasten to his study in the White House:

> It is not for the President to determine criminal guilt or render judgment in civil cases. That is the function of the courts. It is not for him to prejudge. I

shall do neither; but when facts are revealed to me that require action for the purpose of insuring the enforcement of either civil or criminal liability, such action will be taken. That is the province of the Executive. . . . Counsel will be instructed to prosecute these cases in the courts, so that if there is any guilt it will be punished; if there is any civil liability, it will be enforced; if there is any fraud, it will be revealed; and if there are any contracts which are illegal, they will be canceled. Every law will be enforced and every right of the people and the Government will be protected.

The "counsel" he mentioned were to be two independent lawyers, one from each political party, appointed by the president. For the Republicans he appointed a lawyer from Philadelphia, Owen J. Roberts, who later became an associate justice of the Supreme Court. For the Democrats he appointed Thomas W. Gregory, attorney general in the Wilson administration.

On 1 February, Doheny returned to testify and, irritated by the committee's questioning and by Walsh's posturing, said that he had employed four former members of President Wilson's cabinet: Secretary of the Interior Franklin K. Lane, Secretary of War Lindley M. Garrison, Attorney General Gregory, and Secretary of the Treasury William G. McAdoo, who was Wilson's son-in-law. When Doheny identified Gregory as one of the recipients of his payments, he made Gregory's appointment as counsel impossible, and the president replaced him with a former senator from Ohio, Atlee Pomerene. It was interesting that Gregory did not disqualify himself until Doheny's payment—admittedly a small one, $2,000—was revealed. In McAdoo's case, Doheny said that he had retained him at $50,000 a year, a princely sum. McAdoo was the leading contender for the 1924 Democratic nomination. Asked why he had employed McAdoo and the others, Doheny explained, "I paid them for their influence."

The next day, Fall appeared in a packed Senate caucus room, looking ill, and read, "I decline . . . to answer any questions on the ground that it may tend to incriminate me."

By a partisan vote, the Senate on 11 February asked the president to dismiss Secretary Denby from the cabinet. Four hours later, Coolidge put off the committee with another statement. "As soon as special counsel can advise as to the legality of these issues and assemble for me the pertinent facts . . . I shall take such action as seems essential for the full protection of the public interests. The dismissal of an officer of the Government . . . other than by impeachment, is exclusively an executive function." The president annexed the opinions of Presidents James Madison and Grover Cleveland—the one far enough back to be considered bipartisan (although the word was not yet in use in the 1920s), the other a member of the Democratic party.

After this second statement, the president discovered that he could not save Secretary Denby, who resigned on his own volition, with no presidential pressure that has ever been recorded. Denby may have realized that by signing over jurisdiction of the oil reserves without making an issue of it, he had implicated himself in the resultant scandal and therefore harmed his position if not with Harding then with his successor. He may also have sensed that even if Coolidge had protected him at the moment, the president would not do so in the future, and surely after the forthcoming election would have made him walk the plank. Denby manfully explained his resignation: "I am able to fight my own battles, but I cannot fight slander protected by senatorial immunity." He thanked the president with "deep appreciation" for the "strong message." Coolidge wrote a farewell letter that he must have composed himself: "It is with regret that I am to part with you. You will go with the knowledge that your honesty and integrity have not been impugned."[10] But it is difficult not to conclude that Coolidge was cutting his losses, surrendering to the Senate so that with the help of Roberts and Pomerene he could fight another day.

Just what happened to remove Teapot Dome from the front pages is uncertain. Fortunately for Coolidge, by May it was all over. The public may have seen too much politics in the bellowing of La Follette, followed by Walsh's journey to Florida, the twists and turns of the principals; after a while, it was difficult to keep up interest. It is possible, too, that the war's benefits for capitalists and corporations, some of which had emerged by this time, made the payments to Fall of $100,000 (Doheny's) and $304,000 (Sinclair's) seem bagatelles. Moreover, it was news that had to compete with other sensational events. Too, the very appearance of the new president in the White House—the man who had lived at 21 Massasoit Street, Northampton, a side-by-side double house, and, during his presidency, feared that his rent, $30 a month, might be raised—created an atmosphere in Washington that assisted in dispelling the miasma of the oil scandal. He was a dour man, and his facial expression—the way in which both sides of his mouth turned down—seemed to say that he had nothing to do with scandal and the nation could rely on him.

The investigation was virtually finished by spring 1924. When the Senate committee held its last hearing early in May, not a single spectator was present. In June, the president's investigators recommended the prosecution of Doheny's son (the bagman), Doheny, Sinclair, and Fall. A few years were necessary to organize and conduct the trials. A household servant murdered the son in 1929, removing him from prosecution. In 1930, the father went free on the claim that he had not intended to bribe Fall. Sinclair received six months in jail for contempt of Congress and jury tampering, not for bribery. In 1931, the former secretary of the interior went to prison for one year.

Teapot Dome flared up again in 1928, suitably before the presidential election. It came to light that Harding's postmaster general, Will H. Hays, who had retired from the cabinet in 1922 to head the Motion Picture Producers and Distributors of America with the task of "cleaning up" the movies, had allowed oil money to pass into the coffers of the national committee of the GOP. Hays received the money in the form of liberty bonds, which he assigned to leading party members to exchange for cash; he asked Secretary Mellon to exchange $50,000 worth of bonds, and Mellon chose not to undertake this laundering task, replying that he wished to make a personal contribution to the party in the same amount. He did not see fit to inform anyone of the request nor chide Hays for making it. Hays suffered a memory loss and could not recall the details of how he had accepted the bonds or what had happened to them.

The third scandal that arose after Coolidge assumed the presidency involved Attorney General Daugherty. Actually, the scandal was attributable to Daugherty's closest friend, Jess W. Smith, of Washington Court House, Ohio. When Smith was a youth, Daugherty had virtually adopted him, and Smith in turn attached himself to Daugherty like a dog. When Daugherty went to Washington to join Harding's cabinet, Smith accompanied him. Daugherty's wife was an invalid and was often hospitalized or in Florida, so Daugherty arranged for Smith to stay in his Wardman Park Hotel apartment and to have a desk in the Department of Justice, although he was not employed there. Neither of these arrangements was wise. Smith was a loud-talking, obnoxious individual and gave the impression that he was close to the attorney general. The desk in the department seemed to confirm it. It is possible that word got to President Harding that Smith was involved in an illegal scheme involving the alien property custodian, Col. Thomas W. Miller. In any case, Harding learned that Smith was acting improperly and told Daugherty to get him out of Washington. Smith was about to leave but changed his mind and shot himself in Daugherty's apartment one morning while the attorney general was at the White House. After Smith's death, it became evident that he had taken $224,000 of a $391,000 bribe paid by a German national to obtain reimbursement for the confiscation and sale of a family-owned firm during the war. In fact, the seizure and sale had been altogether proper, and the German had a fraudulent claim—hence the need for the bribe. In addition to Smith's involvement, John T. King, a Republican fixer who died before he could be sent to jail, took $112,000. Miller took $50,000 and eventually went to jail. No one was able to trace what happened to the balance of the bribe—$5,000.

The Daugherty case was first taken up by a special Senate committee headed by a freshman senator, Smith W. Brookhart of Iowa. The committee was dominated by another freshman senator, Burton K. Wheeler of Montana. Brookhart was a Republican, Wheeler a Democrat; both were political mavericks. Brookhart was proud of his middle name, which was Wildman, and Wheeler was to be La Follette's vice-presidential running mate on the Progressive ticket in the presidential election. Wheeler in particular was a wild card in the deck of American politics, and for a short time in the spring of 1924, he created almost as much newspaper attention as did his fellow Montanan Walsh. Indeed, that might have been his purpose.

The investigations of the Brookhart-Wheeler committee were sheer melodrama. Wheeler's memoirs of forty years later relate how he took a train to Columbus, Ohio, and subpoenaed the ex-wife of Jess Smith and personally brought her back to Washington to testify before the committee as its first witness. Roxie R. Stinson was an impressive redhead, and for a while, her stories made good newspaper copy, although what she knew was less important than she claimed. What she did not claim to know, Wheeler filled in with the testimony of a former Department of Justice employee, Gaston B. Means. The latter weighed three hundred pounds and possessed a baby face and a convincing, even authoritative manner. A few years later, after a prison term for violating the Volstead Act, Means wrote *The Strange Death of President Harding* (1930), in which he intimated that Florence Harding, whom he had never met, told him that she had poisoned her husband. After this publication, he obtained $104,000 from Ned McLean's gullible wife, Evalyn, to give to the kidnapper of the Lindberghs' baby. When the child was found dead, the kidnapper identified, and Means failed to give the money back, Evalyn McLean took him to court and sent him to prison a second time.

For all its activity, the Brookhart-Wheeler committee never secured anything on Daugherty. A U.S. attorney for the southern district of New York, in whose jurisdiction the former attorney general was tried, attempted to show that because Smith took $224,000 and King $112,000, it stood to reason that Smith had divided his take with Daugherty, but there was no proof. Indeed, Daugherty was neither the fool nor the knave he was drawn to be. As Harding's campaign manager, he had been highly effective. No friend of Forbes, he had warned Harding about him. He and Fall disliked each other. Chief Justice Taft liked Daugherty, who consulted with Taft on the appointment of federal judges and accepted Taft's choices. When Daugherty died years later, his estate amounted to $175,000.[11]

Coolidge sought valiantly to regain control over the Daugherty issue, and it was difficult work. He had to treat the matter with care, if only because he was also receiving demands for Denby's resignation. Another reason was that he knew that Daugherty was unbalanced and needed protection. Dr. Boone may have spoken to the president about this, for he was seeing Daugherty professionally and was convinced that the attorney general had suffered a stroke in the spring of 1923. Boone had gone to Florida and North Carolina with Daugherty for several weeks to care for him. In public, it was said that the attorney general had suffered a breakdown. For months he was irrational. Boone took him to the dentist early in 1924 and he talked in tirades, said that he was running his own office, letting his lawyer handle the Senate investigation. He seemed to resent any claim that he was physically unable to carry on. He wanted Boone to tell the press that he was in fine shape.[12] After the investigation began, Coolidge called one of Daugherty's principal critics, Sen. William E. Borah of Idaho, to the White House and asked his views on the attorney general. Borah advised the president to dismiss him. Within minutes, Daugherty appeared; the president had summoned both men to fight it out. Daugherty remarked sarcastically to Borah, "Well, don't let my presence embarrass you." Borah responded, "I think I should be the least embarrassed person here." For an hour the two argued.[13] The White House social secretary, Mary Randolph, described how "I sat in the White House at my desk in the alcove over the great front door, saw Daugherty come up the grand stairway and go into the President's study—his jaw set and his eye like flint. With my own ears I heard his vociferous denials—his loud and angry protestations—as President Coolidge and his advisers strove with him in the President's study. And I saw him come out again, white with rage—watched him stamp angrily down the stairs and out of the house."[14]

Mark Sullivan called on Coolidge to urge him to get rid of Daugherty. The president said, "In confidence, the trouble with Daugherty is mental." He said also that Daugherty's son was "defective." The son, an alcoholic and a wastrel, was causing trouble; he eventually was committed to an asylum. The president told Sullivan, "I wouldn't be surprised to see a blowup any time."[15]

Coolidge finally had to demand Daugherty's resignation. The attorney general went to the White House again, this time by himself, and spoke roughly to Coolidge, refusing to resign. Coolidge's Massachusetts friend, Butler, was staying at the mansion, and after Daugherty left, the president said to Butler, "He should not have talked to me as he did." Butler advised sending Daugherty a note telling him that he was dismissed, and on 27 March, that is what happened. The president's private secretary, Slemp, sent a note saying that "the president directs me to notify you that he expects your resignation at once."[16] The nominal reason was the issue of giving records of his department to the Brookhart-Wheeler committee.

The business of handling the resignation, with its appearance of having been forced by a Senate committee as irresponsible as that of Brookhart and Wheeler, had been as complicated as Teapot Dome. Two days after Daugherty's dismissal, 29 March, Mrs. Coolidge told Boone that she felt badly about it. The next day, the president explained himself. Daugherty, he said, was a strong man, courageous, won people to him; the department was in fine condition, and his accomplishments and achievements were remarkable. But Coolidge needed an attorney general free from attack, disinterested in the investigation of himself and his office.[17]

The Daugherty affair did not end in 1924. It went on in private for years, ending with Daugherty's death in 1941. Not long before Coolidge left office in 1929, by which time the Harding scandals had receded in public memory, Dr. Boone received a letter from Daugherty enclosing a sealed letter addressed to the president. The physician talked it over with Slemp's successor, Sanders, who took it up with the president. Coolidge called Boone and Sanders into the office, weighed the matter, and said, "Do not reply to H.M.D. but if necessary to say anything to him you can tell him you delivered his letter to the president but do not know whether he read it or not." He added to the men in the office, "I will tell you, however, that I do not intend to open the letter." He read Daugherty's cover letter to Boone, gave it back, and explained, "I do not know whether you know it or not but Daugherty is not mentally sound." By this time, Daugherty had been tried twice in federal court, and each time the jury failed to convict him, although the second failure was by a single vote. Ten years later, in 1939, six years after Coolidge's death, Daugherty sent Boone a copy of the Coolidge letter, in which he had asked the president to "say in a public way that time, trials and court actions and findings, as well as unquestionable facts, have proven my integrity and faithfulness."[18] It was a pathetic request.

Coming into the White House, Coolidge managed a standoff with the imperious Senate. At the same time, he was bolstering his personal political position, looking to the Republican nomination in 1924 and the election the following November. In handling both tasks, the president showed that all the years beginning with ward politics in Northampton had not been wasted. It is possible that some of the calculation he seemed to display was just another case of Coolidge luck, but there was too much success for it to have been only that.

Quietly he disposed of his competitors for the nomination. The first episode in their disappearance came in the autumn of 1923, when there was a strike in the anthracite coal fields of Pennsylvania, timed before winter, when householders and industrial users would need Pennsylvania's prime product. This gave the president an opportunity to assign the task of mediating between strikers and mine owners to Governor Pinchot, of Ballinger-Pinchot fame, who had presidential ambitions. Coolidge knew that something had to be done and that whoever did it would attract the dissatisfaction of both parties. Pinchot wanted to step in, and Coolidge let him.

The way in which Coolidge handled Pinchot was so typical of Massachusetts politics writ large on the national scene that it deserves mention in detail. It not only showed how Coolidge got rid of Pinchot but also illustrated one of the president's favorite aphorisms: never do something yourself that you can get someone else to do. At the outset, to be sure, Coolidge knew that he was dealing with the man who in 1902 had advised Roosevelt to bring miners and operators to Washington and mediate a strike that seemed destined to last forever. Roosevelt had been given great credit for his role in that affair, and Pinchot, observing the success of his advice, was likely to try it again. Sure enough, the Pennsylvania governor, anticipating a strike on the miners' deadline of 1 September 1923, spoke with the president on the day after Harding's funeral and offered his cooperation. Perhaps under the influence of grief, Coolidge did not seem to be concentrating on the Pennsylvania matter. Thinking how Roosevelt might have reacted, and certain that Coolidge suffered by comparison, Pinchot on 15 August urged arbitration, including announcement of the members of the arbitral board. On 23 August, beside himself over presidential inaction, the governor telephoned the president's secretary and said that if Coolidge would do nothing it was the duty of the governor to act. Coolidge might have smiled when he learned of the telephone call, and he certainly did nothing, except to invite Pinchot to lunch the next day, along with mining engineer John Hays Hammond, chairman of the United States Coal Commission, which had been established in 1922 as strictly an advisory board. The luncheon went off as planned—a social occasion. After Coolidge took Pinchot and Hammond upstairs for cigars, Hammond gave Pinchot a rundown on the nation's coal problems that ensured that any settlement of the prospective strike would be according to the Coolidge plan, not the Pinchot plan that the governor appeared to have in his pocket. After the meeting, a White House press release related that Governor Pinchot was going to act in "cooperation" with federal authorities. According to Hammond's autobiography, "President Coolidge many times referred to this as our 'coup.'"

Everything worked out as Coolidge planned. After the luncheon, Pinchot was on his own. The strike began on 1 September and was over on 7 September. The settlement for 150,000 miners, obtained in the approved Rooseveltian manner, with Pinchot as Roosevelt, gave the miners a 10 percent wage increase. "It is one of those things," Pinchot wrote, "that happened to work out just exactly right. Of course I am perfectly delighted." Congratulatory letters came from friends and national leaders. Coolidge sent "heartiest congratulations" and told the governor that he could not commend his service too highly. "It was a very difficult situation," the president said, "in which I invited your cooperation." The president added a handwritten note inviting him to be a guest at the White House soon. But Pinchot gained the undying enmity of the conservatives of his own party, whose authority centered in Pittsburgh's best-known resident, Secretary

Mellon, whose coal company was involved. "Old Andy Mellon," as Coolidge privately described him, appears to have made sure of the Pennsylvania delegation's lack of enthusiasm for Pinchot at the forthcoming convention. Coolidge, who must have smiled all the time to himself, would have smiled again when the anthracite settlement that worked out exactly right ended in 1925 in another strike that lasted six months and that the ambitious governor was in no hurry to settle.[19]

Pinchot was the first intraparty antagonist that Coolidge separated from the nomination, and one by one the other contenders dropped out. Governor Frank O. Lowden of Illinois had lost the Republican nomination in 1920 because he and his principal opponent, Maj. Gen. Leonard Wood, not merely fought each other to a standstill but also spent too much money in the process. In 1923, Lowden was busy arranging conferences with wheat producers in the Midwest, seeking an agreement that would allow them to propose a government program to raise the price of wheat. Coolidge seems not to have thought on this subject beyond his Vermont experience, where wheat was not a farm product. He decided against such a program, except for palliatives, and must have known that Lowden would be able to do little more than produce a cacophony of suggestions for allaying the farmers' plight. The governor received headlines, but his program never developed, and he had no time to contest the nomination with the president.

General Wood was in the Philippines, where Harding had sent him to take back the political power the Wilson administration had given to the Filipinos. The task was so large that he had little time to think of the nomination. Moreover, he suffered from a brain tumor and would die in 1927 during an operation to remove it.

The most likely candidate for the nomination, other than the president, was automobile magnate Henry Ford. Harding had feared a Ford candidacy, and on his cross-country trip to Tacoma and Alaska, he apparently was calculating not in terms of showing himself to the people of Alaska, who could not vote, or taking a vacation, which he needed, but in displaying his attractive personality to the people of the western states. Mrs. Harding had an acute political sensitivity and wrote to a friend just before the trip that many westerners did not know they had a president, and Warren was about to show them. Ford was a danger. Indeed, when Harding died in the early evening of 2 August in San Francisco at the Palace Hotel, his wife was supposedly reading a magazine article to her husband about himself and entitled "A Calm Review of a Calm Man," out of the *Saturday Evening Post,* but she was actually reading an article about Ford out of the *Dearborn Independent.* Even in his last moments, Harding was thinking of Ford.

The father of the Model T excited people everywhere, especially westerners, whose distances the automobile promised to conquer. Straw votes made him the voters' first choice. But something happened to Ford. In December 1923, he and Coolidge met at the White House, after which the president sent a message to Congress offering a plan for the sale of two wartime government nitrate plants, a steam generating plant, and a dam at or near Muscle Shoals in Alabama—a plan that fitted an offer Ford had made to turn Muscle Shoals into a great place for the production of fertilizer or perhaps electric power. Not long afterward, on 18 December, Ford punctured his own presidential balloon by declaring himself for Coolidge: "I would never for a moment think of running against Calvin Coolidge for president." There was talk of an arrangement. Probably his decision was only more evidence of Ford's shifting ideas and the vagaries of his enthusiasms. Politics may have left his mind, if it was ever there, in favor of a great new chapter of industrial leadership at Muscle Shoals, in which case he would consign the lesser prize, the presidency, to Coolidge.[20]

Although he supported the industrialist's interest in Muscle Shoals, Coolidge sat back and watched Ford make one mistake after another. In 1921, Ford had journeyed to Muscle Shoals in his private railway car, the *Fair Lane*, but real estate operators had gotten in ahead of him and bought up land in the area he proposed to turn into a rural megacity, seventy-five miles long, next to the factory he would build to supply nitrates to the nation's farmers, or perhaps it was electricity to the megacity. Soon everyone was confused, and a certification of that fact was a drop in real estate prices. Ford blew hot and cold on Muscle Shoals. As he moved in other directions, his incessant anti-Semitic remarks so irritated Wall Street lawyer Samuel Untermeyer that the latter published a slashing attack:

> The man is so densely ignorant on every subject except automobiles and so blinded by a depth of bigotry that belongs to the dark ages from which he has not emerged, that he is fool enough to publicly exploit this madhouse bug of his about the international bankers owning the gold of the world. He imagines that the great international bankers of the world are Jews, which is not true. . . . Why can't the people realize that a cheap, petty, ignorant man who has grown rich can get just as crazy as any poor devil of an inmate of a lunatic asylum? The only difference is that the one is locked up for the public safety, while the other is permitted to roam at large to the great peril of the public.[21]

In such ways Coolidge dispatched his rivals, or they dispatched themselves. Meanwhile, in a wise move two days after the state of the Union address, that is, on 8 December 1923, he made his own move for the nomination. His trustworthy friend Stearns announced that the president's friends were organizing to place his name before the party's convention in Cleveland. It was a wise move, for three reasons. First, Stearns made the announcement, not the president; if anything immediately went awry, Coolidge could have disowned the statement. Second, the president in his address had declared his platform, which, with the possible exception of his opposition to the soldiers' bonus, was a good program—basically, that of Harding. He would have known that La Follette, who was being coy about his own candidacy, would take the opposite program. That would leave the Democrats in the middle with no program except for the scandal in the Veterans' Bureau, which had not come to much; Teapot Dome had not yet developed. Third, by announcing half a year before the convention, the president could gather delegates, force them to commit their votes in advance of the occasion. If they did not commit, they would lay themselves open to retribution. Thus, with the assistance of Stearns and, as the statement read, "organizing under the guidance of William M. Butler, who will act as the President's personal representative," the president soon tied up the delegates. By April 1924, Butler had a majority, all Coolidge needed. By that time, nothing—not even Teapot Dome and the Daugherty affair—could displace him.

The Republicans held their convention in June, at the new Cleveland Public Auditorium. The huge hall gave the appearance of a giant horseshoe because of its long, almost encircling balcony. Coolidge might have interpreted this as a sign of good luck. Upon assembling, the delegates did what they were supposed to do, which was listen to the necessary speeches and nominate the president. Coolidge did not attend; he remained in Washington. The convention had its moments. Some of them involved the presentation of laurels to the Ohio presidents, Ulysses S. Grant, Rutherford B. Hayes, James A. Garfield, McKinley, Taft, and, of course, Harding. The high point of the speeches may have been the remarks of Addison G. Proctor, an eighty-six-year-old from St. Joseph, Michigan, the last survivor of the convention that had nominated Lincoln in 1860. Proctor told the delegates in what Rep. Joseph Martin of Massachusetts considered a fine piece of understatement, "In the nomination of Lincoln, it seems to me, we builded better than we knew."[22] To be sure, all these honored representatives of the GOP brought luster to the convention's choice of 1924.

The only remaining business lay in the choice of a vice-presidential running mate, in which the president took as much advantage as he could. He dangled the vice-presidential nomination before whatever party leaders might think it attractive. After the election, the president's secretary, Slemp (who knew something of the presidential mind; upon retirement, he edited a collection of Coolidge documents entitled *The Mind of the President*), told Dr. Boone during a trip down the Potomac on the *Mayflower* that Butler had behaved "terribly" at Cleveland by supporting former senator William S. Kenyon of Iowa, Congressman Theodore E. Burton of Ohio, and Secretary of Commerce Hoover. It is possible that Slemp was indirectly criticizing his chief, with whom he had differences. But he should have understood Butler's tactics. Burton was anxious for the vice presidency and required a little flattery. Kenyon and Hoover had the advantage of being western men and could help the ticket's geographic spread. Even if they did not make it at the convention, they, like Burton, would feel better. The president spoke favorably of Governor Arthur M. Hyde of Missouri and Representative Sanders of Indiana, soon to become his secretary.

Coolidge made a serious attempt to get Senator Borah on the ticket. The Idahoan would have helped the spread and was a well-known progressive who needed to be kept away from the La Follette insurgency. He enjoyed enormous popularity in his state. It was said that he only had to send home a notice every six years that he was eligible for reelection; his campaign fund once consisted of only $200 he had put up. Nationally, he was attractive. The Lion of Idaho parted his hair down the middle; he had a voice as big as Bryan's and was a similar spellbinder. He had a way of touching whatever seemed close to the national psyche.

But Borah refused to go on the ticket. In November 1923, he told Mark Sullivan that Coolidge's friends were urging him, but he was uncertain. He would have to forfeit his Senate seat, which he had possessed since 1907, as he was up for reelection in 1924.[23] At that time, although he did not say so, he could not have been at all certain that Coolidge could win. Moreover, if Coolidge did win, carrying Borah into office, he would have to keep his mouth shut during the next four years, as Coolidge had done for two and a half. Borah was no man to do that.

As the months passed, Coolidge pressed Borah. Washington reporter Frederick William Wile observed in his news column that "by every means at the President's command the Coolidge steam roller at Cleveland is to be lubricated with western grease."[24] On 12 June, Borah was summoned by the president. Coolidge said that the convention was going to nominate the senator, that no one had ever declined a nomination for vice president, and that he did not see how anyone could. According to Sullivan, Borah told the president that he could and he would; he had sent a letter to Cleveland to that effect, which was in the care of a friend, former senator Albert J. Beveridge of Indiana.[25] Coolidge asked Borah to telephone Stearns in Cleveland and repeat what he had said to the president, which he did. At that juncture, something may have gone wrong between Coolidge and Butler, but probably not. Remembering his own possible declination of the vice presidency through Crane in 1920 and his receptivity to a draft, Coolidge may have told Butler to go ahead, which Butler did.

The convention drafted Borah, and the senator did as promised, turning the nomination down. Boone, present on the second floor of the White

House, sat with Mrs. Coolidge listening to the radio. The president was walking in the garden looking for wild rabbits, playing with the dogs, occasionally passing the radio and making humorous remarks. When Borah refused, Coolidge gave the impression of having suffered a severe blow and during a silent prayer before the convention's noon session sat with closed eyes in the west sitting room.[26]

About the rest of it, including finding a running mate, Coolidge gave the impression of utter boredom. Governor Lowden was nominated, and Ted Clark came over from the executive offices, only to discover that the president had gone to sleep in his room. He said to Mrs. Coolidge, "I must confer with the president immediately!" Mrs. Coolidge went in and woke him up, and a sleepy president came out into the west hall and sat down in a large chair with his feet on the radiator or sill. Clark told him of the nomination, and Coolidge said nothing. Clark said, "I know you wish to and should send Governor Lowden a message of congratulations." Coolidge dictated a brief one. Then Lowden turned the nomination down. The convention finally nominated General Dawes. The general was like an Illinois Borah—earnest, jowly, sharp-eyed, hair similarly parted down the middle—and although he did not balance the ticket, he was acceptable. Like Borah, he was hardly a Coolidge intimate, but he would do. Meanwhile, Coolidge had gone back to sleep. Again Clark came over and asked for the president. Mrs. Coolidge smiled broadly and pointed toward the bedroom and said, "Asleep."

Clark said, "He will have to be awakened, for it is very necessary that I confer with him."

Upon being told that Dawes had been nominated, the president said nothing for a while; he pulled out a Corona cigar and started smoking and seemed to be deep in thought. Clark finally said, "Mr. President, you now have to send General Dawes a message of congratulations."

The president maintained silence and then in his nasal voice said, "Send him the same message I sent Lowden."

Clark composed another message, and all was well. The president was not enthusiastic about Dawes, however. Mrs. Coolidge, who was careful about political matters but who must have heard from her husband in this regard, later told Boone that she did not like Dawes, but it was necessary to work with the tools at hand.[27]

Such were Coolidge's troubles obtaining a vice-presidential nominee, but they were nothing compared with the Democrats' troubles. The major problem was Doheny's testimony on 1 February before the Teapot Dome committee that their principal contender for the presidential nomination, McAdoo, was in his employ. The testimony had been provoked by the committee chairman, a Republican, acting on instructions from Sen. James

A. Reed of Missouri, who was himself campaigning for the Democratic nomination and wanted McAdoo out of the race. By chance, McAdoo was in Washington because of the fatal illness of his father-in-law. A few days after Doheny mentioned his name, McAdoo went before the committee and put the best face he could on his cupidity. Tall, wiry, and bright, he could make his points forcefully. But he had taken too much money, and it turned out that his law firm had also received a $100,000 fee from Doheny, with the oilman promising a total fee of $1 million if the McAdoo partners could alleviate his difficulties with the Mexican government over his enormous holdings south of the border. A cartoon of the time showed McAdoo as a waiter, serving a salad to a lady labeled "McAdoo Democrats." "Is there too much oil?" he asked. "O, William!" was the answer. "It's perrfectly de-e-licious."

With McAdoo weakened, it was the party's further ill fortune that Governor Smith of New York put himself forward, in the belief that his remoteness from Washington scandals might bring him the presidency. To many northern Democrats ,the raspy-voiced governor from the sidewalks of New York was their favorite. Franklin Roosevelt introduced him to the convention as "the happy warrior." He seemed the ideal representation of the "city man" in a nation that, by 1920, had become more urban than rural. "There ain't no oil on Al," sang his supporters. Years later, in the 1980s, it was discovered that Smith may have taken $400,000 from a prominent New York City lawyer who desired a rise in the city's nickel subway fare.

After McAdoo and Smith canceled each other out, there was not much choice. Senator Walsh was receptive, but by this time he had shown himself to be sufficiently partisan in the conduct of the Teapot Dome investigation that he remained in the Senate. Another Democratic hopeful was former governor Samuel Ralston of Indiana, sixty-eight years old and corpulent. His physician advised him not to try for the nomination, and he died the next year.

In sheer desperation, after weeks in steamy Madison Square Garden, the Democrats nominated Davis, who had been ambassador to London in the last months of the Wilson administration. He had gone to New York from West Virginia and traded weakly on his onetime residence in that hardly illustrious state, hoping that it would remove the stigma of Wall Street. He was a poor choice in 1924, and he knew it. He took the nomination as a testimony to his virtues, if also to his party's bankruptcy.

To lend even more unlikelihood to the Democratic ticket, the party leaders joined Davis with Governor Charles W. Bryan of Nebraska, brother of William Jennings Bryan. By this time, the better-known Bryan had lost out in American politics, after running in 1896, 1900, and 1908. Sullivan described him in 1923 as a troubadour going up and down the country making speeches that were unreported in the newspapers, with no hearing outside the communities in which he delivered them.[28] Charley Bryan did not look like his brother. Six foot one, he had a mustache and wore oval, rimless glasses. He wore a black silk skullcap because light shining on his bald head gave him pain. He had a staccato speaking style. He added nothing to the ticket and in a vague, undefined way lent it a crank aspect.

Confirming the forthcoming defeat of the Democrats was appearance of the hastily organized third party, the La Follette Progressives, who accepted a platform written solely by their leader. It condemned everything Coolidge would run on. It spoke of the current "mercenary system of degraded foreign policy," whatever that meant—perhaps a criticism of the World Court. It condemned the Mellon tax program. It favored a soldiers' bonus. La Follette's running mate was Senator Wheeler.

The only question about the Progressive party of 1924 was whether it would remove the presidential choice to the House of Representatives. Or, put slightly differently: how strong was progressivism? After Wilson espoused it in the New Freedom program in 1912, in opposition to Theodore Roosevelt's New Nationalism, the progressives had divided between the Democrats and Roosevelt's new party. The Rooseveltians returned to Republicanism in 1916. The world war turned attention elsewhere, and in 1924, the Progressives were not numerous enough to make the new party a lively organization. The bond that held it together was La Follette, who was no Roosevelt. He confused his anti-Coolidge platform by talking about issues of the 1890s, when he had entered public life, about the trusts and the money power. Wheeler talked about the Harding scandals, another dead issue.

Republican speech making that fall was mostly by campaigners other than Coolidge. Calvin, Jr., had died in July. Coolidge made a few set-piece speeches and left the campaigning to Dawes, who took over. Dawes traveled 15,000 miles in a special train, made 108 speeches, and obtained 350,000 listeners, not counting radio audiences for night speeches. It was enough to make one dizzy. He gave audiences a choice. "Where do you stand?" he shouted, his Hoover collar shaking. "With President Coolidge on the Constitution with the flag, or on the sinking sands of Socialism?" Davis sought to get off the sands onto Teapot Dome and other subjects. The less Charley Bryan said the better. La Follette and Wheeler shouted their irrelevancies, and Dawes made fun of them. "The voices of the demagogues are like the faint, plaintive cries of the peewit in the wilderness," he said. The country laughed at the comparison to the chirping of a tiny bird.[29]

Victory was visible from the beginning. Dawes sent Coolidge a poll from Fairbury, Nebraska, in a county with 5,200 registered voters. It was Charley Bryan country. The Fairbury newspapers polled 3,000 visitors to the county fair, and the result was Coolidge 1,700, Davis 800, and La Follette 500. Nationally, it was 15.7 million for Coolidge, 8.3 million for Davis, and 4.9 million for La Follette.[30] In the electoral vote, the result was overwhelming; the president received 382 ballots to 136 and 13, respectively. The decisiveness of the electoral vote occurred because the Republicans carried the border states along the South. The Solid South may have been solid, but it was an enclave against all the rest of the states that voted Republican.

4

★ ★ ★ ★ ★

INDUSTRY AND LABOR

"While anything that relates to the functions of the government is of enormous interest to me," Coolidge wrote in his autobiography, "its economic relations have always had a peculiar fascination for me." He rightly sensed that in politics it was safer to deal with economics, if only because economics were visible; one could see the results, for good or ill. Voters could see the results. Other issues on which a politician might attempt to base policy could have a greater initial attraction, they might stir souls, yet there was the danger that the more ethereal, the more removed from the visible they were, the more likely it was that some other politician might claim the result. In the peroration to his state of the Union address to Congress in December 1923, the most important speech of his presidency, Coolidge announced, "We want idealism. We want that vision which lifts men and nations above themselves. These are virtues by reason of their own merit. But they must not be cloistered; they must not be impractical; they must not be ineffective." He might as well have added that they should, if possible, be economic. Throughout his presidency, these were the issues that he usually advanced.

People would make fun of the president of the 1920s, saying that he was the author of statements that looked too much to the nation's economy. Coolidge, the critics announced, did not understand that twentieth-century Americans needed idealism. They pointed out his best-known remark, offered in a speech to the Society of American Newspaper Editors in January 1924, that "the chief business of the American people is business." Although it was true that he liked to address economic issues, he

61

said other things as well. Wealth, he remarked in the speech to the editors, was not the chief end of man. It was a means to "well-nigh every desirable achievement." He spoke of "the multiplication of schools, the increase of knowledge, the dissemination of intelligence, the encouragement of science, the broadening of outlook, the expansion of liberties, the widening of culture." He was too intelligent to rest his ideas on William Graham Sumner, the well-known economic determinist. "So long as wealth is made the means and not the end," he said, "we need not greatly fear it."

Critics of the nation's thirtieth president often noticed that despite Coolidge's interest in economic issues, he did not advocate many novelties in this regard. Why was he willing to accept what he found? The answer is that he became president when American industry was thriving. In his mind's eye, he looked across the country and beheld a nation that, economically speaking, was in the midst of a boom. He thought that he should leave well enough alone.

That the economy was thriving could not be disputed. Measured in current prices, which fluctuated narrowly during the Coolidge years, national income in 1923 stood at $71.6 billion; in 1928, his last full year in office, it was $81.7 billion. Consolidation of manufacturing firms may have had something to do with this result. In 1923, the 1,240 largest firms sold 69 percent of goods produced by American corporations; by 1929, when more than 92 percent of all goods were products of corporations, the 1,289 largest accounted for 76 percent. The increase in inventions also had something to do with this result. In the decade ending in 1890, there were 208,000 patents granted in the United States; in successive decades, the numbers were 221,000 , 314,000, 384,000, and, for the 1920s, a total of 421,000. The increase in engineers in the country was startling, showing the application of inventions. In 1880, the nation boasted only 7,000 engineers. The figure rose to 43,000 at the turn of the century, 136,000 by 1920, 226,000 by 1930.

Perhaps the most important factor in the industrial changes of the twentieth century was the rapid increase in the use of electricity, which became the prime source of power. In earlier years, the typical factory bought coal, made steam in a hand-fired boiler, and carried the power to workplaces by a series of shafts, pulleys, and belts—a cumbersome system at best. The substitution of individual electric motors marked a great advance. In 1914, 30 percent of manufacture was electrified. In 1929, the figure stood at 70 percent. Another advantage of electricity was that factories could now be located anywhere, not necessarily close to water power or supplies of coal; technical advances had joined the huge generating plants and created reservoirs of power that sent it across the nation. Between 1919 and 1929, power per wage earner increased 50 percent in manufacturing, 60 percent in mines and quarries, 74 percent in steam railroads. Efficiency went up so rapidly that between 1920 and 1929, manufacturing dispensed with the labor of thirty-two out of every hundred employees necessary for each unit of output. It reabsorbed twenty-seven from increased production. In manufacturing, coal mining, and railroads, 3.2 million employees proved unnecessary. Increased production took back 2.2 million. The net decline of 1 million meant a turn to service employment.

The wonderful state of industry pleased the president, and he could explain it by remarking that American industry had entered a second phase of development, quite different from the first that had started before the Civil War. His time, industrially speaking, differed from the time of Rockefeller and the Vanderbilts and all the other titans of industry who seized opportunities and made themselves rich. John D. Rockefeller, Jr., was looking at business enterprise quite differently from the way his father had. Young Rockefeller declared industry an association of owners and workers rather than a congeries of empires. As for the Vanderbilts, they had become harmless inhabitants of New York and Newport and travelers to Europe. Few large industrial titans dominated empires in the 1920s. There was the flivver man, Ford, and in steel, a big name was Charles M. Schwab, one of Andrew Carnegie's lieutenants who single-handedly created an empire known as Bethlehem Steel. Schwab visited the president in the White House in 1926 and dazzled Coolidge.

> I had a very agreeable call from Charles M. Schwab yesterday. I could not help but think as he came in and went out how well he represented the result of America. Beginning, as he did, with no property and with meager opportunities he has developed a great manufacturing plant for the service of the people of America and is doing considerable business abroad. He told me that he started the Bethlehem Steel works with $12,000,000 capital and now it represents $800,000,000 capital. I have forgotten how many employees he said, they run into the scores of thousands.[1]

Schwab was quite different in outlook from Coolidge. He was a conspicuous spender; he constructed an estate in Pennsylvania that occupied a thousand acres, a townhouse in New York that filled a city block. He was an immoral man in his preference for women other than his wife. Coolidge saw his business side, which was efficient. But apart from Ford and Schwab and a few others, the titans were gone. The controllers of American industry, the president knew, were faceless men such as Judge Elbert H. Gary of U.S. Steel and Alfred P. Sloan, Jr., of General Motors. They were the managers—he believed responsible managers—of the enterprises over which they presided, managing them for the good of their owners and of the workers who produced the goods. The firms he saw making the manifold products of American industry were managed rather than run.

For the Coolidge administration, the government figure who carried out the president's policy toward industry was the secretary of commerce. Hoover was an administrative whirlwind. A business periodical singled out phrases characteristic of his language: reason, knowledge, the facts, patience, goodwill, quiet negotiation, restraint of passion, moderation, calm and prudent common counsel. He, of course, was a doer, not a philosopher. He had little time for books. He once told Mark Sullivan that it was hard to find a book that would occupy a man: "I rarely spend more than an hour in a book." Sullivan responded that he had been reading a book by James Harvey Robinson, *Mind in the Making*, which he considered excellent. Hoover made a note of the title and author but may not have spent more than an hour with it.[2] Nothing could keep him from getting to work, and when he did so, he made everything move. Each morning he ate the same breakfast of bacon and eggs, dressed in the same-color suit and tie, and hurried from his house at 2300 S Street NW down Connecticut Avenue to his office, where he smoked twenty big, black cigars a day and worked to assist American business and businessmen. He transformed his department, which had given his Democratic predecessor, Oscar S. Straus, little to do except "putting the fish to bed at night and turning on the lights around the coast."[3] At the end of his first five days in office, Hoover had created an information service to distribute statistics and pamphlets on business opportunities. By the end of his eight-year tenure, his department was the largest customer of the Government Printing Office. He made the Bureau of Standards "the agency of the department of commerce for research and testing for the industries."[4] The Federal Specifications Board organized business standards involving measurements, carrying on the wartime effort in that regard.

Hoover hoped to make the Commerce Department "more nearly meet the needs of the American business public." He took the tiny Bureau of Foreign and Domestic Commerce and multiplied its budget by a factor of five, increasing its domestic offices from seven to twenty-nine and its offices abroad from twenty-three to fifty-eight. Much of this activity was under the direction of a Harvard professor of Latin American history and economics, Julius Klein, who organized the bureau along commodity lines, turning its personnel into experts in their specialties, in accord with the fact that American business itself, at home and abroad, had become specialized.

The bureau under Klein obtained a great deal of publicity, and Hoover named it as one of his leading accomplishments. Yet it may not have accomplished as much as Hoover and Klein hoped. In 1929, when Hoover became president, the proportion of American manufactures exported was 6 percent. This compared with 5 percent in 1913 and the same in 1899.

Despite the country's booming economy during the 1920s, exports did little more than keep up with industrial growth.

Perhaps more important than reorganizing the Commerce Department were Hoover's attempts, which met with considerable success, to develop a business philosophy. Here he stressed individualism. In 1922, he published a little book entitled *American Individualism,* reprinted in 1928 when he was running for the presidency. In the book he said that it was up to individuals to stand up to competition. It was the duty of government, he wrote, to ensure everyone that opportunity.

As secretary of commerce, Hoover tirelessly advanced the need for "associational progressivism" or "corporatism." This was a grand idea of society organized as independent economic units, decentralized and yet self-governed. The units would work harmoniously out of a sense of social responsibility and need for efficiency. Government would be largely absent from this harmonious community, for it would be unnecessary. All would be voluntary, for force meant "statism," which could destroy everything. The idea was not original with Hoover. It had appeared in government efforts during the war, notably in the work of the War Industries Board headed by Bernard Baruch, who saw that he could obtain more through cooperation than through enforcement, because he did not have the time to develop the machinery for enforcement, and there was some question of his legal power. The National Civic Federation and other promoters of social cooperation had advocated the same thing. It was akin to prescriptions offered by engineers and efficiency experts and the new trade associations of special industries.

When independent economic units, perhaps trade associations, sought to govern themselves, there was the danger that they would go beyond what Hoover had in mind. He once talked with Sullivan about that. The trouble was the professional secretaries and professional organizers of the associations, he said, who always tried to make them "open price" organizations, which was against the law. In response to a question whether the government would give trade associations immunity—that is, allow them to fix prices—Hoover answered as follows: "I want to cease to be Secretary of Commerce for a few minutes now. I want to speak as a private American citizen. Speaking in that role, you know that price fixing is illegal and you ought not to attempt to practice it nor want to practice it. You know what the twilight zone is and you ought to get out of it."[5]

From his own sense of engineering efficiency and Quaker service, Hoover did his best to set everything in perspective, and the Hoover perspective included foreign affairs. The "justification of any rich man," he informed the New York State Chamber of Commerce, "is his trusteeship to the community for his wealth." Wealth did not merely mean trusteeship to the nation: "the justification of America . . . is her trusteeship to the world-community for the property which she holds." In an era when the issue of war debts inflamed the country's foreign relations, Europeans needed to know that Americans had more in mind than dollars. He told the New Yorkers, hoping that his words would go abroad through the newspaper reporters present, that "the money which has come to us . . . is money in trust, and unless America recognizes this trust, she will pay dearly and bitterly for its possession." His conclusion may not have been quite as impressive to Europeans, but it meant much to Hoover: "The requital of the obligation which comes with riches . . . should not be alone her duty, but should be her crown."[6]

Hoover's accomplishments in commerce were many, and he deserved credit for them, but there was also a debit side. He poached on the territories of other cabinet members. He saw that the secretary of labor, Davis, was not inclined to exercise his authority, and as early as 1922, Hoover turned the Department of Labor into a "cooperative satellite." He attached to his own department much of the Interior Department, annexing its bureaus of mines and patents. By sending his department's representatives abroad, he encroached on the Department of State. For a while, he fought Secretary of Agriculture Wallace.[7] He managed his replacement by Jardine, who became a member of the Hoover team.[8]

Coolidge made a curious proposal when Secretary Wallace died and agriculture needed a new chief. He offered the department to Hoover. One wonders whether Hoover refused because he believed that the president was attempting to cut down his empire. By putting him in agriculture, Coolidge would be giving Hoover a department whose supporters were demoralized, because farmers were in economic want during the 1920s. Then Hoover could start all over again.

In addition to Hoover's poaching, there was his too obvious ambition. This alone would have antagonized Coolidge, and the only question is when the antagonism began. An admirer who was keeping a diary wrote that he liked Hoover personally, but "politically . . . I am desperately afraid of him." This supporter saw a campaign that was being pushed by Hoover himself, "making him the great figure in American life, the one man in the administration who has completely at heart the good of the American people." He saw Hoover as "insanely ambitious for personal power."[9] When Hoover's presidential ambition became evident in 1927, confirming any doubts the president may have had, Coolidge appears to have turned almost immediately against him.

In observing the attitude of the Coolidge administration toward industry, a question might arise about the federal government's administrative agencies other than cabinet departments. These were the regulatory commissions, which represented the hope of the American people for protection from business excesses. They could stand apart from politics and address the subtleties of particular industrial abuses. It was one thing to have on the books the Sherman Antitrust Act of 1890 and the Clayton Antitrust Act of 1914, but such laws needed administrative enforcement, and the commissions seemed the ideal way to do it. The commission approach for the regulation of portions of industry was an invention of American administrative practice, beginning in 1887 with the Interstate Commerce Commission (ICC). The Tariff Commission was organized in 1916, and in the 1920s was given the duty of assisting with the administration of the Fordney-McCumber tariff of 1922. The Federal Trade Commission was the centerpiece of progressive era legislation during the Wilson administration, authorized in 1914 for the purpose of administering antitrust policy.

Unfortunately, the regulatory commissions amounted to far less than the public expected of them, for several reasons. For one, bureaucracy tended to overwhelm them. They could start out with the most admirable of programs, and the bureaucrats would take over. For another, "most of the regulatory commissions were merely captured and neutralized by the businesses they sought to regulate."[10] As business enterprise increased and mergers created giant firms, businesses captured their regulators. The Coolidge administration did its part in this descent of the commissions into irrelevance, for the president of 1923–29 did not think that business needed regulation.

Consider what happened to the venerable ICC. In its initial years, it managed to bring railroad rates under control. Still, the commission continued to focus on rates when it should have been looking at other railroad problems. In a word, it became bureaucratic, unable to get out of the rut it had fallen into. As Judge Learned Hand observed, commissions tended to "fall into grooves and when they get into grooves, then God save you to get them out of the grooves."[11] Among the railroads' problems was increasing competition for freight—their principal business—from river and Great Lakes transport that was subsidized by the federal government through dredging and the construction of locks and other assistance. They would also soon encounter massive competition from trucks using taxpayer-supported roads. The commission needed to look into this government-subsidized competition and, if it did nothing else, sound the alarm. The railroads were losing business for other reasons as well. Two depressed industries during the 1920s, agriculture and coal mining, were principal sources of railroad freight, and their problems were bound to become the railroads' problems. The railroads were rapidly losing passenger traffic to the new automobiles. During the 1920s, it fell by 44 percent, despite a population increase of 15 percent. But nothing happened in the ICC to bolster the railroads' position against these problems. The ICC refused to lift its eyes above its routine business of rate adjustment.

The nation's rail network had been haphazardly flung across the United States before and after the Civil War, and the ICC needed to confront this problem. Superfluous, uneconomical railroad lines could remain in operation only by tying themselves to economically healthy lines. Railroading in the United States had broken down during World War I, when the government took over the entire rail system, and after the war, there was every reason to force reorganization into economical regional systems. Congress passed the Esch-Cummins Transportation Act of 1920, which sought to sponsor reorganization; it was a compromise between what its authors desired and what Congress would accept. Much of it had been written in conference committee, subject to trade-offs, but the possibility inherent in the legislation was a complete reorganization of the country's railroads. The Supreme Court heard a case contesting its constitutionality and supported reorganization. Speaking for a unanimous Court, Chief Justice Taft was completely on the ICC's side. Taft declared that the new act "seeks affirmatively to build up a system of railways," that it "aims to give the owners of the railways an opportunity to earn enough to maintain their properties and equipment," and that to "achieve this great purpose, it puts the railroad systems of the country more completely than ever under the fostering guardianship and control of the commission." A strong group of commissioners on the ICC might have managed reorganization, but the commissioners could not see beyond the ICC's past. The 1920 act increased their number from nine to eleven, but as in years gone by, they continued in the business of regulating rates. The staff of two thousand employees accomplished their work under five divisions. In fiscal year 1928, Division 4 decided 469 rate cases and 548 finance cases, or four cases each working day. They saw their mission as control, not structural innovation. They let the chance for a major reorganization of the nation's railroad system go by.

Another problem that the ICC should have faced and failed to was railroad finance. This problem had several parts. One was the railroads' failure to reduce their bonded indebtedness, perhaps governed by the belief that it was necessary to keep stockholders happy by paying out surplus in dividends. The Wheeler-Truman Committee of the Senate in the 1930s believed that the railroads preferred to issue bonds rather than stock because so many investors in railroads had been hurt by earlier bankruptcies, and there was competition for available funds by other companies seeking to sell stock. Furthermore, bonds could not upset current managements. The continuance of bonded indebtedness and the resort to more bonds was a very bad sign that should have been seen by the commissioners of the ICC, for any sort of economic downturn would throw the heavily bonded railroads into bankruptcy.

There was also the matter of railroad holding companies, which the ICC chose not to look into because the Esch-Cummins Act referred only to operating companies. Holding companies were the devices of the best New York and Chicago legal firms and of such speculative buccaneers as the brothers Mantis J. and Oris P. Van Sweringen of Cleveland, who in a few years created a huge railroad empire valued at $3 billion. The brothers started as real estate developers of suburban Shaker Heights. For commuters to downtown Cleveland they needed a high-speed electric line instead of the leisurely streetcar lines, as well as a terminal. The Nickel Plate Railroad, owned by the New York Central, was for sale because the Justice Department in Washington had asked the Central to sell it. The price was $8.5 million for the controlling shares. The Van Sweringens did not have that kind of money, but they formed a holding company and sold enough preferred—that is, nonvoting—stock to cover the first payment on their purchase. Having gotten into railroads, they went further, borrowing from the Union Trust Company and piling holding company on holding company, creating the Vaness (Van Sweringen) Company on top of the General Securities Corporation on top of the Alleghany Corporation. Each of the twenty-four layers in the pyramid was smaller, so very little money was necessary at the top to control operating railroads at the bottom; the brothers controlled the Hocking Valley Railroad at a cost of one-fourth of 1 percent of its worth.

In the course of empire building, the brothers reconstructed the center of Cleveland, with three eighteen-story general-purpose buildings, a large department store building that they filled by purchasing the Higbee Company, and the Cleveland Hotel to serve travelers to the city. The centerpiece of the collection was the new Cleveland Terminal, placed between Higbee's and the hotel, topped with a seven-hundred-foot tower with a huge golden spire at the summit. For their railroad empire, they engaged an excellent manager. But their financial pyramid was susceptible to collapse because of the same problem that plagued the more conventional financing of railroads by bond issues; if payments from one holding company to the next higher one failed, the failure could destroy the pyramid. When destruction of the Van Sweringen empire came in the mid-1930s, it reduced the brothers' combined personal fortune of $120 million to a personal indebtedness of $70 million and "a tangle of financial legal debris" that took years to sort out.[12]

Coolidge gave little attention to the ICC, making no effort to rejuvenate the commission's membership and expand its purview. Similarly, he made little use of the Tariff Commission, making no effort to obtain tariff changes beyond moving rates upward. As with the ICC, the tariff problem was a lack of vision, a feeling that what seemed to be working did not require change. The tariff was an ancient American institution, and as late as 1913, with the Underwood-Simmons tariff, it constituted the principal source of government revenue. With passage of the federal income tax, the tariff's importance diminished, and in the last years of the twentieth century, it provided little more than 1 percent of federal revenue. Increasingly important in tariff making—or so the Coolidge administration believed—was protection, and the 1920s certainly manifested that outlook in regard to the Tariff Commission. The president had considerable opportunity to become a tariff reformer, because section 315 of the Fordney-McCumber tariff authorized the president to raise or lower rates by as much as 50 percent to equalize costs of production between the United States and other countries. The act of 1922 averaged a 38.5 percent tariff on dutiable imports, compared with 27 percent for the Underwood-Simmons Act and 40.8 percent under the Payne-Aldrich tariff of 1909. In the 1922 act, the opportunity for more liberal trade was present, but the president and probably most of his countrymen believed that it was more advisable to "buy American." American businessmen felt that way, and they had the support of American farmers, who feared that foreign nations would dump agricultural products. There was also support from U.S. producers of oil, copper, and anthracite coal, who feared competition from rich deposits in new lands (such as copper in Rhodesia and the Congo), depreciation of foreign currencies, or state-promoted exports from Russia.

Coolidge moved carefully but firmly to create a protectionist majority on the Tariff Commission. He was safe enough with the chairman, Thomas O. Marvin, an active member of the Home Market Club of Boston; with William Burgess, who had been a lobbyist for pottery manufacturers; and with E. B. Brossard, who was an agricultural economist chiefly concerned with the highly protected sugar beet industry. He had to be careful with the three antiprotectionists, for early in his presidency they went public with their concern for freer trade. He waited until after his election in 1924 and then dismissed David J. Lewis, contending justifiably that the commission was a fact-finding group and not a semijudicial agency; after the commissioners studied a given tariff, they could only make a recommendation to the president, who decided what to do under section 315. In 1925, he obtained the resignation of a second low-tariff commissioner, William S. Culbertson, whom he appointed minister to Romania. The third antiprotectionist, Edward P. Costigan, was cornered and resigned in 1928, remarking that Coolidge had raised rates on thirty-three items and reduced them on five: millfeeds, live quail, paintbrush handles, cresylic acid, and phenol. One suspects that the president's puckish sense of humor had a hand in choosing the items for reduction.

The fate of the Federal Trade Commission (FTC) was the most obvious symbol of presidential disdain for regulation. There had been such high hopes for the FTC. The theory that led to its establishment was that anti-trust laws lacked full effect because they came into operation only after monopolistic practices had become entrenched and because only the cumbersome processes of litigation could enforce them. The FTC received unprecedented powers to investigate, publicize, and prohibit "unfair methods of competition." The act of 1914 defined unfair competition as involving "substantial lessening of competition or tendency to create monopoly." But what happened to the FTC during the 1920s showed how a Republican administration could subvert Democratic legislative designs of large promise, how theory was no substitute for vigilance.

Admittedly, the FTC was in trouble before Coolidge's intervention. The war had prevented antitrust prosecutions, because production had been far more important than regulation. After the war, Congress intervened when the FTC threatened action against the meat packers, the so-called big five; the Packers and Stockyards Act of 1921 removed the packers from the FTC's jurisdiction. The courts turned against the FTC in a series of decisions denying the commission's right to define "unfair methods of competition." They took over this power of the commission—an extraordinary invasion of a congressional right that Congress might have looked into if it had not been too busy asserting its general rights against the presidency. The courts also insisted on their right to review procedure and findings of fact. This meant that any FTC ruling might be subject to constricted interpretation, given the courts' generally conservative outlook, as well as time-consuming litigation over procedure and findings of fact. Soon the courts were passing judgment on all sorts of business practices. Contrary to the FTC, the Supreme Court held that oil companies could force gas stations to sell only their own products, that the Beech Nut Company could fix retail prices for its products, that manufacturers could give lower discounts to wholesalers or chain stores even if other buyers ordered the same quantities, and that manufacturers could prevent any dealers who became agents from handling products from competing companies.

But it was President Coolidge who turned the FTC into a shell of a regulatory body. Coolidge in 1925 appointed William E. Humphrey to the FTC, thereby achieving a majority of Republican commissioners. With the appointment of Humphrey, a former member of the House of Representatives from Oregon who was connected with lumber interests there, antitrust regulation became all but impossible. Humphrey's appearance marked a change of commission rules. Beginning in March 1925, there had to be allegations of unfair practices instead of investigations that might turn up such practices. A second change was the decision to settle most cases by "stipulation," or informal agreement, rather than by formal action; presumably, this would make changes easier. A third rule gave defendants the opportunity to present arguments informally and confidentially. A fourth, adopted a few weeks later, made stipulation agreements confidential, without any public announcement. Humphrey was soon bragging of his accomplishments. "I certainly did make a revolutionary change in the method and policies of the commission," he said. "If it was going east before, it is going west now." When someone raised the subject of the new rules, he asked defiantly, "What of it?" He defended himself by asking another question and giving the answer: "Do you think I would have a body of men working here under me that did not share my ideas about these matters? Not on your life. I would not hesitate a minute to cut their heads off if they disagreed with me. What in hell do you think I am here for?"[13]

The collapse of the FTC was illustrated by what happened to an antitrust investigation of the Aluminum Company of America (Alcoa), begun after the war and lasting into 1925. It was politically sensitive, because Secretary Mellon was a large shareholder in Alcoa. The investigation was suspended in 1922, and the statute of limitations applied after one year. In 1924, the commission reported to Attorney General Stone that Alcoa had violated a decree by a federal court. Stone agreed that the charge warranted consideration, and the commission renewed its investigation. But when Stone asked the commission for the results of the investigation, he discovered that because of the changes instituted after the appointment of Humphrey, he could not obtain the results without the written consent of the company, which had supplied evidence voluntarily.

Commissioner Humphrey in 1926 created a trade practice conference division within the commission staff to encourage industrial self-regulation. The division allowed an industry to "make its own rules of business conduct . . . in cooperation with the commission."[14] It was akin to Secretary Hoover's efforts to get government out of business, to avoid statism.

Regulation in the Coolidge era was thin to the point of invisibility. A sign of the times was the new building of the Chamber of Commerce of the United States, erected on Lafayette Square in Washington, on the site of the old Eustis-Corcoran House. The heavy neoclassical structure was designed by Cass Gilbert, who later designed the Supreme Court building on Capitol Hill. The Chamber of Commerce building dominated its square, and some observers said that it dominated the eighteenth-century edifice on the other side of Pennsylvania Avenue.

The 1920s saw the triumph of American industry, for its accomplishments stood at every hand. Its organization reached across the continent, its efficiency was known worldwide, its production was nothing short of astonishing. Its relation to American government was so intimate that it could be described as dominating government. And in regard to American labor, its relation to laboring men and women, it was similarly dominant: nominally equal, managing a Hooverian cooperation between its purposes and those of the workforce that achieved them, industry controlled its labor force more closely, tightly, than in any previous era in American history.

The domination of labor by industry was evident in statistics of the time. Labor's lack of power was apparent in the weakness of union membership, which declined from 5.1 million in 1920 to 3.4 million in 1929. The greater part of the drop occurred by 1923, when membership was 3.5 million. This was in a nonagricultural workforce of more than 30 million—meaning that union membership in the 1920s averaged one worker in ten, or 10.2 percent, a drop from 19.4 percent in 1920.

One reason that workers did not enroll in unions was that they were doing much better in the 1920s. Real wages rose, the workweek declined, unemployment was low. Real wages for industrial workers were 8 percent above the base year (1914 = 100) in 1921, 13 percent above in 1922, and 19 percent above in 1923. For the next two years, the figure remained at this level and then increased, reaching 32 percent in 1928. The workweek declined from 47.4 hours in 1920 to 44.2 in 1929. This meant a five-and-a-half-day week. Henry Ford introduced a five-day week in his plants in 1926, but few industrialists followed; a survey two years later found 216,000 workers with five-day weeks, but many of them were working as many hours as they had with six-day weeks. All the while unemployment was a low 3.7 percent between 1923 and 1929. This compared with 6.1 between 1911 and 1917, a fairly prosperous time for workers.

Another reason for low union membership during the 1920s was the unions' unwillingness to organize unskilled workers in the basic industries. Unions did not exist in steel, electrical equipment, rubber, cement, textiles, chemicals, and food. There were no effective unions in nonferrous metals or petroleum. Motor transport had a smattering of membership. Utilities, banking, insurance, retail and wholesale trade, the professions, and domestic and personal service were unorganized. Union leaders ignored the sudden rise of the automobile industry.

The union movement had long dealt with skilled workers and flourished in two sheltered occupations, railroads and construction. The former had been an object of government regulation for many years, since the creation of the ICC. Construction was a peculiar occupation in which each of its urban centers was relatively immune from competition and whose conduct in the large cities was tied up with local political machines. In 1927, when construction across the country slowed, railroad and construction workers represented half the total membership of American unions. Trade unionism was strong in street railways, water transportation, printing, and music. In competitive occupations, at the beginning of the 1920s, unions were strong in clothing and coal mining. The garment industry maintained union membership throughout the decade, but the coal industry did not, suffering a tremendous loss.

Leadership of the American Federation of Labor (AFL) during the 1920s was conservative. The AFL's perennial president, Samuel Gompers, dealt with skilled workers all his life and could not envision the organization of any other workers. After his death in 1924, his successor, William Green, thought largely in terms of preserving the union movement rather than entering into novel efforts of organization. Green symbolized the union movement's lackluster leadership. He looked the part: "A placid, colorless man who belonged to both the Elks and the Odd Fellows, Green wore rimless glasses, a large gold watch chain in his vest, and a diamond ring on his finger."[15]

The result of the increasing well-being of laboring men and women and of the unwillingness of labor leaders to be adventuresome was a sort of settling down of labor in its relation to industry. Labor accepted the dominance of industry. Strikes were dramatically down. The average per year between 1916 and 1921 had been 3,503. In 1930, there were 637. In 1919, one worker in five left his or her job in an industrial dispute; in 1925, one in fifty. Between 1925 and 1928, that figure diminished. After the anthracite coal strike of 1923, there was no strike of any size that caught national attention and drew newspaper readers to the plight of workers and to community attitudes toward unions until the textile mill strike at Gastonia, North Carolina, in 1929, after Coolidge left the presidency. Most workers had come to accept the domination of the managers of American industry; if they did not love big business, they decided that they could live with it.

President Coolidge took the condition of labor at face value: it was better than it had been in recent memory. Intervening in economic matters was against his philosophy, as he had shown in his attitude toward regulation. It would interfere with what he thought should be a free market. His outlook was evident in regard to the wages of government workers in Washington. In executive departments in 1926, salaries were 91 percent of what they had been in 1914. When postal employees sought a bill on their own behalf, Coolidge was against it. He called Sen. James Couzens of Michigan, a member of his own party, to the White House and made a considerable argument. When the senator told Coolidge that a postman could not raise a family on $1,500 a year, the president replied, "In Northampton, Massachusetts, you can have a first-rate house to live in for $30 a month."

"That's no argument!" said Couzens. "All of our postal employees can't live in Northampton, Massachusetts!"

"I had an uncle in Northampton," continued the president. "He sent his children through high school and college and he never made more than $1,500 a year in his life."

Couzens banged his fist on Coolidge's desk. "That's the trouble with you, Mr. President! You have a Northampton viewpoint, instead of a national viewpoint!"[16]

The Coolidge administration had little desire to get into labor issues, as was evident during the troubles in the bituminous coal industry, which arose in 1923 about the same time as the short-lived anthracite strike in Pennsylvania. Coolidge handed the anthracite strike to Governor Pinchot, and for the bituminous mines, he did little more. The situation in those mines was deplorable, for there were too many mines and the operators were pressing their men: pay scales were falling, and safety regulations were often breached. Workers in the industry needed protection until there could be a shaking out of marginal mines. The president first placed his hope in the Coal Commission, which late in 1923 submitted a report of three thousand pages that described the industry in great detail but failed to advise any legislation—after the commission had spent $500,000 and issued press releases about its progress and conclusions. Its chairman, John Hays Hammond, completely in sympathy with the president's purposes, explained, "We did not solve the coal problem, nor did we expect to. In presenting our report we uttered the warning that the solution of the coal problem could only grow out of a sustained and thoughtful effort over many years by the public, by Congress, by industry, and by students generally. The problem is almost unbelievably complex and there is no easy short-cut to a solution."[17] The administration next turned to an effort that bore the cachet of Secretary Hoover and took headlines and gave the impression of activity. Hoover produced the Jacksonville agreement, worked out in February 1924 by the coal operators and the head of the United Mine Workers (UMW), John L. Lewis. The UMW *Journal* declared on the day of signing that it "will go down in history as one of the red letter days." The editorial writer announced that it was the best pact the union had ever obtained in the fields. A front-page cartoon showed Lewis bringing home the bacon.[18]

The result of Coolidge's inaction and Hoover's action in regard to the bituminous coal industry was not immediately apparent. At the outset, there were higher wages, but they did not last, because they penalized unionized operators facing competition from nonunion mines. High wage rates in union fields were paralleled by the refusal of owners of many weakly organized mines in Kentucky and West Virginia to adhere to them.

Southern coal entered midwestern markets, prices dropped, mines suspended operation, and miners were laid off. In many closed mines, operators waited a few weeks or months—long enough for miners to move away or take up other occupations—and then reopened with nonunion scales. The Mellon-controlled Pittsburgh Coal Company took this course. Secretary of Labor Davis called a conference of bituminous operators and the UMW in December 1927, but few operators attended, and the conference collapsed. All in all, 3,300 bituminous mines closed, and 250,000 miners lost their jobs.

In loss of jobs and harm done to the UMW, it was possible to see purposeful behavior by Coolidge's negotiator Hoover, who from the beginning may have desired nonunion mines. Perhaps he hoped to subject the sick soft coal industry to a ruthless reorganization that would allow domination by a few large coal concerns. In Hoover's view, labor disputes encouraged inefficient mining, and a substantial period of labor peace was necessary to make changes, hence the Jacksonville meeting that calmed the waters so that natural economic forces could prevail.[19] But such an interpretation seems devious to a fault, too logical, and it fails to give Secretary Hoover credit for good intentions.

One can argue that Lewis behaved ineffectively in the belief that he had to do something for the large portion of his membership mining soft coal. Lewis was a conservative Republican and voted for Hoover in 1928. Yet it seems more reasonable to conclude that he took his losses because he had to. Blaming him for not making much of an effort to organize southern mines seems wrong, for the South was inveterately antiunion, and organization would have been nearly impossible in a region where basic civil liberties would be violated, as was proved at Gastonia in 1929.

In looking at the Coolidge administration's attitude toward labor, one might note its tolerance toward company representation schemes, but like the insufficient measures taken in the soft coal fields, it would have been difficult to expect anything else. The 1920s, with their rising good times for workers, dulled feelings about antiunion activities. Economist Thomas N. Carver in 1925 opined that labor and capital had finally grasped the fact of mutual dependence, and he predicted harmony between them. The tide of good feelings would wash away rancors of the past. Company representation plans proved industry's good intentions. By 1929, 2 million workers were enrolled in plans, from simple shop committees to grand schemes of "congressional" representation, with spokesmen for workers, supervisors, and management imitating the three branches of the federal government. The mass production industries saw many such experiments. Secretary Hoover admitted that representation schemes were capable of misuse, that industrial managers might employ them to head off unionism, but he did not follow up on this possibility. Labor historian Robert H. Zieger has pointed out that at a time when organized labor was woefully weak, Hoover had no suggestions to oppose representation. "Forceful and articulate in his exposure of problems of production and efficiency, he was silent and acquiescent in his attitude toward representation." Traditional society and socialism were both bankrupt, Hoover said; society had to find a way to increase productivity, and this would be the application of the science of management within a setting of individualism and voluntarism. "Government, he held, would inevitably play a key role, but primarily as a coordinator, mediator, and information-dispenser, not as a coercive or restrictive force."[20]

In dealing with one important part of the labor force, railroad labor, the Coolidge administration showed that it could have a policy, and a judicious one. Here there was precedent for government action. The Adamson Act of 1916 mandated a workday of eight hours for railroad employees, with time and a half for overtime. It was the first instance of federal intervention in the wages of employees of private corporations. During World War I, the government took over the railroads. The Transportation Act of 1920 sought to ensure the profitable operation of the railroads, once they were returned to private ownership, and provided machinery for settling labor disputes through a Railroad Labor Board. The latter seemed a step forward, with its nine members sitting as a tribunal for the adjustment of disputes. But by late 1923 it was clear that the labor board was not working. The chairman was a former Republican governor of Tennessee, ruggedly individualistic Ben W. Hooper, who managed to antagonize the railroad brotherhoods. Hooper told Coolidge that the board had done much, "really served a useful public purpose." He said that in 1922, when Attorney General Daugherty obtained an injunction against a railroad strike that forbade almost any effort on the part of strikers, the injunction was a necessity, that everything nicely conspired to put the board in control. He predicted a period of peace on the railroads.[21] Recognizing bad advice when he heard it, Coolidge two weeks later in his annual message commented on the board's limits and asked for something new. With the Watson-Parker Act of 1926 he obtained it, a victory for the brotherhoods. The act endorsed collective bargaining and was a skillful retreat from Daugherty's solution. In later years, when mediation and arbitration failed, the act's cooling-off procedures prevented work stoppages. By means of hearings and negotiations, it headed off a threatened strike on western railroads in the summer of 1928.

Finally, in examining the labor situation during the Coolidge administration, mention must be made of the work of the courts in this era of industrial prosperity and labor decline. Labor, it would seem, was controlled in part by the unseen hand of prosperity and by the temper of the times, which was against union organization. But there was also the application of legal sanctions. In this regard, two special devices proved of value. One was the continuing use of the injunction, an invention of English equity courts long before the existence of labor organizations. The injunction had been twisted from its original purpose, which was to prevent physical damage to property while a suit was in process. American courts after the Civil War invoked it against strikes and, in the 1920s, extended it to embrace intangible property. In the half century from 1880 to 1930, state and federal courts issued 1,845 orders, half of them in the 1920s. A second legal device of the decade was damage suits against labor unions; like injunctions, they had been employed before but were now remarkably broadened. Common law held that an unincorporated association such as a union was not a legal entity and could neither sue nor be sued. The courts reduced this protection through fine-spun theorizing.[22]

The courts, notably the Supreme Court, displayed a general hostility toward anything that favored labor. Some of this was the result of Harding's appointment of former president Taft as chief justice. One biographer described him as "conservative, if not reactionary." He seemed to be a stereotypical chief justice, physically impressive, large of frame, with what Alpheus T. Mason described as "more than a little bay window." Mason related the remark of Justice David J. Brewer that Taft was the most polite man alive: "I heard that recently he arose in a streetcar and gave his seat to three women." But behind the avoirdupois was a legal reformer who avowed that he had been chosen "to reverse a few decisions." Of labor, he wrote privately, "That faction we have to hit every little while."[23]

Taft devoted much attention to what he described as getting politics out of court appointments, but in reality, he was looking to appoint conservatives like himself. Good conservatives would know what to do with labor. Political appointments might bring in compromisers who, under the claim of dispensing law, would split the difference in quarrels between industry and labor. The political appointment of judges almost obsessed Taft. He lobbied unashamedly against the intrusion of politics—successfully with Harding, but not so well with Coolidge. With Harding he worked through "Dear old Harry Daugherty—much as they damned him, he did most excellent work in standing off Senators."[24] Daugherty converted Harding, even though Taft admitted that the conversion required continual applications of holy water. With Coolidge, he was not so successful but was willing to go to lengths. At the outset of the Coolidge administration, he heard that Senator Kenyon of Iowa wanted a nominee and had gotten himself on the Harding funeral train for that purpose. Taft got on the train and spoke his piece to Coolidge, he thought sufficiently. As time passed, he saw that Coolidge was not answering requests and was listening to the siren calls of senators. Coolidge also appeared to take the position that a lawyer was a lawyer, perhaps because of his own elevation to the bar by virtue of reading law rather than attending an Ivy League law school. The work of building the courts became increasingly hard. "They pay no attention to me at the White House," he complained. But he should not have worried, because whatever the quality of Coolidge's appointees, they were almost certain to be conservatives. Clerks hedged the poor lawyers among them and cleaned up their opinions, and the Coolidge result was the same as the Harding result.

On the Supreme Court, Taft through Daugherty placed three conservatives, Justices George Sutherland, Pierce Butler, and Edward T. Sanford, and grouped them with three previous appointees, Willis Van Devanter, James C. McReynolds, and Joseph McKenna. The Taft Court easily countered the liberalism of Justices Holmes and Louis D. Brandeis. Coolidge made only one Supreme Court appointment at the beginning of his presidency in 1925, when Daugherty's successor Stone took McKenna's place. In a series of decisions in the early 1920s, the High Court duly resolved labor cases. It extended application of the Sherman Act and removed labor's protection under the Clayton Act. It was clear that no child labor law would stand up under review, and proponents turned to a constitutional amendment, which after passing Congress in 1924 achieved five state ratifications by 1929. In *Adkins* v. *Children's Hospital* (1923), the Supreme Court declared a District of Columbia minimum-wage law for women unconstitutional; thereafter, the few state laws were dead letters. Labor issues of importance in the Coolidge administration's later years were few.

Taken as a whole, the 1920s Court was antilabor. The Tri-City case in 1921 imposed severe restrictions on picketing. The case went back to 1914, when the Tri-City Central Trades Council at Granite City, Illinois, struck American Steel Foundries for recognition and posted pickets. There was no violence. Taft ruled that picketing by three to four groups with four to twelve persons in each group was wrong, "methods which however lawful in their announced purpose inevitably lead to intimidation and violence." The word "picket" was "sinister," suggestive of a military purpose.[25] The Court limited pickets to one at each gate. This restrictive interpretation of what constituted picketing became the federal law defining one of the most important union weapons against employers, and state courts followed it. The other notable decision on labor was the Bedford Stone case in 1927, which involved denial of an injunction against the journeymen stone cutters for refusing to handle nonunion limestone. The majority on the Court desired reversal of the lower court decision, and Taft managed it, although it was heroic work. Holmes and Brandeis were opposed, and Stone and Sanford seemed ready to join them, making a five-to-four decision instead of Taft's usual "massing" of the Court. There had been mounting public criticism of the Court's labor decisions, and such a close decision would raise questions about reversals. The chief justice brought the two straying sheep back into the fold, and for the moment, all was well.

The position of labor was weak from the side of unionism and government policy and weak in support from the courts, with some sign that the latter might change. The possibility of change was evident inside the Supreme Court but not outside. Meanwhile, labor's weakness was industry's strength.

5

★ ★ ★ ★ ★

AGRICULTURE

American industry during the 1920s not merely flourished but triumphed, and American labor accepted the portion of the national income that industry considered suitable for workers, but the farmers of the country felt left out, ignored. The felt that they were not receiving what the nation owed them, and they were correct: their labor was not being properly recompensed.

The trouble was overproduction. For a while after the Civil War, American farm products that were not consumed domestically found ready markets abroad. But wheat began to enter Great Britain and western Europe from Russia, Romania, Canada, Australia, even India. Cotton became available from Egypt. Overproduction was easily visible by the time the war broke out in 1914. The war years brought back the markets of Britain, France, and Italy for American grain, because war with Germany, Austria-Hungary, and Turkey closed off Russian and Romanian supplies and shipping was unavailable for long hauls from Australia and India. A year or two after the war, however, the nations of western Europe resorted to their former suppliers. Moreover, within the United States, the war taught housewives to use less bread because of the need to ship wheat to Europe; having resorted to substitutes such as fruits and vegetables, they failed to return to the heavy use of bread that had marked prewar diets. Per capita wheat consumption in the United States declined from 217 pounds in 1909 to 180 pounds in 1925. Consumption of potatoes was also down, four pounds less in 1925 than in 1919—a drop of 8 million bushels, or between

2 and 3 percent of total production. Declining population growth, caused by the end of unlimited immigration and the beginning of the trend toward smaller families, affected demand for farm products.

The precipitating event for the farm problem of the 1920s was the virtual depression of 1920–21. It was more than what in the nineteenth century was known as a panic, such as those of 1819, 1837, 1857, 1873, and 1893. It was the worst such experience for farmers until the Great Depression. The 1920–21 downturn affected millions of farmers in the summer of 1920, and prices of farm commodities began a decline that continued for almost two years. Number 1 dark northern wheat brought $2.94 a bushel in Minneapolis in early July—what farmers considered a good price. In succeeding months, the drop appalled them. By December, wheat was down to $1.72. A year later, in December 1921, it had plummeted to ninety-two cents. Using 1909–14 as a base period—which farmers remembered fondly as a time of peak incomes, a time just before the inflation of the war years—the farm dollar in 1920 was worth eighty-five cents; by 1921, it was down to sixty-nine cents. Put up against all commodities, not simply farm products, the farm dollar looked a little better—ninety-three cents in 1920 and seventy-nine cents in 1921.

One factor that proved a boon to farmers in the 1920s also became a source of overproduction, although it was not yet apparent during the depression of 1920–21. This was the great increase in the use of tractors, especially small tractors. It had begun before the war. The big event was the introduction of the 2,500-pound Fordson by Henry Ford, who demonstrated it personally in a plowing exhibition at Fremont, Nebraska, in August 1915. It boasted a wheel base of sixty-three inches and could turn in a twenty-one-foot circle; it possessed a four-cylinder, twenty-horsepower engine that ran on kerosene. In 1917, the inventor of the Model T organized a separate corporation, known as Henry Ford and Son, and the first Fordson for domestic use came off the assembly line in April of the next year. By the time of the armistice, Ford had produced 26,817 of the tractors. By 1924, he was turning out 750 Fordsons a day. Production rose to 486,800 in 1925 and 650,000 in 1927, making Ford responsible for half the tractors made in the United States up to that time.[1] The result of the introduction of these small tractors was a decline in the horse and mule population from 26.4 million to 19.5 million during the 1920s. That freed 30 million acres that had been devoted to oats and hay for animal feed, and most of that acreage went into other crops, leading to overproduction. There were other problems with the Fordsons and their competitors, in that tractors raised costs and, unlike animals, did not breed their successors. One might contend that tractors gave farmers more leisure to consider their problems and agitate them. The Fordsons appealed to the small farmers hardest hit by the drop in farm prices—the marginal farmers.

What should be done about overproduction? From the outset, this farm problem became a political problem. In the booming industrial economy of the 1920s, something had to be done about agriculture, if only because the agricultural way of life was such a prominent part of American history and still occupied great numbers of Americans after 1920, despite what the census said about the country becoming more urban than rural. By 1920, urban dwellers represented 57 percent of all Americans. But this did not tell the whole story, for the real city dwellers in the nation were not yet a majority, even by 1930. In that year, 68 million persons were classified as urban, but only 36 million lived in cities with populations of one hundred thousand or more. And as Donald McCoy wrote, many of the people in cities came from the country or small towns and did not yet identify with the city. They identified with the nation's heritage of farms and towns. The cities had grown mightily in the 1880s and 1890s, and most of them, save for a few on the eastern seaboard, were new creations; their existence had not yet fastened itself into the national consciousness.[2] The American people really looked back to Jefferson's apostrophe to farmers in the 1780s, that "those who labor in the earth are the chosen people of God . . . whose breasts He has made His peculiar deposit for substantial and genuine virtue. . . . The mobs of the great cities add just so much to the support of pure government, as sores do to the strength of the human body."

The Republican party in the 1920s had to be careful of the farmers because of their longtime importance within the party and the danger that no program at all might mean their defection. At the moment, the Democrats were in disarray because of their inability to produce attractive presidential candidates. Behind that inability was the party's confusing composition, for it was a coalition of southerners and big-city machines. If the Democrats could resolve their differences and challenge the Republicans, and if the latter lost the support of the farmers, the Republican party could lose control of the federal government.

Acreage restriction was talked about. Industry practiced scarcity by restricting production in bad economic times. This was possible in businesses that dominated markets, as many did. Secretary Wallace considered restriction and believed that his cabinet department had a responsibility to inform its constituents of probable demand. In 1921 he wrote to his son Henry A., who was editing *Wallaces' Farmer,* that "we should cut down production to our own needs, or a little more." The *Washington Post* in 1924 remarked that "the remedy is plain: let American wheat growers quit try-ing to compete with cheap foreign wheat and cut their production down to home needs."[3] A tariff could keep out cheap foreign wheat.

Nothing happened, because restriction was unpopular with farmers. The idea of economic scarcity did not appeal in the 1920s and has never made farmers happy. Voluntary restriction was hopeless; farmers were individualists, and even if some might have been converted to the idea of restricting production, others were bound to take advantage. In 1924, wheat acreage was down; cotton and corn acreage was up. Total crop acreage was 1 million less than in the high years of 1918–19, but the coun-try had 500 million acres in production or pasture and 500 million more in forest; this was not much of a reduction.

One possibility for government intervention considered in the 1920s was export debentures. They enlisted considerable support and were attractive because their administration would be easy. They would provide higher prices for farmers, depending on the height of the tariff, and proces-sors and purchasers of grain would pay the cost. Grain sold in the domes-tic market would be at the tariff price. That sold abroad would be sold at a loss. Exporters would receive debentures equal to the loss, and deben-tures would be receivable for the payment of import duties; importers would buy them from exporters. To farmers, export debentures were attrac-tive because their cost would be in the form of reduced government re-ceipts from imports, which was not easy for nonfarmers to see.

Mulling over the need to do something, Coolidge proposed a confer-ence to consider the financial aspects of government assistance to farmers. The goal was to get something on the table before the presidential election. In organizing the conference, the president consulted Hoover, who rec-ommended that the delegates be drawn largely from the business and financial world, not agriculture: a financial subject required financial peo-ple. Hoover drew up a suitable list and asked for Secretary Wallace's com-ments on it, but the final composition of the meeting followed the Hoover list, except for the addition of officers of the leading farm organizations.

The agricultural conference took place on 4 February 1924, a one-day session, and the results were not significant. Hoover, as chairman, dom-inated the proceedings, guided the discussion, and discouraged unwanted resolutions. Wallace gave a short speech at the opening and took no further part. The conference's recommendations included higher duties on wheat. In accord with a plan advanced by the president of the North Dakota State Agricultural College and introduced into Congress by Sen. Peter Norbeck of South Dakota and Rep. Olger B. Burtness of North Dakota, it called for a Federal Agricultural Diversification Commission consisting of the secre-taries of commerce, agriculture, and the treasury, with an appropriation of

$50 million. The proposed commission would lend money to farmers. Hoover described the purpose vaguely as "some change in the basis of agriculture by diversification."[4] Just what that change might be, or how $50 million might eliminate the farm problem, he did not say.

The conference adopted a plan for the expansion of rural credit, and this proposal might have reminded the conferees of the Federal Farm Loan Act of 1916, which was not proving remarkably successful. The act had established a Federal Farm Loan Board, which supervised two mortgage systems. One consisted of federal land banks to supply money at cost to farm loan associations organized on a cooperative basis. The act divided the country into twelve districts with a federal land bank in each. The other system consisted of joint-stock land banks, privately owned. The two mortgage systems did not begin operation rapidly and were of little use in the depression of 1920–21. For a while, the federal land banks could not sell their bonds, and the treasury supported them. The public and private systems clashed. The federal banks were supposed to support cooperatives and thereby keep the loans out of politics. But politics and nepotism surrounded mortgages however they were financed, and three of the federal land banks and five of the privately owned joint-stock land banks got into trouble and had to be reorganized. Between 1923 and the end of the decade, loans under the two systems increased 50 percent, to $2 billion. Farm loans from life insurance companies were about the same in volume, and they increased similarly. The net result of the federal programs and the life insurance companies' program was arguable. By shifting mortgages from local banks or individuals, they brought lower interest rates for farmers. They apparently did little for the liquidity of local banks, however, which in farming areas went under by the hundreds during the Great Depression.

In his acceptance speech for the presidential nomination in 1924, Coolidge asked for a separate commission to investigate conditions of farming and make recommendations to Congress. One of the farming advocates suggested that the president place Secretary Wallace in charge of this commission, and the secretary made suggestions about the composition of the group, writing to the head of the Iowa Farm Bureau that if there had to be a general commission, it had better be a good one. Coolidge again followed Hoover's recommendations and made the appointments not long after Wallace's death in October 1924. Nothing came of the commission.

After the presidential election, Coolidge turned to the idea of farm cooperatives. It appeared during a press conference, after a reporter asked for a "slant" on the new secretary of agriculture to replace Wallace. The president had installed an interim secretary, Howard M. Gore, who had been an assistant secretary and was leaving to become governor of West

Virginia. "The trouble with agriculture at the present time," Coolidge said, "is in the marketing end." He said that secretaries of agriculture had been of two sorts: one was a practical farmer; the other was from an agricultural college, perhaps an economist. What he now wanted was "a man that can organize the business of agriculture." Production was getting along well (he might have said too well). Colleges were emphasizing production. The "marketing end" needed organization so that the farmer could secure the results of his industry. "That is a great economic problem," he said. "It is *the* great economic problem, to my mind, of the present time—how to secure for our farming population the rewards that they ought to have as a result of their industry."[5] He said that many results of the farmer's industry were "dissipated" between the farmer and the consumer, raising the issue of middlemen. Cooperatives would allow an escape from middlemen. He may have received some of his information from Secretary Hoover, who about this time was showing that farmers often dealt with representatives of large corporations. Three large tobacco companies bought nearly half the nation's tobacco crop. Thirteen flour mills purchased half the wheat crop. Three packers bought one-fourth of the cattle and hogs. A half dozen manufacturers produced the farm machinery. As Hoover put the solution, cooperatives would "give a larger part of the consumer's dollar to the farmer."[6]

It is doubtful that Coolidge thought much about cooperatives. His outlook on the farm problem was based on his Vermont experience, which of course had made him leave the farm. Vermont farming was subsistence, except for such cash crops as wool and cheese. In 1890, Coolidge's father had gone in with neighbors to establish the Notch's cheese factory, but it probably was no more lucrative than sheep. Coolidge's outlook was of no advantage to the generality of American farmers. He liked to talk about the farming business, and behind that talk was a sense that farming was a business that should have a balance sheet, and in event of loss, the farmer ought to get off the farm. Senator Wheeler discussed farm problems with Coolidge, who asked, "When a man can't make any money in a business, what does he do?" Coolidge told the chairman of the Federal Farm Loan Board, Robert A. Cooper, that the life of the farmer "has its compensations." He added, "Well, farmers never have made money. I don't believe we can do much about it. But of course we will have to seem to be doing something."[7]

When Coolidge came out for cooperatives, he was supporting a plan that appealed greatly to Secretary Hoover, and the question is why Hoover was so enthusiastic. It may have been because of his inveterate unwillingness to look as closely at solutions as he did at problems. Hoover had a tendency to think that everything had a solution, somewhere, somehow. His solution for manufacturing and mining was in ever larger foreign markets, which his assistant secretary, Klein, would discover. Like everyone who looked at agriculture, Hoover saw the overproduction, and like any intelligent and emotionally uncharged individual, he could not see any possibility of increasing exports. He was no politician and would not have said, as Coolidge did to the head of the Federal Loan Board, that a palliative was necessary. Hoover was not one to stall, to wait out a problem. When Coolidge saw ten troubles coming down the road, he waited until nine had run off the road and then dealt with the tenth, but this strategy would never have satisfied Hoover. Instead, in regard to the farm problem, he seems to have believed that the cooperatives would help, and eventually population growth in the United States would expand the domestic market.[8]

The president's proposal of cooperatives, seconded by Hoover, became known as the Jardine-Tincher plan, after the new secretary of agriculture and Rep. J. Napoleon Tincher of Kansas. Jardine argued that cooperatives armed with liberal credits could stabilize farm prices by purchasing and holding excess production. He was careful to avoid any notion that he was attempting to raise the price of farm commodities. Rep. Gilbert N. Haugen of Iowa asked whether he was "really for increasing the price." The answer was, "I am for stabilizing the price." Jardine was a conservative like Coolidge and Hoover and did not see his role as raising prices.[9]

The principal present-day student of American farming, Gilbert C. Fite, has asked how Secretary Jardine could have believed that cooperatives would solve the farm problem. He concludes that Jardine ended up supporting cooperatives because he was so fearful, because of his doctrinaire beliefs, of government aid to agriculture. Fite believes that Jardine was not stupid, but was stubborn and naive. "Even a casual look at recent agricultural history with which he was presumably familiar would have told him that voluntary arrangements had been dismal failures." Individual farmers would take advantage of any effort by a cooperative to control prices of such commodities as cotton, tobacco, and wheat. Members would have to pay storage fees, and nonmembers could profit by selling at the same prices. Public opinion meant nothing to them, for they were too remote on their farms. Members themselves would break contracts to deliver if it was advantageous, that is, if markets went higher than delivery prices. A cooperative would be weak in disciplining members. In any event, time would be necessary for pursuing lawsuits. The whole situation would quickly become impossible.[10]

The administration's solutions were of no help to farmers and their families in the 1920s, who were not living well. Eight million farm people lived within five miles of towns or cities with more than twenty-five hundred inhabitants and had access to schools and hospitals, but 20 million lived in isolation. In the middle of the decade, 10 percent of farms had water piped into the houses, 7 percent enjoyed gas or electric lighting, and 38 percent had telephones. Farmers were considered hayseeds, rubes, incapable of enjoying life. As radios became available—their cost with batteries amounting to a few dollars—farmers purchased them, and the radios helped relieve the isolation of farm life. City wiseacres pointed out that this proved that farmers preferred radios to taking baths, because only one farmer in ten had a bathtub. The latter was an impossible luxury without running water, which in the country meant not merely piping water from a well but also purchasing a pump and a gravity or pressure tank and installing drainage.[11]

Coolidge's palliatives for agriculture, supported by Hoover and Jardine, found little favor among farmers, who late in 1922 had begun turning to what became known as McNary-Haugenism, that is, legislation to export farm surpluses. Once the surpluses were gotten rid of, that would be the end of the farm problem.

The father of the several McNary-Haugen bills was an official of the Moline Plow Company, George N. Peek. His grandfather had been the brother-in-law of John Deere—a name every farmer knew—who was the inventor of the famous steel plow and whose company had long stood for marvelous farm inventions. Peek and a collaborator, former brigadier general Hugh S. Johnson, undertook to solve the farm problem because they could not sell plows to "busted customers," and by the end of December 1921 they had prepared a plan.

Most of the ideas for McNary-Haugen were Peek's, and their expression in a pamphlet printed early in 1922, *Equality for Agriculture,* was Johnson's. Johnson was a wordsmith; he could say whatever was on his mind in sharp, vigorous language. The ideas quickly obtained a hearing. Late in 1923, Secretary Wallace came out for them. With assistance within the Department of Agriculture—while Coolidge was busy with Teapot Dome and arranging his nomination—Peek's ideas became a congressional bill sponsored by Sen. Charles L. McNary of Oregon and Representative Haugen of Iowa.

Peek, Johnson, Wallace, McNary, and Haugen all believed that a fair domestic price for farm produce was needed, with the same ratio to the nation's current general price index that prewar agricultural prices bore to the general price index. The ratio price would require computation each year and protection by a fluctuating tariff. Industry had used the tariff to receive "the full tariff differential over world price."[12] It controlled its production and took the differential. Agriculture, without control, saw its production forced down to the world price. Farmers needed the tariff to make the plan effective. A government-sponsored corporation would buy up surpluses and dump them over the tariff at world prices. An "equalization fee" would charge farmers with losses. If one took, for example, the ten years from 1904 to 1914 and established the ratio between prices of farm commodities and nonagricultural goods, or used the general price index that included farm goods and compared it with the current ratio, it would be possible to get a domestic price that would raise the purchasing power of farm commodities to prewar levels. In December 1921, when wheat should have been bringing $1.53 a bushel, its price was ninety-two cents. If the United States produced 800 million bushels of wheat and consumed 600 million, 200 million would have to be sold abroad. The difference between the ratio price and the world price in 1921 was sixty-one cents. The export corporation would lose $122 million on the 200 million bushels. A tax or equalization fee on each of the 800 million bushels sold, the total crop, would be fifteen cents. For all his crop, a farmer would receive $1.38 a bushel, a lot better than ninety-two cents.

The scheme caught on, "swept like a cyclone across the western prairies in late 1922 and 1923." A leader of the Montana Farm Bureau wrote to Senator Walsh that he had never seen anything gain favor so fast, "spreading like wildfire from mouth to ear among the farmers and smaller businessmen." Peek and Johnson got into a personal argument over management of the plow company and went their separate ways, but Peek continued in the parity fight throughout the 1920s, moving to Washington in 1925 to be at its center. Wealthy, he put his own money into the fight and obtained assistance from Governor Lowden, who had married the daughter of sleeping car magnate George Pullman; from Wall Street speculator Bernard Baruch; and from the chairman of General Electric, Owen D. Young. The "man from Moline" was a veritable evangelist in what he and his many supporters believed was an invincible cause. He preached for agriculture as if he were the late Dwight L. Moody or his own contemporary, the Reverend Billy Sunday. He said that nothing could stop his proposal. "I believe it is just as impossible to stop this movement as it would be to undertake to flag a cyclone with a pocket handkerchief."[13]

The plan changed as opportunity presented itself. The first bill appearing in 1924 was a proposal for a gigantic agricultural export corporation capitalized at $200 million to purchase specified commodities when surpluses depressed their markets. It could sell the surpluses abroad or hold them for higher prices at home, with farmers paying the losses through the fee.

The first bill did not work, and McNary reintroduced it in February 1925. Reported favorably from the agriculture committee, it was too late in the winter session to go any further. On the session's final day, it was tacked to the Omnibus Naval Bill, an inconvenient place for Republican and Democratic naval enthusiasts, and lost by a vote of sixty-nine to seventeen.

Fite has written that what gave militancy to the farm relief campaign of the 1920s was concern for protecting agriculture and the country from industrial domination. "Without such a philosophical basis, the drive would have been impotent and without real foundation. Not to recognize this is to miss the true significance of the McNary-Haugen movement." There was the fact that farmers bought in a protected market and sold at world prices. The McNary-Haugen bills' two-price system only resembled the situation created by tariffs protecting domestic manufactures. United States Steel and Standard Oil commonly dumped products abroad. Farmers insisted on retaining their foreign markets, and suggestions that they give them up only reminded them of how industry acted. When Hoover told the agricultural conference that "the fundamental need is balancing of agricultural production to our home demand," critics attacked his concept of balance: "non-export for the farmer and aggressive export for the manufacturer," Mark Sullivan wrote.[14]

What made the Peek-Johnson plan, encapsulated in the McNary-Haugen bills, a serious matter for the Coolidge administration was the drastic drop in cotton prices beginning in 1925 that brought southern farmers scurrying to support what previously had been a midwestern and western program. In the summer of 1924, the chances of picking up support in the Cotton Belt had not been good. Cotton had been thirty cents a pound in December 1923, when much of the crop went to market. It declined but was still more than twenty cents, above the ratio price advocated by McNary-Haugenites. The reasons for the high price were three successive short crops, 1921–23; decreased foreign production; and more demand from U.S. mills and other consumers as the country lifted itself out of the depression. But then, as happened with wheat and other commodities, cotton received its comeuppance. It became subject to competition from mills using the nonagricultural fiber rayon. A larger crop in 1925 made prices fall. Next year, a record crop of 17 million bales, together with large carryovers from 1925, broke prices to a ruinous level, twelve cents a pound. Peek in early 1926 offered cooperation to the southern farm leaders, telling the American Cotton Growers Exchange to "write their own ticket." He was frank about it, saying that he would meet southern wishes in return for "cooperation in helping us get what we want."[15]

Unlike the wheat people, the cotton people did not favor an export-dumping plan, but rather a central agency to keep surpluses from depressing prices. They liked the notion of cooperatives under federal assistance. And so the third McNary-Haugen bill introduced in January 1927 included a farm board working through cooperatives to dispose of surpluses of basic crops. This version of McNary-Haugen was diplomatic in other ways. The fee to finance orderly marketing, whether holding or dumping, was to be collected through middlemen instead of producers, in the "transportation, processing, or sale" of a crop, and until the fee could be collected, Congress was to provide $250 million. Yet the bill did not speak of a special price objective, parity. McNary used the language of his enemies, stressing the surplus problem, the "unduly depressing" nature of surpluses.

To the Coolidge-Hoover-Jardine forces, the joining of southern farmers with those in the Midwest and West must have seemed frightening. Republican control of Congress, especially of the Senate, had been insecure beginning with the Harding administration, for the parties were closely matched and plagued by the wobbling of progressives. Now there was this alliance of farmers, whose congressional supporters had become known as the farm bloc. The bloc had come into being in May 1921, when Senator Kenyon invited a group of midwestern and southern senators to discuss the needs of agriculture. The meeting was held in the Washington offices of the Farm Bureau Federation. A dozen senators were present, together with advisers from the Department of Agriculture. By 1927, senators from other farm states had brought the total in the bloc to between twenty and thirty. In the House, there was less formal organization of a hundred farm-state congressmen.

Sen. George H. Moses of New Hampshire, where farming was about as important as in Vermont, heaped ridicule on the farm bloc, describing it as twenty lawyers, an editor (Capper of Kansas), and a well digger (Norbeck). The bloc, he claimed, had a padded membership; when it became popular with rural constituents, some senators "came in for cover." He liked to tell how Senator Kellogg, who was in trouble in Minnesota because he preferred Washington to St. Paul, attended a meeting for five minutes and received a great deal of publicity in Minnesota.[16]

But the bloc was a matter of deep concern to the administration. Coolidge tried to play up to farm bloc senators. Conservative senators complained that Norbeck, McNary, and Capper were more welcome in the executive offices than were the president's majority leader, Sen. Charles Curtis of Kansas, and the faithful Sen. James E. Watson of Indiana.

Unfortunately for farmers—midwestern, western, and southern—and their bloc in Congress, they faced a clever opponent in the White House, who had spent years calculating political forces in Massachusetts. Measurements on the national scene were more complex, but Coolidge was an experienced calculator. When his own nostrums for the farm problem broke down in the face of McNary-Haugen enthusiasm, he was able to look into what he faced with the farmers. McNary-Haugen did not become serious until 1926–27. Confronting it, Coolidge saw that there was no such thing as a united group of farmers, even though southerners had joined; farmers were as different as the commodities they produced. Growers of wheat, raisers of livestock, dairymen, cotton and tobacco farmers, and vegetable raisers had little in common. There were regional differences, and cattle feeders, for example, did not want higher grain prices. Peek's inability to bring in the cotton farmers until the break in the price of cotton showed the diversity of interests.

Too, the McNary-Haugen bills had plenty of loose ends, which were obvious to everyone who read them. There was the complexity of administering a plan. Crops differed in percentages exported—20 or 25 percent for wheat, 50 percent for cotton. Corn was usually fed to hogs, and the latter went to market rather than the former. Peek admitted that administrative problems required study and took the position that "if the plan was applied to wheat alone it would inspire such confidence as to immediately stimulate general activity."[17]

Coolidge believed that higher prices would increase surpluses, which was the position of most economists. Historically, this always happened, and there was no reason to suppose that it would not happen again. Jardine put the case sharply, saying that McNary-Haugen "might create an artificially high price for wheat for one year. But . . . the guaranteed high price would bring in all the marginal acreage; our exportable surplus would double and treble, and the structure would come toppling down of its own weight." The McNary-Haugenites never faced this criticism. Peek admitted it privately: "I think it is true that a substantial increase in price will bring additional production and that unless the situation is intelligently handled there is danger of breaking down the plan."[18]

In the latter 1920s, the farmers' position vis-à-vis their antagonists, the industrialists, was improving. After 1921, nonagricultural goods dropped in price, and prices of farm products increased. The farm dollar rose from sixty-nine cents in 1921 to ninety-one cents in 1928.

Coolidge must have known that many supporters of McNary-Haugen in Congress were lukewarm and offered their support for reasons other than conviction. There had been vote-trading with supporters of a branch banking bill. Some were making a record for themselves. A story was told of Senator Watson's explanation of why he voted for McNary-Haugen when at first he opposed it. Someone asked, "Jim, how come?" His answer: "Well, you know there comes a time in the life of every politician when he must rise above his principles."[19] Senator Curtis, although majority leader, voted as Kansas desired. Watson and Curtis expected a veto.

Secretary Mellon cast his influence against farm legislation. He lined up opponents of McNary-Haugen: businessmen of all sorts beyond small-town merchants who dealt with farmers, laborers concerned about the cost of groceries, southern Democrats other than cotton and tobacco farmers, economists, editors of many farm journals who knew a nostrum when they saw one. In a speech of June 1926, Mellon told them why putting the government in the business of caring for farmers was wrong. McNary-Haugen's effect, he said, "will be to increase the cost of living to every consumer of five basic agricultural commodities." He averred that "we shall have the unusual spectacle of the American consuming public paying a bonus to the producers of five major agricultural commodities, with a resulting decrease in the purchasing power of wages, and at the same time contributing a subsidy to the foreign consumers, who under the proposed plan will secure American commodities at prices below the American level." With European labor living off American labor, foreign competitors could undersell U.S. manufactures in U.S. and foreign markets. Farmers would ruin American industry and labor.[20]

McNary-Haugen passed twice, and each time Coolidge vetoed it. On the first occasion, February 1927, Coolidge's secretary, Sanders, asked Jardine "whether there is any objection to its approval." That same day, Jardine sent the president a twenty-one-page memorandum that virtually revealed its authorship: Hoover.[21] The first half of the resultant veto, a fourteen-thousand-word document, followed the Hoover-Jardine memorandum. The rest was repetition with as much hyperbole as the traffic would bear, and perhaps a little more. In his first annual message, the president had said that "no complicated scheme of relief, no plan for government fixing of prices, no resort to the public treasury will be of any permanent value in establishing agriculture." The veto message ornamented these words with statements that the bill was unsound, unconstitutional, a violation of "the philosophy of our government" and "the spirit of our institutions." The equalization fee was a "vicious form of taxation." Higher prices would encourage production.

The McNary-Haugenites regrouped, modified the bill in light of some of Coolidge's objections, and repassed it by large majorities in May 1928, only to receive a second, harsher veto. The bill was bureaucracy gone mad, autocracy, ponderously futile, a preposterous economic and commercial fallacy, full of vicious devices, delusive experiments, and fantastic promises.

An apparent solution was the Agricultural Marketing Act, signed by Coolidge's successor, Hoover, on 15 June 1929. It passed the House by a vote of 366 to 35. The Senate passed a similar measure with an amendment adding export debentures, but the conference committee removed them. It provided government funds to support prices and had no dumping proviso. A radical proposal had worn itself down through compromise with southerners and efforts to placate Coolidge. When Hoover signed the marketing act, he was flanked by McNary and Haugen. The president gave each one a pen. A constituent excitedly wrote to Haugen, asking if he had received his pen, and the answer was a little sharp: "Yes, I received the pen with which the President signed the Federal Farm Bill. I also received the pen used by the Speaker in signing the bill which was vetoed by Mr. Coolidge, so I am well supplied with pens."[22]

One might contend that the long struggle for McNary-Haugen was a waste of time. In none of its forms would it have worked, for the reasons cited by intelligent foes and friends. Still, something had to be done, whether McNary-Haugen or the Coolidge-Hoover-Jardine palliatives, for the farm problem of the 1920s was a political problem that demanded attention. Unhappily, the only other courses were politically impossible. One would have been to follow the economics of Adam Smith and let farmers take their punishment, a process that would have been equivalent to early-nineteenth-century England under the Corn Laws. To be sure, this procedure would not have worked in a democracy, which England was not in the nineteenth century. The other unacceptable procedure, given the outlook of Americans during the 1920s, would have been subsidies for farmers, with adjustment for commodities they produced. Americans had not yet learned the meaning of "entitlement," a word that received currency in the 1960s in the flush of post–World War II prosperity. Even proponents of McNary-Haugen were hesitant about subsidies and found them acceptable only if disguised as equalization fees or debentures.

6

★ ★ ★ ★ ★

SOCIETY

In several important aspects of American society, the Coolidge administration made its presence felt—in one aspect positively, albeit on a remarkably small scale, and in the others negatively in one way or another. This record was in accord with the traditional view of the federal government's involvement in social issues, a view that had marked the government since its institution in 1789. The single positive program of a social nature advocated by the Coolidge administration was road construction. Actually, it had been anticipated by the Republican president's Democratic predecessor Wilson in the Federal Aid Road Act of 1916. Throughout the 1920s, the government in Washington sponsored a matching program with the states for the construction of roads. The other involvements of the administration in issues of American society were all negative. The Eighteenth Amendment to the Constitution forbade "manufacture, sale, or transportation of intoxicating liquors within, the importation thereof into, or the exportation thereof from the United States and all territory subject to the jurisdiction thereof, for beverage purposes." Many Americans considered the legislation of enforcement, the Volstead Act, an outrage, depriving them of their right to take a drink. The administration virtually agreed and enforced Prohibition in such a lackadaisical way as to make it ineffective. The federal government did little for civil rights and liberties, consigning those concerns to the conservative courts, which did little. On immigration it went along with the obvious desire of Congress and the American people to close off the large influx of previous years and made its own special contribution by excluding Japanese immigrants. Lastly, it looked with a jaundiced eye toward the decade's proposed great social experiment of using the wartime facilities at Muscle Shoals in Alabama to lift the entire Tennessee Valley out of that region's decades-old poverty.

The Coolidge era was a time of small government, evident in the nearly complete lack of federal social programs. The idea of old-age pensions had hardly entered the national consciousness; in 1928, 1,221 persons in the United States received pensions, and the total benefits were $222,589. At the time of the stock market crash in 1929, neither the federal government nor the states had a program of unemployment compensation. During the depression of 1920–21, John R. Commons of the University of Wisconsin drafted a bill for such compensation that received support by the Wisconsin Federation of Labor and progressives in the legislature. It was introduced at every session thereafter, opposed by employers, and defeated every time.

Most surprising was the primitive state of federal welfare provisions across the nation. *Recent Social Trends* made a point about this. One of its chapter writers proudly noted that in 1928 the public welfare expenditures of the federal government reached a total of $752 million, considerably greater than the public welfare spending of all other public agencies of the country put together. After this statement, the author explained that 96 percent of the sum represented expenditures for former soldiers and sailors. Excluding aid to veterans, the federal government spent $30 million on public welfare. Of that amount, $11.5 million was for hospitalization and other care for American Indians under its several dozen agencies, $6.4 million for maintaining prisons, $4.9 million for medical treatment of merchant seamen, and $2.9 million for regulation of immigrants. In appearance, the federal government was busily engaged in welfare, with the creation of the Children's Bureau in 1912, the Employment Service in 1917, the Woman's Bureau in 1920, and the Apportionments for Infancy and Maternity Hygiene in 1921. But the Children's Bureau and the Woman's Bureau may have been reactions to the imminent passage of the Nineteenth Amendment giving women the right to vote, and the work of those bureaus was neither exciting nor important. The maternity services were discontinued in 1929. The term "public welfare" itself had appeared only in 1914–15 in departments in Chicago, St. Louis, Cincinnati, and Cleveland, followed by Los Angeles in 1916, Detroit and Richmond in 1919, New York and Philadelphia in 1920, and Milwaukee in 1922. Cities and counties spent $500 million on welfare in 1928.

Of all the social changes of the 1920s, by far the most important was the appearance of vast numbers of automobiles. It introduced what historians of the phenomenon described as "automobility." To be sure, the decade during which Coolidge was president did not mark the introduction of automobiles. In 1921, there were 9.3 million cars registered. Indeed, in the early 1920s, popular magazines were filled with discussions of the question, "Is the auto market saturated?" In 1921, the well-known economist of the Cleveland Trust Company, Leonard P. Ayres, announced that "very nearly all Americans who can afford to have cars now own them."[1] But consider what happened over the next years. By 1929, registrations reached 26.7 million. The nation possessed more autos than radios (10 million) or telephones (19.9 million). The number of passenger cars produced annually rose from 1.5 million in 1921 to 5.3 million in 1929. Of the total number of registrations in 1929, 23 million were passenger cars, which meant that the entire population of the country might be speeding along the roads, that is, if there were sufficient improved roads or the weather was good enough to navigate the unimproved ones.

Production of so many cars changed the economy of the United States. In 1926, automobile manufacturing ranked first in value of product. Motor vehicle factory sales had a wholesale value of $3 billion, and motorists spent $10 billion in operating expenses, traveling 141 billion miles. The car industry was the lifeblood of the petroleum industry, a leading customer of the steel industry, and the largest consumer of plate glass and rubber.

Automobiles raised questions as to their meaning for society. In the first decade of the century, President Wilson of Princeton University expressed his concern that the motorcar would stimulate socialism in the United States by inciting the poor to envy the rich.[2] He was partly wrong: auto envy did not lead to socialism, but cars led to envy everywhere, which the manufacturers and their advertising agencies exploited.

Accidents rose rapidly, with 23,600 deaths (including the deaths of 10,000 children) in 1924, 700,000 injuries, and $1 billion in property damage. *Motor Age* regarded these losses as "one of the big economic problems of the day." Unfortunately, the automobile industry dominated the National Safety Council, which had been founded in 1913 to combat all kinds of accidents. The council did not take an active role in preventing automobile accidents, announcing that there was little possibility of change until "those using the highways come to have a better understanding of what the laws are."[3]

The impact of the "car revolution" or the "automobile age," however one wishes to describe it, was large. For farmers, the automobile age meant ease of travel and in performing farm tasks. On the 6.5 million farms in the United States in 1924, there were 4.2 million automobiles and 370,000 trucks, not to mention all the Fordsons and other tractors. City dwellers celebrated their liberation from the unsanitary horse, which had left filth everywhere. Few people realized that automobile exhaust was going to "prove even more detrimental to public health than horse exhaust once had been."[4] The car revolution became the driving force in the creation of such residential suburbs as Beverly Hills (which grew 2,485 percent in 1920–30), Glendale (363 percent), Inglewood (492 percent), and Huntington Park (444 percent), all suburbs of Los Angeles; Cleveland Heights (234 percent), Garfield Heights (511 percent), and Shaker Heights (1,000 percent—this, of course, was the Van Sweringens' creation), suburbs of Cleveland; and Grosse Pointe (724 percent) and Ferndale (689 percent), suburbs of Detroit.[5] There were continuing problems in transportation, and the new suburbs exacerbated them. Only in later years did it become apparent that urban transportation required a mix of trucks and buses and rail transportation rather than mass ownership of cars. In the 1920s, parking in cities became difficult, sidewalks had to give way to more street, and traffic jams appeared everywhere, reducing and sometimes ending automobility.

The sudden appearance of millions of automobiles vastly changed life in the United States, and without the public construction of local, state, and national roads, the new automobiles would have been useless. Just to describe the poor condition of roads across the length and breadth of the United States in the decade before the road building of the 1920s is to relate the unbelievable. It was a different age. In 1915, a farmer living near Kansas City undertook to convey his mother and uncle to a place named Mone-gaw Springs. As he informed his fiancée after the experience,

> we almost reached the springs without an accident. We got within a half mile of them and ran over a stump. I spilled Uncle Harry over the front seat and threw Mamma over my own head. . . . I backed Lizzie off the stump and ran her into town with a badly bent axle. Mamma and I started for home at 6:00 A.M. on Monday. Got within seventy-five miles of it and it began to rain. Had the nicest slipping time you ever saw. What with a crooked axle and a bent steering wheel I could hardly stay in the road. Five miles south of Harrisonville Lizzie took a header for the ditch and got there.

A farmer came along and took his fellow farmer and "Mamma" to his house, where they stayed the night. The next morning, the friendly farmer hitched his team to the car and pulled it out of the ditch. The driver, Harry S. Truman, got home at 3:00 P.M. Tuesday.[6]

In 1919, a U.S. Army officer helped supervise a cross-country tour by a convoy of seventy-five trucks, ambulances, automobiles, and repair cars. In addition to rating the vehicles, the tour was to be a test of the nation's highways. Both achieved minimum standards; Maj. Dwight D. Eisenhower's convoy averaged fifty miles a day. The trip of 3,242 miles required two months.

The initial action of the government in Washington to improve the nation's roads was the Federal Aid Road Act of 1916, which appropriated $75 million over five years, in conjunction with at least equal amounts appropriated by the states. The money was spent, but most of it had to be spent after the war, by which time the need for roads was far more pressing than the sponsors of the act could have imagined. Beginning in 1916, the annual production of passenger cars was over a million a year.

The need for a larger program was evident in the Federal Highway Act of 1921, which stipulated an annual appropriation of $75 million, reaching $690 million by the end of the decade. And unlike the act of 1916, that of 1921 created a national system of roads. Under the matching grant arrangement, the act's appropriations could be used only for the construction of roads, not for maintenance; the latter cost, which came to one-fourth the cost of construction, was picked up by the states. The act of 1921 called for a road system not exceeding 7 percent of the total road mileage of the states. The 7 percent figure meant 200,000 miles of road, of which 102,000 became the federal system. Eventually the country's national highway system totaled 350,000 miles. Its purpose was to arrange a network of arterial highways serving every city of 50,000 or more.

Gasoline taxes, imposed by the states, paid for much road construction. Oregon, New Mexico, and Colorado enacted the taxes in 1919, and they spread to the last holdout, New York, in 1929. That year, the combined revenue of state gasoline taxes was $431 million. Rates of three or four cents a gallon were common. By 1929, twenty-one states no longer used any general property taxes for main roads. The reason was that "the gasoline tax was superior as a user tax because the amount of gasoline consumed in a vehicle was a good measure of the use of the road and also of the damage that a vehicle did to a road."[7] Moreover, there was little complaint about the gasoline tax. The chief collector of the gasoline tax in Tennessee exclaimed in 1926, "Who ever heard, before, of a popular tax?"[8] Unlike licenses, it taxed "foreign" vehicles in interstate traffic. It was exceedingly easy to collect; the cost was less than 1 percent. It was collected in dribbles and was unnoticeable. In addition, the gradual reduction in the price of gasoline during the 1920s, caused in part by new methods of refining, made the tax less apparent; gasoline in 1920 cost 29.38 cents a gallon, and by 1931, it was 16.98 cents. The first federal gasoline tax did not come until 1932.

The cost of American roads under the 1921 act and under taxing or bond issues by states, counties, and municipalities was surprisingly high. In 1929, the last year of the automobile boom in the United States, when Detroit factories turned out more cars than would be produced annually until 1949, government at all levels spent $2.23 billion on roads.

Between 1921 and 1930, the total mileage of roads and streets increased only 3 percent, or 100,000 miles; a similar amount of road was added in the next decade. The mileage of surfaced highway doubled in the 1920s, and again in the 1930s. The year 1945 saw mileage of improved roads exceed that of unimproved for the first time.

It is interesting that the act of 1921 led almost immediately to the numbering of the new federal highways and the creation of a uniform system of road signs, an important if secondary task in creating a road system. At the suggestion of the American Association of State Highway Officials in 1925, Secretary of Agriculture Jardine appointed a joint board of state and federal highway officials "to undertake immediately the selection and designation of a comprehensive system of through interstate routes and to devise a comprehensive and uniform scheme for designating such routes in such manner as to give them a conspicuous place among the highways of the country." This resulted in the numbering of federal roads, with even numbers for east-west roads and odd for north-south. The board designated the more important transcontinental routes in multiples of ten, beginning at U.S. Route 10 south of the Canadian boundary, through U.S. Route 40 across the midsection of the country, to U.S. Route 90 traversing the southern states from coast to coast. The historic north-south road on the East Coast became U.S. Route 1, and numbers increased into the west up to U.S. Route 101, the West Coast road familiar to all Californians. The federal role in road construction meant the adoption of uniform signs for stops, railroads, turns, and curves—a system of hexagons, oblongs, and, much later, triangles with which all Americans became familiar.

With the numbering of federal roads, such projects as the Lincoln Highway, organized in Detroit in 1912–13, virtually came to an end. Vestiges remained, recalling the initial effort to promote coast-to-coast travel before the federal government stepped in. In common with other named roads, the Lincoln Highway was reduced to road signs bearing the likeness of the Civil War president. It approximated U.S. Route 30 east of the Mississippi and west to Salt Lake City.

The nature of improved American roads, compared with those in Europe in the interwar era, was unremarkable. In the nineteenth century, road surfaces were improved by use of cobblestones, planks, wooden blocks, bricks, asphalt, and crushed stone. The first mile of concrete road was built in Wayne County, Michigan, the county of Detroit, in 1909, and people came from all over the United States and Canada to see it. Beyond concrete surfacing and the continued use of asphalt and crushed stone surfacing, American road building seldom went. Curiously, special-purpose roads first appeared in Westchester County and on Long Island outside New York City. They were conceived in 1906 and completed in 1923, and they were created to alleviate congestion and were exclusively for noncommercial vehicles. Most roads of the 1920s were constructed in conventional form, with no access control, and they were predominantly two-lane. After 1924, there were stretches of multilane road in heavily traveled areas, but they seldom had center divisions and frequently were three lanes, not four. The turnpike era came in the 1930s, with the Merritt Parkway in Connecticut and the Pennsylvania Turnpike. There was no attempt to construct such imaginative systems as the German autobahn. To be sure, the German system had other purposes than American roads. It was primarily to alleviate unemployment and looked to military use. Germans possessed far fewer cars than Americans: in 1927, 196 people per motor vehicle, versus 5.3 in the United States.

In retrospect, it is possible to see that the presence of the federal government in the first years of the automobile age was far smaller than it should have been. Here was a revolutionary change in the way Americans lived. "America became the world's first true consumer-oriented society during the early part of this century because its citizens were eager literally to reshape their land and their everyday lives to accommodate the gasoline powered motor car." While other industrial nations suffered wars and revolutions, Americans "built a new kind of consumer-oriented capitalism around the production, sale, and use of tens of millions of automobiles."[9] The 1920s were a time when a vision of the future should have been possible; the car boom was clear to all adults of that decade. But the leaders of the federal government seem to have virtually ignored it, other than spending $75 million a year. Coolidge never had a car until after he left the White House. Even then he did not drive it, employing a chauffeur. As with other aspects of government, he observed the car revolution rather than doing something about it. In his acerbic manner, he may have thought that Secretary Hoover would do something about it. As it happened, no one did anything except officials of the states, counties, cities, and towns. State officials received a small amount of federal money and guidance on the numbering of national roads and on road signs, but little else. No one offered advice about alternative modes of transportation.

The second social problem in which government took a hand in the 1920s was Prohibition, the Eighteenth Amendment and its legislation of enforcement. The Volstead Act of 1919 construed intoxicating liquor as that containing as little as 0.5 percent alcohol by volume. It fixed penalties for the sale of liquor, provided injunctions against establishments found to be selling liquor, contained a search and seizure clause, and permitted retention of private stocks bought before the act went into effect. Curiously, many contemporary and later Americans described Prohibition as the most outrageous example of government intrusion into the social lives of citizens, but in reality, enforcement of Prohibition was so light as to have been virtually nonexistent.

To understand what happened during the dry decade, it is necessary to understand that Prohibition replaced the saloon, with all its attendant evils—an institution that few Americans living today have any connection with. The saloon can be traced back to frontier days, when life was hard and society was difficult to enjoy. It may have obtained a new lease on life when the "new immigration" beginning in the 1880s brought in great numbers of people who yearned for society and had grown up with the unrestricted but often more discreet drinking of Europe. By the turn of the century and after, the saloon was a lively part of American towns and cities, with 178,000 across the country, in addition to scores of thousands of "blind pigs" selling liquor in dry towns and in cities that were fully wet.

The saloon led to unacceptable public behavior. The assistant attorney general in charge of Prohibition enforcement in the 1920s, Mabel Walker Willebrandt, had been a moderate drinker before the Volstead Act. But she remembered that in 1911–14, when she was attending law school in Los Angeles, she had to wait late at night, after the law library had closed, on the corner of First and Main Streets for the interurban car. "Indelibly impressed on my mind is the fact that scarcely a night—never a week—went by without several drunken men reeling past me from the five saloons near that corner."[10]

Moreover, industrial America needed more discipline—enforced by government, if necessary. Economically if not politically, Henry Ford was one of the leaders of his era. In his remarks about Prohibition, he was not far off the mark in relating how alcohol and machinery did not mix. Typically he exaggerated, but his commentaries brought much contemporary agreement from industrial leaders. "I would not be able to build a car that will run two hundred thousand miles if booze were around," he asserted, "because I wouldn't have accurate workmen."[11] An even more important problem of drunkenness was the huge loss of life because of drunk driving.

In the latter 1920s, as evasion of the law became organized, it was possible to contend that what President Hoover would describe as "a noble experiment" had been anything but that. Contemporaries and some historians claimed that Prohibition made drinking fashionable, especially among young people, who were too unsophisticated to understand sophistication. It built up a criminal class that profited from selling bootleg liquor.

There was no real proof of these results. Young people are always willing to try forbidden fruits. The criminal class was already there; the notorious Chicago gangster Alphonse Capone may not have made much money on liquor, for he had to pay enormous bribes. His basic industries were probably those he had taken over before the era of Prohibition—gambling and prostitution.[12]

There is no doubt the law was defied, although the stories were so piquant, sometimes so amusing, that they may have made the defiance seem larger than it was. In Philadelphia, a bottle manufacturing plant filled large monthly orders for Pinch bottles and other antique shapes with trademarks of old companies blown in the glass; the bottles would be filled elsewhere with synthetic products that gave evidence of age. A drug concern in a Texas town secured medicinal permits for two hundred barrels of Jamaica ginger, which was 90 percent alcohol; as Mabel Willebrandt wrote, two hundred barrels would have cared for a quantity of old-fashioned tummy aches. Investment bankers advertised an issue of securities of an industrial alcohol company by informing investors that demand for the product was constantly increasing, from 1 million gallons in 1906 to 90 million in 1928. In Chicago, the state attorney revoked the licenses of fourteen hundred soft-drink parlors and twice as many speakeasies, testifying to confusion over what was sold under local signboards and to the existence of many more places in need of revocation. All the while, liquor came across the Canadian border, or Americans crossed the border to obtain it. According to the *Congressional Record,*

> Four and twenty Yankees
> Feeling mighty dry
> Took a trip to Canada
> And bought a case of rye.
> When the case was opened
> The Yanks began to sing—
> "To hell with the President
> God Save the King!"[13]

If one did not wish to purchase substitutes or patronize speakeasies or cross the border, it was possible to do everything at home. Congressman Fiorello H. LaGuardia demonstrated before moving picture cameras in front of the Capitol how he could produce beer with 4 percent alcohol by mixing two parts of malt tonic and one part of near beer. Before Prohibition, the Department of Agriculture had published bulletins on making alcohol from apples, oats, bananas, pumpkins, and parsnips, and after Prohibition, it continued to distribute them.

Family physicians frequently diagnosed and treated cases of thirstitis; in 1929, druggists filled 11 million prescriptions. A religious awakening accompanied Prohibition; during the first two years, the demand for sacramental wines increased by eight hundred thousand gallons.[14]

For the most part, the highest officials of the federal government observed the law. President Harding kept a private liquor supply at the White House and served friends, although the often quoted description of a White House party by Alice Roosevelt Longworth was probably a gross exaggeration.[15] Many times Dr. Boone was on the second floor of the White House during the Harding administration and said that he never saw a bottle. Reporter Mark Sullivan told a story or two of having a drink with Harding, but the president had to enter a dressing room and pull out the bottle, and the presidential cache hardly sounded like the display Alice Longworth recounted. As for President Coolidge, he served no alcohol. In his college years, he was known to drink beer, but he offered no drinks to White House guests. When the artist Frank O. Salisbury arrived to paint the presidential portrait, Coolidge offered him a cigar, and Salisbury explained that he did not smoke. The president said, "Well, there is very little in these days that we can offer you."[16] It is true that when Coolidge was having indigestion and gaining weight, Boone found that Elixir Lactopeptin was beneficial. That, however, was not illegal. The president liked its flavor, and the physician believed that its small amount of alcohol gave him a lift. Coolidge would ask for it frequently, even when Boone and his fellow physician, Dr. James F. Coupal, did not prescribe it.[17] Coolidge's successor Hoover served no liquor. One story had it that at the outset of Prohibition, Lou Henry Hoover broke all the bottles in the Hoover household.

Members of the cabinet during the 1920s were something else. Secretary of State Kellogg supported Prohibition and had voted for the Volstead Act as a member of the Senate. He sent a telegram to the executive secretary of the Republican Woman's Club in St. Paul, "Have not only voted for all prohibition legislation, but am heartily in favor of the enforcement of the prohibition law."[18] Nonetheless, he told Boone that when he came from St. Paul to Washington, he was fortunate to acquire a good butler from the previous occupant of his Washington house. Whenever Kellogg went out to dinner, the butler would hold out a tray with one martini if it was going to be a wet dinner, and two or three martinis if it was going to be a dry dinner.[19] When the secretary played eighteen holes of golf on Washington courses, which he frequently did, he always looked forward to the nineteenth hole.

Secretary Mellon followed the lead of the secretary of state. According to the diary of William R. Castle, Jr., "All these Pittsburgh people are very cordial and friendly. Our table consisted of the Reeds [Sen. and Mrs. David A. Reed], Mr. Andrew Mellon and Mr. and Mrs. Dick Mellon [the secretary's brother]. It was very pleasant to get to know the Secretary well and in quite an unofficial way and amusing to give a drink to the Chief Prohibition Enforcement Officer of the United States."[20]

Secretary Mellon was not always attuned to politics, and if a story of Sullivan's can be believed, he came very close to an embarrassment that might have forced his resignation from the cabinet. According to the story, two writers for the *Ladies Home Journal* interviewed him about Prohibition enforcement, and one of them, an old-fashioned newspaperman, undertook to "get around" him. The secretary naively said that when he came to Washington he brought his liquor with him, that he personally was not obeying the spirit of the law, and that many others were not. The writers' editor realized the story's import and sent one of the reporters back to Mellon with the article to tell him that out of consideration the magazine would not print it. Mellon did not grasp the position he was in and did not seem especially grateful. The editor instructed his writer to leave the article with the secretary with the understanding that if Mellon ever felt moved to say such things publicly, he should let the *Ladies Home Journal* have the story.[21]

Stories involving violation of the law by senators and members of the House of Representatives were legion. Mabel Willebrandt heard tales of members of both houses drunk on the floor. The irrepressible Jim Watson of Indiana espoused the dry cause but was walking along the corridors of the Senate Office Building and asked Walter E. Edge of New Jersey for a drink, as he had had a long afternoon. Edge refused but invited Watson to his house. Edge had another story about coming back from Europe aboard the *Leviathan* with Sen. Elmer Thomas, the well-known Oklahoma dry. Thomas had been to Russia and produced a bottle of vodka. "We made sure that he would have none left to embarrass him at the port of New York."[22] All Washington was amused by Rep. George Holden Tinkham of Massachusetts, a life member of the Society of Mayflower Descendants, whose long black beard made him look like the big-game hunter he was. He had what his friend Joe Martin described as "a virulent hatred" of Prohibition. On the walls of his apartment in the old Arlington Hotel, he hung stuffed heads of hyenas and other ferocious animals he had shot during his trips to Africa, each head named after a prohibitionist. One time Martin took a leader of the Woman's Christian Temperance Union and her daughter, wife of the governor of New Hampshire, to see the apartment. "This is Andrew J. Volstead," said Tinkham, pointing to an ungodly-looking beast. "And this," he said as they approached the next head, "is Wayne B. Wheeler, of the Anti-Saloon League."[23]

But amidst all the evasions of Prohibition was a fairly obvious fact that displayed political judgment but said little of political morality. What seems to have happened during the Prohibition era is that political leaders gave in because they felt they had to, and then they followed an exquisitely inattentive course toward enforcement, sensing that Prohibition would either gather support and make itself effective or lose support and go down to defeat. Many politicians did not much care which way the decision went. If necessary, they would support the law; if convenient, they would not. The advance of local and state option during the decade before national Prohibition created an issue that the leaders did not want to face. It reflected rural and small-town sentiment, and within cities there was much support. The support cut party lines and could derange allegiances. Prohibition came to the fore during World War I and its aftermath, concomitant with passage of the Nineteenth Amendment giving women the right to vote. For a while, the latter created great uncertainty, for leaders feared that a concentrated women's vote could derange all their calculations. It seemed wise to let the Prohibition experiment proceed and attempt to deal with the Nineteenth Amendment. Two experiments at the same time were confusing.

Federal enforcement was a joke. When President Harding brought Mabel Willebrandt into the Department of Justice, it was to undertake duties in addition to enforcement, such as supervising income, estate, and corporation tax cases. Congress in 1922 gave the Prohibition Bureau $6.7 million for three thousand employees, including clerks. The country was divided into federal districts, each headed by an administrator with a salary of $6,000 a year, and agents were paid $1,800. Field agents were untrained, and there were insufficient numbers. In the district for New England, there were 91 agents; in the New York City district, 129. In Oklahoma—a few years removed from the oil boom, when the state was filled with wildcatters—there were 18 Prohibition agents.

The states behaved shamelessly. They passed the task of enforcement to the federal government, merely notifying federal officials of illegal activity. In Maryland, there was no provision for enforcement. The New York State Assembly in 1923 voted to repeal the enforcement law, and Governor Smith signed the bill. Governor Pinchot of Pennsylvania, being a prohibitionist, sought enforcement; he insisted on daily reports of arrests and quantities of liquor confiscated, and in four years the police made 13,368 arrests and padlocked many saloons. Enforcement meant draconian measures in Philadelphia, where in 1923 the mayor borrowed Brig. Gen. Smedley D. Butler from the U.S. Marines. Butler had proved himself in China during the Boxer Rebellion and in Haiti during the occupation, when marines under his supervision and Haitian labor had built a remarkable number of roads in a very short time, thereby pacifying the unruly republic. During his first five days in Philadelphia, he closed 973 saloons, but the citizens turned against him, making his task difficult. At the end of 1925, his leave of absence from the military expired. Pinchot went to Washington to ask President Coolidge for a two-year extension. Coolidge sent Butler back to China to command the marine contingent permanently stationed there. The general issued his final communiqué, saying that "trying to enforce the law in Philadelphia was worse than any battle I was ever in." State legislatures in 1926 appropriated $698,855 for enforcement, estimated to be one-eighth the amount they spent to enforce laws for the control of fish and game.

Even with the lack of enforcement, most citizens chose to respect the law. Some respected it because they had no alternative. Bootleg liquor was three to six times its pre-1920 price. A student of Prohibition has concluded that the consumption of liquor dropped radically during the years when the Eighteenth Amendment was in force. A report for Congress in 1972 showed that annual per capita consumption—with beer, wine, and distilled liquor converted to gallons of absolute alcohol—stood at 2.6 for 1906–10, before state dry laws had national effect. After the end of Prohibition, in 1934, the figure stood at 0.97; in 1940, it was 1.56. Only by 1970 had it risen to the level of 1906–10.[24]

Unfortunately for the experiment, when memory of the old-time saloon dimmed and the Great Depression made the revival of an old industry attractive, Prohibition came to an end.

Civil rights and liberties took a backseat among social issues of the 1920s. In the case of civil rights, this was understandable, if only because the rights of black Americans had seldom concerned their white brothers and sisters. The Civil War had disposed of the issue; not until the late 1930s did civil rights come to the fore. The doctrine of separate and unequal had never been given up in the South, and things were not much better in the North, not out of a tradition of racial inferiority, but because black Americans lived in city ghettoes and rarely appeared in small towns and villages. City political machines solicited black votes, but for the most part, blacks did not disturb citywide equations and had little importance in state office-holding. The influx of black workers into northern cities during the war would have major importance; 300,000 to 400,000 blacks went north to replace the labor of white immigrants who moved up the economic scale or entered the army. The wartime influx may have been the most important event for black Americans since emancipation, but in the 1920s, it had not yet acquired political importance. Within black society, a debate went on between followers of the late Booker T. Washington of Tuskegee Institute and the Harvard-trained W. E. B. Du Bois of Atlanta University, between those who believed in the need for blacks to make themselves useful to white Americans through hard work and thereby receive respect, and those who believed in political activism. The debate hissed and sputtered, but the mass of blacks did not know of its existence.

For most Americans, the lynchings in the South that occurred year after dismal year did not seem to bother them. Perhaps this was because such events went virtually unreported or were subsumed under the rubric of actions of posses. People who did pay attention were made to feel better by the fact that lynching diminished markedly. *Recent Social Trends* treated the decrease in clinical fashion, relating that for thirty years before 1920, the annual average had been eighty-four. Since 1920, the trend was "sharply downward averaging only 16 per year from 1925 to 1929." Lynching, the authors of this sometimes sociological treatise opined, fluctuated with the economic cycle, being more frequent in periods of depression. Perhaps for that reason there were only nine lynchings in 1929.[25]

A congressman from Missouri introduced an antilynching bill in 1922, which passed the House but was prevented from coming to a vote in the Senate. The opposition was mostly southern. Senator Pepper of Pennsylvania argued that because the proposed child labor amendment would allow the federal government to exercise a special guardianship over children in industry, an antilynching bill was reasonable: "there is no good reason why it should not extend protection to our Negro fellow-citizens in the South."[26]

What black Americans needed was the right to vote, and the National Association for the Advancement of Colored People (NAACP) saw the beginning of victory in the case of *Nixon* v. *Herndon* (1927), in which the Supreme Court ruled against a white primary in Texas. Justice Holmes, speaking for the Court, said that "color cannot be made the basis of a statutory classification." After the southern states attempted a series of subterfuges, this landmark decision led to *Smith* v. *Allwright* (1944), which avowed that constitutional rights "would be of little value if they could be thus indirectly denied."

In the 1920s, the irrepressible Representative Tinkham annually cheered supporters of black rights by introducing a bill providing that representation in the House of Representatives be based on number of voters rather than population. Had the bill passed, it would have reduced the South's representation drastically. This led to a denouement that was not especially amusing. Tiring of Tinkham's efforts, the southerners solicited the help of western representatives with a bill to exclude aliens from population figures. This struck at New England; the trans-Mississippi West contained few blacks. Representative Martin of Tinkham's state suggested that Republican leaders further amend the bill with Tinkham's proposition—no aliens, no blacks. The next day, the North and South got together and dropped both propositions.[27]

One might have thought that the progressives in Congress, of whatever party, would have shown their high-minded principles by standing up for black rights, but the very fact that southerners could ally with westerners to try to exclude aliens showed how foolish such a hope was. The principled progressives would have little or nothing to do with American blacks. Senator Walsh of Montana, so keenly against Teapot Dome, said that he would "make very little showing to the colored man." Norbeck of South Dakota wanted "to send all the Negroes back to Africa." Hiram Johnson thought that "perhaps our idea of the fatherhood of God and the brotherhood of man as applied to our citizens of African descent may be a little wrong." He described blacks as "a shiftless and stupid set." As for the Lion of Idaho, he claimed that after "extended study" of the South's treatment of blacks, he believed that no southern law contradicted the Constitution. He put his faith in the Eighteenth Amendment, not the Fourteenth and Fifteenth.[28]

Coolidge may not have seen many blacks in Vermont or even in Massachusetts, and his position on injustice did not stand out on the grand tablet of presidential utterances on that subject. Harding had at least shown some interest and said some good things and, if only in contrast to Wilson, looked good on the issue. Coolidge's predecessor had gone down to Birmingham, spoken to a mixed audience of whites and blacks, and said, "let the black man vote when he is fit to vote; prohibit the white man voting when he is unfit to vote." He advised his audience to "lay aside any program that looks to lining up the black man as a mere political adjunct" and asked for "an end of prejudice."

Coolidge frequently advised Congress on the need for antilynching legislation but otherwise expressed himself privately. Theodore Roosevelt, Jr., liked nothing better than to advise Republican presidents and was often in the Harding White House. Until he left Washington in 1924 to run for governor of New York, he also seems to have been in the Coolidge White House fairly often. In October 1923, he sent a memorandum to the new president on civil rights, to the effect that "the only way to treat the colored people is on a basis of merit, giving the good colored man the position regardless of his race and let it stand there." Politicians, Ted Roosevelt believed, were "too apt to either give no colored man a position or to simply give the job to the rather disreputable politician," and both procedures were wrong. He received a note saying that Coolidge had liked the memo, and Slemp at the White House said that the president had asked for the memo a second time "just before he saw a bunch of the colored brethren who were down representing the equal rights association." Roosevelt went to the White House and met the delegation coming out "in a black cloud." He knew some of the members and "had to stop and talk." He was uncertain what they wanted, but he believed that it was "in general to give the colored man a square deal." Roosevelt informed his diary that he too was in favor of that. He explained his belief to Coolidge and suggested that at the next cabinet meeting the president should ask if there were any positions that could be given to "colored people." Then a search should be made throughout the country (not in Washington, because that would only bring in the unworthy black politicians) for competent blacks to fill the positions. President Coolidge, he added, "agreed and explained at some length how he felt on it."[29] What more the president did about it is unknown, although it is clear that the Coolidge administration did not make any notable appointments of black Americans.

In the 1924 election, Coolidge had no great trouble, but it is worth pointing out that GOP strategy toward the rights of black Americans four years later was clever in the short run but catastrophic in the long run. In 1924, the lackluster Democratic candidate Davis received one-fourth of the black vote. He had promised that if elected he would make no distinctions on the basis of race, even though there was not a single black delegate to the convention in Madison Square Garden, or even an alternate. In the 1928 campaign, Hoover's strategists, probably with his consent, made a bid for southern support, which meant making peace with southern leaders. Although the result was electoral votes from border states, it convinced black leaders to leave the party of Lincoln. In the next election, 1932, they were gone.[30]

James Weldon Johnson, executive secretary of the NAACP, and Walter White, who followed Johnson in the secretaryship, stressed corrective education, legislation, and, when possible, litigation. They focused on antilynching legislation, and although that campaign was without result, their advocacy heightened awareness of the violence against blacks. During the 1920s, the NAACP established itself as the national representative for black Americans.

For Native Americans, the situation in terms of civil rights and liberties was as confused as that of black Americans. The Dawes General Allotment Act of 1887 gave citizenship to Indians born within the United States who had received allotments of land, as well as those who had moved away from tribes and adopted "the habits of civilized life." The act had alienated millions of acres of Indian land, destroyed the security that landownership had given, and produced acute social disorganization. In the 1920s, new proposals looked to abandonment of the allotment program. One bright spot was passage of an Indian citizenship act in 1924; two-thirds of Native Americans were already citizens, and the act made all Indians citizens. Indians nonetheless continued to possess attenuated privileges. A study released in 1928 recommended schools near the houses of Indian youngsters and abandonment of off-reservation boarding schools. As for the right to consume liquor, so generally disputed during the Prohibition era, there was little talk about any change in the prohibition of liquor for Indians that had gone into effect in 1832, and it would not be repealed until 1953.

Black Americans and Native Americans thus knew what their political pasts had been—wildernesses in which civil rights did not carry the same meaning as for other Americans. The two groups languished in their uncertainties. Meanwhile, many white Americans turned to the Ku Klux Klan, an incarnation of which rose and fell during the Coolidge years. A half century earlier, the Klan had hated blacks, but the successor organization, founded in Atlanta in 1915 and organized in 1922 by Dallas dentist Hiram W. Evans, in what an observer described as "the great bigotry merger," took on two other enemies: Jews and Catholics. Naming himself the Imperial Wizard, Evans sold memberships for ten dollars, and for a while, members joined at a rate of 3,500 a day. The revived Klan achieved a membership of perhaps 3 million. It called political tunes in such states as Oregon, California, Texas, Alabama, Georgia, Oklahoma, Kansas, and Indiana. It elected a Texas senator and governors in Oregon, California, Alabama, and Georgia. It was estimated that seventy-five members of the House of Representatives owed their elections to the Klan. The organization was nonpartisan; in the South it was Democratic, in the North, Republican. In Indiana, where it thrived in farming areas and southern hill towns close to Kentucky, it swallowed the GOP.

At the Madison Square Garden convention, the Democratic party refused to disavow Klan support, although Davis later made an anti-Klan statement, as did La Follette and Wheeler. General Dawes went to Maine, which was a notable Klan bastion, and told six thousand people at Augusta on 23 August that "I first desire to speak . . . relative to the Ku Klux Klan," whereupon he made himself clear: "Government cannot last if that way, the way of the Ku Klux Klan, is the way to enforce the law in this country. Lawlessness cannot be met with lawlessness if civilization is to be maintained." He had been told not to do so by party managers, but received an ovation. Afterward he visited Coolidge at the Notch, where political writers assumed that he was to be "spanked" for his Klan utterances. He later said that the president did not mention the Maine speech; the visit was a courtesy call.[31] That fall, slogans adorned billboards, "Keep Kool with Koolidge," and Klansmen were telling one another that the Episcopal cathedral being built on Mount St. Alban's in Washington was going to be the pope's new home, where he could command the nation's capital with field guns.

But 1924 proved a turning point in the Klan's fortunes. The Indiana Grand Dragon sexually assaulted a former schoolteacher, which drove her to poison and death, and financial scandals involved eminent Klansmen. By the next year, the Klan's popularity was on the decline. In the summer of 1925, while Coolidge was at Swampscott, forty thousand Klansmen, unhooded, paraded down Pennsylvania Avenue in Washington. Upon his return, he journeyed out to the Denver convention of the American Legion and chose the occasion for some very courageous words. Progress, the president told the legionnaires,

> depends very largely on the encouragement of variety. If we all believed the same thing and thought the same thoughts and applied the same valuations to all the occurrences about us, we should reach a state of equilibrium closely akin to an intellectual and spiritual paralysis. . . . We shall have to look beyond the outward manifestations of race and creed. Divine Providence has not bestowed upon any race a monopoly of patriotism and character. . . . Whether one traces his Americanisms back three centuries to the Mayflower, or three years to the steerage . . . we are all now in the same boat.

Supreme Court cases of the Coolidge era were devoted mostly to protecting business against what seemed to be confiscatory laws, but the Court was watchful against state laws infringing on constitutional rights. The case of Benjamin Gitlow came to the Court in 1925 and involved the publication of a supposedly subversive newspaper and other materials contrary to a New York state law of 1902. Although the case went against the defendant, Justice Holmes argued for free trade in ideas: "if what I think [is] the correct test is applied, it is manifest that there was no danger of attempt to overthrow the government by force on the part of the admittedly small minority who shared the defendant's view." That same year, the Supreme Court reversed a conviction under a Kansas criminal syndicalism law. Up to that time, any activity by a member of the Industrial Workers of the World (IWW) had been automatically punishable. The defendant was an IWW organizer who by speech and pamphlet had been soliciting membership. It was true that by the 1920s, the IWW was shattered, no longer a threat to the Constitution or to anything else. It was also true that Justice Sanford did not dispute the constitutionality of criminal syndicalism laws. He dodged the constitutional issue by ruling that the Kansas statute's application infringed on the defendant's liberty in violation of the due process clause of the Fourteenth Amendment. Nonetheless, the Court had taken a stand modestly in favor of civil liberties.[32]

A permanent change in immigration policy occurred in 1924, and it was assuredly a negative change. From the beginning of American history, the country had been a refuge, furnishing virtually free land to anyone who desired it. The character of immigration and its origins never seemed to matter, except during the nationalist "Know Nothing" era before the Civil War. In the years after that war, it was said that the country was a melting pot in which national qualities disappeared. The "new immigration" that began around 1880—immigration from southeastern Europe—changed things, and by the time of the Wilson administration, there was a desire for restriction. President Taft vetoed a literacy requirement in 1913, and Wilson vetoed similar measures in 1915 and 1917, but by the latter year, the restrictionists were strong enough to pass the bill over his veto. Outwardly, it added only an educational qualification to the physical, mental, and moral requirements for immigrants, but it marked the end of free immigration. It set the stage for the immigration acts of 1921 and 1924.

The act of 1921 showed the sort of limits the country wanted. It confined immigration to 3 percent of the number of foreign-born of each European nationality residing in the United States in 1910. This reduced European immigrants to a maximum of 355,000 a year—55 percent from northwestern Europe and 45 percent from southeastern. The act effectively lowered the latter immigration by 20 percent of the total entering in 1914. Enacted for one year, it was extended for two more. Congress passed it in the belief that millions of Europeans, unable to come over during the war and suffering from the war and its aftermath, were about to descend on the United States. By this time, the notion of a melting pot was in disrepute, and there was talk about "alien indigestion." The act passed by sweeping majorities: 323 to 71 in the House, 62 to 6 in the Senate. In the House, the holdouts were representatives of minority groups from southeastern Europe, mostly in cities of the Northeast. Political affiliation had no bearing on the vote; in the House, opposition consisted of thirty-five Republicans and thirty-six Democrats. In the Senate, progressives either did not vote, as in the case of La Follette, Wheeler, and Lenroot, or went down the line for the legislation. Borah, Brookhart, Johnson, George W. Norris of Nebraska, and Walsh of Montana voted in favor. One of Borah's constituents wrote that "immigration should be completely stopped for at least one generation until we can assimilate and Americanize the millions who are in our midst. . . . We no longer receive the sturdy immigrants from northern Europe and those who come from southern and eastern Europe will most certainly degrade the American race."[33] Borah replied that he was in complete agreement.

Debate prior to the permanent legislation of 1924 was bitter, for the lines had been drawn. Nativists that year were ascendant, as evidenced by the large contingent of the Ku Klux Klan at the Democratic convention and by Coolidge's reluctance to speak out. The erstwhile leader of the Democrats, William Jennings Bryan, represented the West and South, favoring restriction. He was sadly out of touch with the party's city faction led by Smith. Bryan had several reasons for leaving Nebraska in favor of Florida, one of which was that Nebraska's "large foreign element may not be only against prohibition but other moral issues." In Florida "there is but little of the foreign born element." The new congressman from one of the poorest districts of New York City, Fiorello LaGuardia, injected an amusing note into the contentions. Restriction, he said, could not accomplish everything. His dog came from "a distinguished family tree," but the animal was still "only a son of a bitch."[34] Napoleon Tincher was one of the worst restrictionists and taunted LaGuardia shamefully.

> Tincher: I think this chamber here is a place where we ought to think, act and do real Americanism (applause). That is what we are elected for and if you thrust open the gates the districts such as we have examples of here will keep increasing until finally when you get up and say "Mr. Speaker" you will have to speak in Italian or some other language. . . .
> LaGuardia: Will the gentleman yield?
> Tincher: Oh hello, there you are, I knew you would come.
> LaGuardia: The gentleman doesn't know what he is talking about.
> Tincher: I think the issue is fairly well drawn. On the one side is beer, bolshevism, unassimilating settlements and perhaps many flags—on the other side is constitutional government; one flag, stars and stripes; a government of, by and for the people; America our country.[35]

The act of 1924, like its predecessor, favored fewer immigrants from southeastern Europe. It increased the restrictions of the 1921 act, reducing the proportion of national groups admitted from 3 percent to 2 percent and changing the base period from 1920 to 1890 (statisticians later discovered that the census of 1890 was too vague on national origins to be usable, so 1920 figures were substituted). It was complicated in its provisions, although the purpose was clear enough. It proposed to limit immigrants to a maximum of 150,000 a year by 1927. The complexity of the act was such that quotas could not be established until 1929. The act would be the country's basic legislation until the Truman administration after World War II.

The 1924 legislation applied only to Europeans and allowed unlimited immigration from the Western Hemisphere and the Philippines. Almost immediately there was an influx from Mexico, and by 1930, it was estimated that "white Mexicans" totaled 65,000 and the remainder of Mexican immigrants, of Indian and Negro descent, 1.4 million. In the late 1920s, Filipino immigration increased. Bills proposing quotas for the Western Hemisphere and the exclusion of Filipinos were introduced in Congress for the purpose of filling these "holes" in the system.[36]

In another respect, the act of 1924 represented a notable miscalculation. A leading argument in favor of restriction was that the country could not support a large population. Restrictionists took pleasure in statistical analyses showing that the birthrate was diminishing, that restriction would slow it, and that the total population was stabilizing. Before the Civil War, the population was increasing by 35 percent each decade. Between 1900 and 1930, it increased by half that, 16 percent. The increase from 1910 to 1920 was 14 million, and the increase from 1920 to 1930 was 17 million, the largest during any decade in the nation's history; it equaled the total population in 1840. But compared with the percentage increase of that earlier period, it was definitely slowing. *Recent Social Trends* predicted that the U.S. population would be between 145 million and 190 million by the end of the century, probably nearer the lower figure.[37] Population reached 151 million by 1950; forty years later, it stood at 249.6 million. In 1990, real per capita income was the highest on record, and rising.

In discussing the act of 1924, one must consider the proviso excluding Japanese immigration. If the legislation had given Japan a quota, it would have permitted 109 immigrants each year. Scholars have grouped this act with other unwise American decisions of the interwar years that turned the Japanese government toward aggression and resulted in the 1941 attack on Pearl Harbor: the inferior capital-ship ratio awarded Japan at the Washington Conference of 1921–22, arraignment of Japan by Secretary of State Henry L. Stimson over occupation of Manchuria in 1931–32, and support of Nationalist China by the United States during the 1930s.

The question arises whether the administration could have stood against the popular desire to exclude Japanese immigrants. The answer is that it might have done so if the issue had not become a matter of Senate pride. There was much feeling in states such as California favoring exclusion. Hoover went home to California in the middle of the exclusion issue and sent a telegram to Coolidge advising against any Japanese quota: "Opposition here is starting vigorous propaganda to effect that Republican administration policy is to negotiate new Japanese Treaty which will weaken exclusion Pact. Think it advisable in acceptance statement to make clear that subject is a closed book and therefore no longer an issue."[38] One suspects, however, that the administration could have pointed out the small quota involved, if the matter had not become a Senate issue.

In its origins, it seemed to be a simple error by the Japanese ambassador, Masanao Hanihara, that the Senate compounded by construing it as an insult. Hanihara had written a letter to Secretary of State Hughes in which he pronounced exclusion, which at the time had only been talked about in debates, as capable of "grave consequences." In the lexicon of pre-1914 diplomacy, grave consequences meant war, and Congress, especially the Senate, interpreted the letter that way. Dumbstruck by its reception and the resultant legislation, Hanihara resigned as ambassador. Hughes, "badly jolted," called upon Coolidge, who was momentarily ill in bed, and declared that "it was enough to make a man [speaking of himself] resign."

The president told him not to think of such a thing, that he agreed with everything the secretary had done.[39]

At the outset, there was speculation by State Department officials about Hughes's part in this tragic blunder. The head of the western European division, William Castle, made a diary entry on 31 May 1924 concerning a conversation with his opposite on the Far Eastern desk, John V. A. Mac-Murray, soon to be minister to China. MacMurray, he wrote, "came in because I wanted to tell him that Dave Reed [senator from Pennsylvania] told me yesterday that Senator Reed of Missouri was spreading the statement that the Secretary wrote the Hanihara note which caused the Senate to blow up about Japanese exclusion." The two discussed the problem, and MacMurray allowed that the secretary actually had discussed the matter with the Japanese ambassador and that everyone would believe that if he was responsible for part he was responsible for all. Half a dozen years later, Castle was ambassador to Japan, and in his diary for 25 February 1930, he set down an interesting piece of gossip related by the embassy's first secretary, Eugene Dooman. The latter had heard from the secretary in the Japanese embassy in Washington in 1924 that the letter "was entirely written by Jack MacMurray, that Hanihara was afraid it was too strong, but yielded to the supposedly greater knowledge of political conditions of the Department of State." Castle remembered the 1924 conversation: "I know that at the time Jack MacMurray seemed surprised at my vigorous protest against sending the note containing the unfortunate phrase to the Senate and that he seemed far more worried over the whole business than he should normally have been."[40]

Hughes later wrote an autobiography, and in correspondence about it he said that the offending words were Hanihara's and that their insertion "was not advised, suggested, or approved, by any member of the State Department." He told his correspondent that MacMurray, who was also retired, would agree with him. A letter to MacMurray elicited a reply that said the same thing, that the phrase of 1924 was "not advised, suggested or approved by any member of the State Department."[41]

The Japanese foreign minister of the 1920s, Baron Kijuro Shidehara, dictated his memoirs late in life for publication in a newspaper in 1950 and confessed authorship of the "grave consequences" note. It was possible that Shidehara was "taking responsibility" for an error principally by Hughes, whose memory (Hughes died in 1949) he did not wish to sully.[42]

Dooman, who had spoken with Castle in 1930, made an oral history in 1962 in which he had the final say about who was responsible for Japanese exclusion. He remarked that in 1924, when the exclusion proviso was in Congress, the one-time president of the American Japan Society of Tokyo, Baron Sakatani, had said in the House of Peers that if the proviso passed it would affect the willingness of the Japanese people to cooperate with the West. He used the phrase "grave consequences." The consequences Sakatani had in mind were not war but abandonment of cooperation with the Western powers in China (see Chapter 8). Hughes and MacMurray, Dooman said, went over Hanihara's draft and had no objection to the phrase.

Now, I can speak from personal knowledge of this episode. I was in Tokyo at that time. But in 1932, when I was in the State Department on temporary detail from London, I had taken over the desk of Mr. Ransford Miller. Mr. Miller had served for many years in Japan and Korea and had been recalled to the State Department to take over the Japan desk just before the Exclusion Act episode. It was while the Council of the League of Nations sitting in Paris had condemned Japan for aggression in Manchuria that Mr. Miller's death had occurred. . . . It was for that reason that I was called over from London. I found in Mr. Miller's desk a copy of the Manchuria [Hanihara] draft, with corrections in the handwriting of both Mr. Hughes and Mr. Mac-Murray. And the thing was so touchy at that time, that I, on my own initiative, destroyed the draft paper.[43]

The Muscle Shoals project championed by Senator Norris originated out of the emergency need for nitrates during World War I. This wartime need resulted in the pouring of $100 million into a dam, a steam generating plant, and two nitrate plants. Nitrate Plant No. 1 at Sheffield, Alabama, employed the controversial Haber process, which did not work out. Fortunately, that plant consumed the lesser amount of money, $12 million. Plant No. 2 at Muscle Shoals, contracted to the American Cyanamid Company, cost $58 million and was ready to operate by October 1918. A test run showed that it would function as planned and produce forty thousand tons of nitrogen a year, but the end of the war made production unnecessary.

The second phase of what was a complicated history proposed peacetime operation under a variety of schemes, the most prominent of which was Henry Ford's offer to purchase Muscle Shoals after his visit in 1921. Ford made an offer that a junk dealer might have proposed, $5 million for everything, and his plans were characterized by vagueness. People could not quite understand what Ford proposed to do, whether he wished to produce nitrates and thereby fertilizer that would assist farmers across the country, or whether he had in mind the production of hydroelectric power. It was possible that Ford himself did not know why he wanted Muscle Shoals. The money was a bagatelle to him, and meanwhile, his name was prominent not merely in Tennessee and Alabama but throughout the country. If he had political ambitions at the time, the offer would have supported them.

During the next years, Ford's ambitions remained uncertain; the Harding and Coolidge administrations were uncertain. Nothing was being produced at Muscle Shoals, and public interest rose and fell. Perhaps the most memorable episode took place during a hearing before the Senate agriculture committee, over which Norris presided as chairman. A woman testified that on a visit to Decatur, Alabama, in 1922, the senator had said that he would vote for the Ford offer if he could kiss one of the beautiful southern belles. "You did kiss one of the girls," she asserted, "and you are against the Ford offer." Norris arose, red-faced, stern of visage. "I know a blackmail plot when I see it," he said. "I did not kiss that girl. She kissed me."[44]

Ford's uncertainty and the government's uncertainty may have arisen because of the "virtual electrical revolution" of the early 1920s—the tying of electric power into huge grids—which raised the question of whether Muscle Shoals was as valuable for nitrates as it might be for electricity. In the confusion, Coolidge did the statesmanlike thing, urged on by Sen. Oscar Underwood of Alabama—he appointed a committee. On 27 March 1925, following a meeting with Underwood, he announced a Muscle Shoals commission of inquiry. That took care of the rest of the year, until the commission reported on 14 November and unhappily announced its disagreement. The president had appointed five commissioners: former representative John C. McKenzie of Illinois, chairman; former senator Nathaniel Dial of South Carolina, a conservative Democrat; Russell F. Bower, appointed at the request of Senator Underwood and officials of the Farm Bureau; Harry S. Curtis, professor of chemical engineering at Yale University; and William McClellan, a noted electrical engineer and past president of the American Institute of Electrical Engineers. The three nonscientists opted for the development of nitrates for agricultural fertilizer and for munitions for national defense, which ignored the power issue. The two scientific members filed a minority report recommending the use of Muscle Shoals primarily to generate electrical power from the excellent fall in the waters of the Tennessee, using the partially constructed dam.

President Coolidge considered the recommendations and in his annual message of December 1927 reversed his position, which hitherto had seemed to favor production of nitrates in the hope that he could raise his sagging stock with America's farmers. Facing the evident scientific verdict that Muscle Shoals was better used for power, he explained the problem somewhat indirectly: "The last year has seen considerable changes in the problem of Muscle Shoals. Development of other methods shows that nitrates can probably be produced at less cost than by use of hydroelectric power. Extensive investigation made by the Department of War indicates that the nitrate plants on this project are of little value for national defense and can probably be disposed of within two years. . . . This leaves this project mostly concerned with power."[45]

In his message of 1927, Coolidge defined the problem but did not offer a solution, perhaps in accord with his experience that the executive proposed and Congress disposed. It was also in accord with his belief that any large fertilizer project at Muscle Shoals would be another subtraction from the taxes that he and Secretary Mellon were collecting to run the federal government and retire the national debt. A project at Muscle Shoals would open the way for water power projects all over the country. In addition, Coolidge did not want to get into Muscle Shoals because the South was hopelessly Democratic, and it seemed foolish to support its political sinfulness when there were possible Republican projects.

Just as Coolidge did not want a solution to Muscle Shoals, neither did the electric companies. Chicago utilities magnate Samuel Insull and other utility company officers were up in arms about Muscle Shoals; they were in favor of free enterprise, which was what had made the country great. A government project would be potentially competitive with and therefore unsettling to their own industry, which had seen sufficient changes during the last years. Moreover, their holding companies, the devices by which they constructed their empires, were uneasy enterprises and needed no surprises from the outside; having faced up to the opportunities of 1921–24, they needed time to ensure that the flow of interest and dividends would keep control in their own hands.

Caught in this vortex, public and private, Norris sought to compromise. In December 1927, he proposed a plan that contained no provisions for unified development of the Tennessee River, calling for public operation of Muscle Shoals for the production of power and for research on fertilizer. He proposed public distribution of the surplus power produced at the project. Congress went along, adding a proposition that the power produced would develop the Tennessee Valley and work out a "yardstick" for measuring private power rates. How serious Congress was about this is difficult to measure, for it must have been clear that Coolidge would not go along. Thus, any congressman who was personally opposed to the Norris bill but from a district or state where there was support could humor his constituents by voting for the bill and let Coolidge take the blame. The president did not go along and managed to pass the entire project to his successor in a way that Norris deplored: the president pocket-vetoed the Muscle Shoals bill and did not have to explain his reasons for opposing it. Coolidge mentioned Muscle Shoals in his last annual message, but the complicated set of proposals was difficult to understand. He favored some production of fertilizer for farmers and nitrates for national defense. He thought that Congress might provide separate leases of the nitrate and power facilities, but he would approve a bill for leasing "the entire property for the production of nitrates." He desired no further construction of dams on the Tennessee River at government expense but allowed that power companies might obtain government loans to construct dams if they paid prevailing rates of interest. Coming from the usually clear Coolidge, who worked on his public addresses with intense concentration so as to say what he meant, this muddle indicated that he did not want his auditors to understand him.

The overwhelming victory of the Democratic party in 1932 ensured that Muscle Shoals would be transformed by the Tennessee Valley Authority Act of 1933 and that Norris would obtain his program, not a compromise. It ensured a much-needed work project during the Great Depression, gave support to farmers who were in dire trouble and seeking any sort of sustenance, and promised a yardstick for the rates of utility companies. This last possibility, however, was of less importance than formerly, for the utility empires were in a state of collapse—Insull's was in bankruptcy—and were willing to do anything the government told them.

7

LATIN AMERICA

In his first annual message, President Coolidge said that "our main problems are domestic problems." His countrymen agreed. That did not mean that they forgot about foreign policy, only that they did not think much about it. As one surveys the three areas in which American foreign policy functioned during the 1920s, the greatest concern was for Latin America, an area of low priority to the United States economically and largely quiescent politically. There was much less concern for the Far East, and least of all for Europe. Americans were interested in Europe, indeed fascinated, although they liked to claim disinterest. They did not consider the Old World a suitable place for policy beyond the nonpolicy of abstention, established by their first policy principle of a century before, the Monroe Doctrine.

Many years after the fact, Coolidge's Massachusetts friend Congressman Martin (whom everyone referred to as "Joe," except Coolidge, who addressed him as "Joseph") told Robert J. Donovan that foreign affairs during the 1920s were "an inconsequential problem." As proof, he offered the fact that the House Foreign Affairs Committee had debated for an entire week, to the exclusion of all other matters, an appropriation of $20,000 for an international poultry show in Tulsa.[1]

Latin America was the only notable area of concern. There is much to the belief of historians that in securing domination of the Caribbean during and after the Spanish-American War of 1898, including domination over Central America, and in intervening in Mexico in 1914 and 1916, the United States was pursuing a canal policy, protecting the canal approaches. When it became clear after World War I that no nation threatened the canal, the time arrived to give up talk of empire, although it would require slowness to avoid the impression of a retreat. The Latin American policy of the Coolidge administration looked toward getting out of Caribbean and Central American countries and concentrating on issues involving Mexico and Nicaragua. The goal in Mexico was to maintain a climate for investment, because U.S. investment was large there. In Nicaragua, the goal was to maintain order, because that nation possessed an alternative canal route, marines had been there since 1912, and revolution would overturn a Central American treaty of 1923 promising changes of government by peaceful means.

In South America, the Caribbean, and Central America, the economic stakes were quite interesting during the Coolidge era. Much of the financing for investment and trade came from the United States. Between 1919 and 1927, Latin America borrowed $200 million from its prewar European creditors and secured six times that sum from the United States. Investment in Colombia increased from $4 million in 1913 to $280 million in 1929; in Chile, from $15 million in 1912 to $800 million in 1929. Exports to the Latin American republics increased from $348 million in 1913 to $986 million in 1929.

Less interesting were the political stakes, except in Mexico and Nicaragua. The overshadowing political issue in South America was the controversy over the provinces of Tacna and Arica, "the Alsace-Lorraine of South America," between Peru, Chile, and Bolivia. During Coolidge's presidency, the United States sought to keep the dispute out of the hands of the League of Nations. The victorious commander of the U.S. Army in France in 1917–18, Gen. John J. Pershing, tried to settle it by heading a commission, but after a few months he resigned because of ill health. His post was taken by another American general, William Lassiter, but there would be no resolution during the Coolidge administration; Peru and Chile signed a treaty in Washington settling the issue on 3 June 1929. Similarly, the administration failed to settle the dispute over ownership of the Chaco region between Bolivia and Paraguay. Known to foreigners as a worthless piece of territory, a green hell of impenetrable jungle, it had been in contention since colonial times, with proposals of arbitration since 1907. The Chaco war lasted until both contestants were exhausted. Peace terms signed 9 July 1938 gave most of the Chaco to Paraguay.

In the Caribbean, the "American lake," marines remained in occupation of Haiti, where they had been since 1915. They withdrew from the Dominican Republic in 1924, and three years later the president of that republic extended his term by two years, without American advice one way or the other. The island of Cuba, whose freedom had been the cause of the War of 1898, remained an embarrassment in terms of capacity for self-government; its citizens, leaders, or both were unwilling to accept American advice. In the early 1920s, Maj. Gen. Enoch H. Crowder put the Cuban government on a business basis, reducing its budget from $130 million to $55 million. The Cuban treasury closed the fiscal year 1922–23 with a surplus of $12 million. After Crowder left, matters went downhill. The president of Cuba, on a salary of $20,000, acquired a $300,000 property in two years; the expense account at the presidential palace listed $10,000 worth of chickens bought in a single month. Gen. Gerardo Machado was inaugurated president in 1925 and in a few years turned himself into Cuba's first twentieth-century dictator.

By the time Coolidge became president, the Mexican problem, as he might have described it, was almost as old as the Monroe Doctrine, and because Mexico was the closest of the Latin American nations and the largest in North America, it sometimes seemed acute. When Mexico became independent from Spain in the 1820s, the government in Mexico City soon passed under the control of dictators. The best known and, to the United States, most obnoxious was Gen. Antonio López de Santa Anna. The United States defeated his regime in the Mexican War of 1846–48 and seized all of Mexico's territory north of the Rio Grande, including California. Then Americans took less interest in Mexico for a while, because of the approaching Civil War. During that conflict, the French government installed Prince Maximilian of Austria as emperor of Mexico. Beginning in 1865, the government in Washington put pressure on France to withdraw its troops, and not long afterward, the empire collapsed; Maximilian was captured and shot by his subjects. During most of the remaining years until 1910, Mexico was ruled by Gen. Porfirio Díaz, whose government welcomed foreign investment in land, minerals, and oil. The revolution that turned Díaz out brought in a one-party revolutionary government that, by the Coolidge era, was bent on taking back many of the concessions granted by Díaz, with indemnities, if necessary.

Coolidge did what he could to safeguard the $1.5 billion in American-owned land, mineral rights, and oil properties, including refineries, in Mexico.[2] Each president of the United States facing trouble across the border doubtless believed that his Mexican problem was larger than those that had preceded. Being a Republican, Coolidge could compare his diplomacy with that of his Democratic predecessor Wilson, and from the outset, he was certain that he did not desire such intervention as occurred during Wilson's presidency. That decided, the question was how to protect the investments.

First was the issue of how those properties had been obtained, and for a short while, it seemed resolved. American marines had occupied Veracruz in 1914, following capture of a boatload of American sailors by Mexican authorities. In 1916, after Gen. Pancho Villa invaded Columbus, New Mexico, Brigadier General Pershing led an expedition into Mexico. The Mexican Constitution of 1917 was hardly gentle on foreigners and raised questions about American investments. But then in the spring of 1923, at the Bucareli Conference (named for the street in Mexico City where the meeting took place), the American representatives, lawyer Charles Warren and former secretary of the interior John Barton Payne, worked out an interpretation of Article 27 of the Mexican Constitution excluding from confiscation land that had been developed prior to 1917. There was to be compensation up to a stipulated amount with Mexican bonds for expropriated property. Warren and Payne signed the agreement on 15 August.

A sign that all was well appeared when the Mexican government asked the United States to lift its embargo on arms and encourage American bankers to lend money to buy weapons. President Coolidge agreed. He said privately, "We'll be the laughingstock of the world if we don't send guns to Mexico. Look what happened when Wilson refused to support [President Victoriano] Huerta. If we allow [President Álvaro] Obregón to be overthrown, we shall be put in a ridiculous position as we have already rendered him some aid and are committed to his cause."[3] The president lifted the embargo early in 1924 and justified what he described as a few muskets and rounds of ammunition as part of ordinary comity between nations. He went so far as to renew President Harding's request to Congress for settlement of Mexican claims resulting from the occupation of Veracruz. The president-elect of Mexico, Plutarco Elías Calles, visited Washington.

Next year, 1925, relations became awkward. President Calles may have remembered the warmth of his visit to the United States and thought that he could push the North Americans. Coolidge's first ambassador, Warren, may have been part of the trouble. He was not the best representative. He wrote to Coolidge that he was doing his best: "While our relations with Mexico will be the cause from time to time of undesirable situations because of the nature of the Mexican people, nevertheless, it is a fact that the American Government can be most helpful to this neighboring State by being in a position to give friendly advice and assistance."[4] Warren may have given the impression that the United States would be extraordinarily patient. Calles was an ardent nationalist and would have needed little encouragement, and he did not wait long before asserting himself. He saw to it that his government did nothing to settle points at issue over land and oil. Claims and debts also were at issue; claims commissions appointed after the Bucareli Conference were inactive, and Mexico failed to pay its debts.

Mexico's bad faith persuaded Coolidge to inform the Mexican government where he stood. On 11 June 1925, Senator Smoot received a telephone call from the president asking him to dinner at the White House at 7:00 P.M. In addition to the president and his wife, Smoot encountered Attorney General Sargent; Ambassador Warren's replacement, James R. Sheffield; and Senator Borah, who had become chairman of the Foreign Relations Committee upon the death of Senator Lodge. "After dinner we discussed conditions in Mexico," the Utah senator wrote in his diary, "and it was decided to issue a warning to Mexico that she must protect American life and property or America would withdraw its support from the present administration."[5] The day after the White House conference, 12 June, Secretary of State Kellogg made a statement that must have angered President Calles: "The Government of Mexico is now on trial before the world. We have the greatest interest in the stability, prosperity, and independence of Mexico. We have been patient and realize, of course, that it takes time to bring about a stable Government, but we cannot countenance violation of her obligations and failure to protect American citizens." What Calles would not have known was that the statement came at the request of the U.S. president. Kellogg does not seem to have been present at the White House dinner that preceded it.

Not long afterward, the Mexican Congress, upon request of the nation's president, passed two laws that were most disagreeable to the U.S. government. One limited oil rights to fifteen years and required application for renewal of rights or the loss of those rights. The other allowed foreigners to own land if they renounced any resort to their own governments to protect their property. This was the Calvo clause, named after the nineteenth-century Argentinian jurist Carlos Calvo. Latin American governments were inserting it into contracts with private foreign corporations. Such clauses waived all right to protection in cases of violation of contracts, giving host governments the right to trap and nationalize foreign businesses that caught their fancy.

By this time, Sheffield was in Mexico City, and if this New York lawyer spoke to Calles and other Mexican officials in anywhere near the way he wrote to Coolidge and private correspondents, it was no wonder that relations between the two countries were souring. Coolidge had no problems following Sheffield's contentions. "The men in Mexican official life are with few exceptions ignorant of government, of economics and of finance," he informed his chief.

> International obligations rest very lightly upon them. The courts are notoriously corrupt and government by Presidential decree, from which there is no appeal, is frequently resorted to. . . . In my talks with the President, I have emphasized our desire to help and have offered any assistance he would be willing to accept, particularly along educational and economic lines. The unpopularity of Americans, especially since the Veracruz incident, probably

deters him from making use of our help because of its possible political effect except when it concerns the question of borrowing money. Back of it all lies the peculiar psychology of the Latin-Americans, or more properly, Latin-American mind.[6]

To President Butler of Columbia University, Sheffield gave his views on the Mexican cabinet:

There is very little white blood in the Cabinet . . . Calles is Armenian and Indian; Leon almost wholly Indian and an amateur bull-fighter; Saenz, the Foreign Minister, is Jew and Indian; Morones more white blood but not the better for it; Amaro, Secretary of War, a pure blooded Indian and very cruel. He shot his groom dead a fortnight ago for riding instead of leading a polo pony—a deed witnessed by at least one Englishman or American. No mention of course in the papers and no punishment. All this is said so you can visualize what I am up against.[7]

Sheffield was a proud man, and at the outset of his duties he was disappointed that the Mexican cabinet did not call on him. He informed Coolidge of this omission and explained that they did not hold receptions. Coolidge told him that "no doubt calls would be made on you if you indicated to the proper persons that you would be pleased to receive them." But he backed up Sheffield. "Of course," he told Chief Justice Taft, "they don't like him particularly in Mexico but how could a man decently act in such a way that they would."[8]

Thus, in mid-1925, U.S.-Mexican relations were in trouble. Over the next year and a half, they worsened because of U.S. involvement, at first apart from the Mexican situation, in revolutionary happenings in Nicaragua. This gave the government of Mexico the opportunity, which it seized, to embarrass the *norteamericanos,* whose investments in Mexico were so tempting to take back and redistribute. Calles intervened in Nicaragua under the Carranza Doctrine (elaborated by one of President Wilson's enemies, Mexican president Venustiano Carranza), according to which Mexico needed to maintain hegemony over the small nations of Central America to protect them from the economic and political hegemony of the United States.

Events of the Nicaraguan revolution of 1925–27 are discussed in detail later, but in short, Juan B. Sacasa had been the Liberal party vice president under President Carlos Solórzano, and both had been displaced by the Conservative party strongman Emiliano Chamorro, who in a series of fast shuffles proclaimed himself acting president. Chamorro paid Solórzano $30,000 out of the Nicaraguan treasury, and Solórzano departed for San Francisco on a leave of absence. Sacasa, a physician, chose not to reestablish his practice but to go to Washington. Sensing that the Liberals were in a strong moral position, he asked the assistant chief of the State Department's Latin American division, Stokeley Morgan, what the United States was going to do to make him president, in light of Solórzano's leave of absence. To Sacasa's exasperation Morgan replied that the United States would resort only to "moral pressure" to restore a legitimate government in Nicaragua.

Sacasa's exasperation was understandable, although had he known the particulars, he would have realized that the State Department was doing its best to get Chamorro out. Sacasa took matters into his own hands, seeking to oust Chamorro by landing a small force on Nicaragua's Atlantic coast, a wild and undeveloped place far from the country's populated Pacific coast. The uprising did not succeed, and Sacasa went to Mexico City.

Once in Mexico, Sacasa arrived at an arrangement with Calles that became known to the State Department. A former financial agent of Sacasa's in the United States obtained the Sacasa-Calles correspondence and presented it to the legation in Guatemala. What was not available for a while, but eventually came into department possession, was the text of the pact, which was not merely in accord with the Carranza Doctrine but was also inflammatory. For Calles to have arranged it was not a wise course. The first three articles called on Mexico to provide financial backing as well as military advisers, arms, and ammunition for an expeditionary force. Beginning in mid-August 1926, ships bearing men and arms cleared Mexican ports. Article 4 provided for Mexican colonization around the terminal points of what might be a future Nicaraguan canal, as well as the Gulf of Fonseca. Article 5 prescribed Nicaraguan abrogation of such agreements as the Bryan-Chamorro Treaty of 1916, which guaranteed to the United States construction of any Nicaraguan canal; the article pronounced the treaty "a menace to the sovereignty and national integrity of Nicaragua" and thus "harmful to Latin American hegemony." Article 7 promised a loan of 10 million gold pesos once the Sacasa regime established itself in Nicaragua's capital, Managua. The loan would be redeemed through bonds issued by Nicaragua's railroad system, an American-financed enterprise.[9] After Sacasa arranged these articles, early in December 1926, the Liberals established a Nicaraguan government at Puerto Cabezas on the Atlantic coast, with Sacasa as president. This was in opposition to the Managuan government then headed by Chamorro's replacement arranged by the United States, Adolfo Díaz, a one-time American-sponsored head of the Nicaraguan nation. Mexico recognized Sacasa.

The crisis in U.S.-Mexican relations in January 1927 has often been described. It opened with Coolidge's message to Congress on 10 January defending his policies in Nicaragua and accusing Mexico of trying to establish a government hostile to the United States, not merely threatening the constitutional government of Nicaragua but also menacing the Panama Canal. Two days later, Secretary Kellogg testified before the Senate Committee on Foreign Relations and left a printed statement, "Bolshevist Aims and Policies in Mexico and Latin America," which was widely published in newspapers. As Kellogg told the committee,

> The Bolshevist leaders have had very definite ideas with respect to the role which Mexico and Latin America are to play in their program of world Revolution. They have set up as one of their fundamental tasks the destruction of what they term American Imperialism as a necessary prerequisite to the successful development of the international revolutionary movement in the new world. . . . Thus Latin America and Mexico are conceived as a base for activity against the United States.

The secretary described a possible "Mexican-fostered Bolshevik hegemony intervening between the United States and the Panama Canal."[10]

The proportions of this crisis were difficult to discern from the newspapers. President Calles ordered General Obregón, in the event of U.S. intervention, to retire to the interior and set up defenses after setting fire to the oil fields, "making a light which they will be able to see in New Orleans."[11] But on the day Kellogg went before the Foreign Relations Committee, the Mexico City press printed a front-page statement from Foreign Minister Aarón Sáenz that Mexico had no political, territorial, or commercial interests in Nicaragua. A few days later, Sacasa told a reporter that there had never been a pact binding Mexico and the Nicaraguan Liberals.

Senator Borah, who according to one of his biographers had a "passion for wreckage" and was "a destructive statesman," entered the equation on 22 January by writing to Calles, asking for particulars of the Mexican government's stand. On 25 January, working with Senator Robinson of Arkansas, he secured passage of a resolution recommending arbitration with Mexico, by a vote of seventy-nine to zero. Borah defended his position in a series of public speeches. In New Haven, a heckler from the gallery charged him with violating the Logan Act, which forbade unauthorized negotiation with foreign governments. "As chairman of the Senate Foreign Relations Committee," he answered, "I have a right to get my information from any source I wish. This I propose to do, and I know of no power that can stop me." In this address he called for an end to name-calling about Mexico and said, "God has made us neighbors, let justice make us friends."[12]

On 25 April 1927, at a dinner of the United Press Association, Coolidge announced what for a short time was known as the Coolidge Doctrine. The doctrine was clear enough: "The person and property of a citizen are a part of the general domain of the Nation, even when abroad." It was a slap at Calles, the Mexican Congress, and the Calvo clause. At the same time he concluded, "we do not want any controversy with Mexico." A few months later, he appointed a new ambassador to Mexico, his Amherst College friend Morrow.

Just why the president chose Morrow is unclear. Morrow had been unhappy with his position at J. P. Morgan and Company, for the work seemed uninteresting. Coolidge must have known this but for four years had done nothing to help him. At the outset of Coolidge's presidency, Morrow had written two letters, one containing recommendations for policy, and the president had virtually ignored them. Years later, Morrow remarked how Coolidge's successor in the presidency had telephoned three times a week, and between 1923 and 1929, Coolidge had telephoned once— and not about a diplomatic matter. Kellogg in 1925 seems to have asked Coolidge to make Morrow undersecretary of state, and Coolidge wrote to a friend that he did not think it wise to appoint a Morgan partner. After Morrow's death in 1931, journalist Walter Lippmann asserted that Kellogg had so confused Mexican policy that Coolidge had to bring in Morrow. By then retired to St. Paul, Kellogg was furious and wrote to a former department associate that he had suggested Morrow's name.[13]

Morrow had much to recommend him. He was a friend of the Morgan partner Thomas W. Lamont, who had been dealing with the Mexican government as head of a foreign bondholders group known as the International Committee. Morrow and Lamont were far removed from the racism of Sheffield. Morrow sensed the nationalism of Mexico's leaders. He probably was paternalistic, but he was careful. After his work in Mexico, Coolidge was so pleased that he recommended Morrow to Hoover as secretary of state.

Coolidge's recommendation at the outset of the mission was "to keep us out of war with Mexico." It was an exaggeration, for war was never a possibility. The Mexicans as well as the Americans knew that. When Morrow's appointment was announced in September 1927, a Mexican newspaper commented, "After Morrow come the marines." The appointment was a move in the opposite direction.

Morrow went to his new embassy determined to change relations, and quickly did. When he left Englewood, New Jersey, he remarked, "I know what I can do for the Mexicans. I can *like* them." His biographer Harold Nicolson described the result:

> His insatiable friendliness, his utter simplicity, the very exuberance of his good will, held them enthralled. He applauded their food, their climate, their agriculture, their hats, their ancient monuments, the bamboo cages in which they kept their tame parrots, their peasant industries, their patriotism, their volcanoes, even their finances. Here at last was a North American who neither patronized nor sneered. His boyish enjoyment of his task

was infectious. In the sunshine of his zest, under the warm breezes of that creative credulity, even the most morose suspicions melted.[14]

He conducted most of his negotiations orally. He telephoned Washington despite knowledge that the Mexicans had tapped his line. Telephone bills were enormous, $5,000 in ten weeks, and he paid them himself.

His negotiation with Calles was over three issues, and in two he was successful. First, he sought a way out of the Petroleum Law, which was confiscatory, and found a loophole in Article 14 of the constitution of 1917 that said that no legislation should be retroactive. Calles opened their second meeting by asking for suggestions about how to end the diplomatic impasse over oil. "Diplomatic?" Morrow answered. "I am a lawyer, Mr. President, and not a diplomatist. The problem suggests itself to me as a legal problem, not as either a political or a diplomatic problem." Calles remained silent, drooping his heavy cheek sideways, turning slowly on his finger a huge silver ring with a large turquoise. He begged the ambassador to proceed. According to Morrow's memorandum of the conversation, "The President then asked me if I thought that a decision of the Supreme Court following the Texas case would settle the main controversy in the oil dispute. I told him that I thought such a decision would remove the main difficulty. He then rather startled me by saying that such a decision could be expected in two months."[15]

Calles was as good as his word. On 17 November 1927, the court ruled that Articles 14 and 15 of the Petroleum Law were unconstitutional. On 26 December, the Mexican president sent a message to his Congress asking emendation of those articles; the law passed on 28 December, the president ratified it on 3 January 1928, and it was in force on 11 January.

It is possible that if Morrow had arrived two or three years earlier, diplomacy with Mexico would have been much different. Certainly by the time he arrived, bringing his considerable diplomatic talents, it was the right time for a modus vivendi. As an American scholar has speculated, when the Bucareli agreements broke down, there was never a united front on the part of American investors in Mexico. Exporters to Mexico, and especially bankers, favored a more accommodating diplomacy. The oil companies were divided between domestic independents and multinationals; only the multinationals took interest in Mexican oil. American public opinion was largely sympathetic, and Teapot Dome had harmed the image of oil companies, whether independent or multinational. The State Department was never the servant of oil, although it disliked retroactive laws and the Calvo clause. On the Mexican side, there was a desire not to frighten away American capital. By 1927, the revolution in Mexico was settling down. Calles had been unduly enthusiastic about the Carranza Doctrine.[16]

Morrow's second success in Mexico, accomplished after Coolidge left the presidency, was to end the church-state crisis that began in 1926 when the Catholic bishops, fearful of the antichurch measures of the Mexican government, closed all the Mexican churches. The revolutionary leaders who took over in Mexico in 1910 were rightfully fearful of the conservative Catholic prelates, many of whom were against the new regime. The leaders disliked the bishops' willingness to take advice from the Vatican, which they considered an intervention in Mexico's political affairs. There was feeling that the church in Mexico had taken advantage of the regime of Porfirio Díaz to become wealthy and had removed itself from the needs of the common people. The standoff beginning in 1926 became violent when priests and many Mexicans revolted against the Calles government. "Vive Cristo Rey!" was the cry. In 1928, a young Catholic fanatic murdered General Obregón while he was attending a banquet in a suburb of Mexico City; Obregón had been designated Calles's successor at the end of the year, and his death raised the question of who might be strong enough to succeed and whether Calles should unconstitutionally succeed himself, despite a pledge to the contrary. Morrow imported an American priest, the general secretary of the National Catholic Welfare Conference, John J. Burke, who helped Calles out of his problem with the bishops. Calles passed the presidency to Emilio Portes Gil, and on 30 June 1929, to the ringing of bells throughout Mexico, the churches reopened.

The problem that Morrow could not resolve was consolidation of the Mexican debt, both foreign and domestic. Mexican bonds that had been floated between 1885 and 1913 amounted to $485 million. They had gone into default in 1914. Lamont in 1930 worked out an arrangement for the foreign bondholders that Morrow disagreed with, for the ambassador believed that all creditors, not merely foreign bondholders, should have a claim on the Mexican treasury. The Lamont arrangement went unratified. A settlement finally came during World War II that reduced the debt to less than $100 million, and in ensuing years, the Mexican government cleaned up the indebtedness. Morrow would have preferred an international commission to consolidate the debt and arrange a balanced budget that would cover it and provide money for government functions, especially the army and education. A month before his death in October 1931, he confided to a friend that he had failed in "the most important part of his mission in Mexico," and he attributed the failure, perhaps unfairly, to his former partners in J. P. Morgan, for his reform would have entailed a fiscal revolution in Mexico.[17]

During the Coolidge era, Nicaragua received even more attention than Mexico. The intervention of the United States in that small country proved effective in the short run but afterward resulted in the dictatorship of the Somoza family, which in turn produced the Sandinista revolution in 1979 and an unsettled political situation that lasted into the 1990s.

Nicaragua was a small place, and its politics were simple compared with those of Mexico. Its territory comprised two distinct portions, Pacific and Atlantic—the one civilized and populated, the other a virtual jungle. Nicaragua was the size of New York State, and in the 1920s its population was seven hundred thousand. Important cities in the western part were Leon, the center of the Liberal party, and Granada, dominated by the Conservatives. The capital, Managua, founded later, was placed between them in an attempt to occupy a neutral position. In the 1920s, Managua had forty thousand inhabitants. It consisted of few buildings of more than one story, and its streets were unpaved and badly drained, making it dusty most of the year. The American legation was in one of the capital's finest houses, but there were no glass windows. Lighting came from unshielded bulbs hanging from high ceilings. U.S. investment in Nicaragua totaled $30 million. The interest of the State Department in Washington was partly a combination of the rivers and lakes that made Nicaragua an alternative canal site, its proximity to the Panama Canal, and the danger that any U.S. intervention in Nicaraguan affairs might be taken critically by the surrounding small countries, by the revolutionary regime in Mexico, and by the sensitive American public that opposed intervention by its government anywhere, but especially in the Caribbean and Central America.[18]

Complicating diplomacy in Nicaragua was the incompetence of ministers assigned to the Managua legation. The first, during the Harding administration, was a Republican from Colorado, John E. Ramer. In the judgment of Dana G. Munro, a State Department official who served in Nicaragua and was later professor of Latin American history at Princeton, Ramer was "totally unqualified." During Ramer's instruction period in the department, "when he showed no desire to learn anything about the problems that awaited him, it became evident that he was probably the worst of several incompetent political appointees who were being sent to replace the equally incompetent Democratic political appointees in Latin America." Ramer went back to Washington for "consultation" in 1924, after writing two dispatches that he did not allow his assistant or the legation clerk to see. He wrote them in longhand and gave them to a marine typist, who followed the minister's spelling and grammar. In one letter he discussed activities of the "heavy politics," that is, the *jefes politicos* or provincial governors. He advised doubling the legation guard of one hundred marines "just for show, as it would make them [the Nicaraguan officials] set up and take notice." In the other dispatch, he said that he had sent word to President Bartolomé Martínez, through the latter's niece, that the department would protest the appointment of a proposed minister of finance because the man was "anti in spirit and praises bolshevism." The dispatches brought Ramer's recall, although he was not informed that it was permanent until after the U.S. presidential election of 1924.[19]

Ramer's successor, Charles C. Eberhardt, was one of the officers of the former consular service, which had been combined with the diplomatic service into a new foreign service by the Rogers Act of 1924. Eberhardt was fluent in Spanish but was unable to fathom the politics of the country to which he was assigned. The department saw to it that he was frequently in Washington and assigned him an assistant, Munro, who ran the legation in his absence.

The takeover of the government by General Chamorro and his defiance of the U.S. government were Eberhardt's immediate problems, which began three weeks after the marine guard left in August 1925. Solórzano and Sacasa were soon gone, Chamorro was installed as interim president, and the problem was to get him out. It looked as if he would prove a tough customer. As Eberhardt wrote to Kellogg,

> In his direct conversations with me prior to January [1926] General Chamorro was always considerate and polite. One of his final statements to me was that he felt certain that the big and strong United States would not undertake to destroy poor little weak Nicaragua, and that he hoped for a benevolent nonrecognition if he could not be recognized. After three months of this benevolent nonrecognition he has become arrogant, if not openly, at least in his conversations with his immediate friends and party leaders. Only recently, one of the latter, remonstrating with him over his attitude toward the deposed judges of the Supreme Court, suggested that he might produce a most unfavorable impression on the United States in general, and the State Department in particular, to which he is said to have replied: "To Hell with the United States, with the State Department, and with its diplomatic representative here!"[20]

Chamorro was supported in Washington by the international lawyer Chandler P. Anderson, who seems to have been in Chamorro's employ, if not in that of American firms doing business in Nicaragua. Anderson had close ties to the State Department, where he had been employed, and he sought to inform it of how Chamorro, the leader of the Conservative party, which had been in power since 1911 until the election of the Solórzano-Sacasa coalition, would be good for business and for the canal treaty of 1916 that he had signed.[21]

Eberhardt went on leave in June 1926, and the department, which critics said always worked for American business, replaced him with a chargé d'affaires, Lawrence Dennis, a tall, young, forceful man who believed that a straight line was the shortest distance between two points. The president of the Nicaraguan Congress, Dr. Carlos Cuadra Pasos, then in Washington, complained bitterly to Kellogg that Dennis had told a justice of the Nicaraguan Supreme Court that the United States had "the firm purpose" to pry out Chamorro, "and he added that if it were necessary to make 10 revolutions in succession to accomplish that end the evil done would not amount to anything if the purpose of separating Senator Chamorro from power was attained." Dennis told Chamorro that if he did not retire voluntarily he would go out by force. "As he felt impelled by his high duties," Cuadra related,

> President Chamorro rejected that imposition which hurts the dignity of the Republic, and maintaining himself within the bounds of the courtesy due to the Representative of this great nation, and of friendship towards the Government and people of the United States, he answered that he must await in the post, which the law has assigned him, the stroke of that force by which he is threatened, without losing faith in the justice which is traditional to the United States in its dealings with weak peoples.[22]

Despite Dennis's pressure, Chamorro managed to remain in office until he had emptied the Nicaraguan treasury, whereupon he departed in favor of former president Díaz, who was inaugurated on 14 November 1926, with the American chargé attending. Three days later, the United States extended recognition. Soon afterward, President Díaz appointed his friend Chamorro minister to the governments of Britain, France, Spain, and Italy. To support this important mission, Díaz offered $20,000. Chamorro said that he did not want it to be generally known that he was leaving with such a sum and would accept $5,000 as an advance; the remainder could be kept secret. Back on the scene, Eberhardt explained this conversation to the department, remarking that "it should be clearly understood that, in the opinion of President Díaz . . . the departure of General Chamorro was cheap at $20,000."[23]

But the scene changed because of Mexican intervention and the Liberals' employment of a better general, José Moncada, than anyone available to Díaz. Under Moncada, real war broke out. Soldiers were easy to recruit; armed parties were sent through the towns and rounded up all men of the appropriate age who did not wear coats. Favorite places for recruiting were moving picture theaters and the cantinas scattered through the outlying parts of towns. Uniforming the troops was uncomplicated, with red hatbands for Liberal soldiers, blue for Conservative. The wise soldier obtained a ribbon of the enemy color to substitute for his own if he was wounded or in danger of capture. There was no quarter. Flocks of vultures cared for the badly wounded not taken by their human enemies.

The Coolidge administration sent the marines back in force. A strength of fifty-five hundred had arrived or were en route by late February 1927, with eleven cruisers and destroyers at Nicaraguan ports.

It was at this juncture that President Coolidge decided that he had to do something about Nicaragua. A map of the Western Hemisphere had gone up in Coolidge's usually unadorned office, and people were asking, "What is Nicaragua?" Among Central American governments, only El Salvador and Honduras recognized Díaz. The Guatemalan government sympathized with the Liberals and Mexico; the president of Costa Rica said that Díaz's election was unconstitutional. Worst of all, Chamorro on his mission abroad appealed to the League of Nations against Mexico's intervention. In the United States, there was more discussion of league interference than of Mexican intervention.

Coolidge invited Henry L. Stimson down from New York and gave him the Nicaraguan assignment. He had been President Taft's secretary of war when the marines first went to Nicaragua. After meeting with Kellogg, Stimson left confused. Later that day, when he conferred with the president at the White House, he asked, "What do you really want? Do you wish me to be simply your eyes and ears and come back to report to you?"

"No, no," Coolidge answered, "I want you to be a lot more than that. Just go down there, and if you can see a way to clean up that mess, I'd like to have you do it. And back up whatever you think is right."[24]

Stimson knew nothing about Nicaragua and, to the amusement of the *New York Times* reporter covering the war, pronounced the country's name "Nicaragew-a."[25] It was just as well. Early in May 1927, he met Moncada at a place named Tipitapa, and the two sat down under a large blackthorn tree near a dry riverbed. The general spoke English, so no interpreter was needed. In less than thirty minutes, all was settled. Stimson gave Moncada a letter:

> I am authorized to say that the President of the United States intends to accept the request of the Nicaraguan Government to supervise the election of 1928; that the retention of President Díaz during the remainder of his term is regarded as essential to that plan and will be insisted upon; that a general disarmament of the country is also regarded as necessary for the proper and successful conduct of such election; and that the forces of the United States will be authorized to accept the custody of the arms of those willing to lay them down including the government, and to disarm forcibly those who will not do so.

The U.S. price per weapon was $10, and a week and a half after Tipitapa, 15 May 1927, a total of 6,200 rifles, 262 machine guns, and 5 million rounds of ammunition had come in.

But as matters turned out, Stimson had the easy part in settling the politics of Nicaragua. The hard part was arranging an election and afterward maintaining peace. For this task, Kellogg had a first-rate group in Managua consisting of Munro for diplomacy and Brig. Gen. Frank R. McCoy to handle the election. Indeed, Munro was really McCoy's assistant.

Frank McCoy's name would never become a household word, but he was one of the many officers that the U.S. Army produced over the years whose abilities were so versatile that military matters never required all their time, enabling them to perform large acts of statecraft. McCoy had graduated from West Point in 1897 and was too young for high command in World War I and too old for World War II. After serving on General Pershing's staff in France and receiving his general's star, he might have become army chief of staff between the wars. He deserved the post, but there were too many good men left from World War I. After that war, he went to the Philippines and distinguished himself under Governor General Leonard Wood, coming to Stimson's attention that way. A small, friendly man with an engaging smile, he was just the person to become the Dwight Morrow of Nicaragua.[26]

In carrying out Stimson's agreement to supervise the 1928 elections, McCoy and his assistants did yeoman's work. No one could have done the job better. The election's intricacies were many. This was the first free election ever held in Nicaragua; from the beginning of the nation's political history, whatever party was in power had secured victory in an election.

Appointed in mid-1927, McCoy had to arrange what was described in his honor (a doubtful piece of praise, for he was an American and needed to be inconspicuous) as *la ley McCoy*. The law proposed exactly how the election was to be conducted—in the manner of a North American election, with no cheating at the polls. There was sentiment for passage of the law, according to a Cuadra Conservative. "What would become of us if our little nation did not have a great nation like the United States to restrain us from our own mistakes?" he asked the Nicaraguan Congress. He answered his own question: "Intervention by the United States is an absolute necessity. The North American Government asked us what was the best way to obtain peace and order in this country. The answer was 'a free election.' "[27] But the congress voted down the McCoy law, twenty-three to seventeen, and adjourned sine die. The Chamorristas were at the center of this maneuver and converged on Managua's cathedral and rang the bells. Undaunted, McCoy urged President Díaz to enact the election law on his presidential authority. The American general said that the law's "strictly legal status" would be of "distinctly secondary importance." The Nicaraguan Constitution, he said, represented "abstract statements of political theory rather than practical and effective guides for governmental action." He admitted that although executive decrees had long been features of Latin American political thought, they were not in "accord" with Anglo-American custom. Enactment of *la ley McCoy* was necessary to the success of McCoy's mission, and carrying it out by presidential authority was preferable to the only other course, which would be for McCoy to issue the law on his own authority. A member of the general's staff drafted the proclamation, and Díaz signed it on 21 March 1928.[28]

In preparation for the election, General Moncada went to Washington "to obtain assurances," as he put it, "that the United States will fulfill the promises made to me by Mr. Stimson."[29] His concern was whether he would be eligible for the presidency under the treaty of fair revolutionary principles enacted by the Central American states in 1923. In its Article 4, the treaty detailed which officers of a government might succeed to the presidency of a new regime. The agreement explicitly barred revolutionary leaders. The State Department decided that Moncada was eligible. There had been some fighting, which he had led, but there had been no change of government by revolutionary means. Thereafter the Liberals were enthusiastic for *el Presidente Coolidge* and *la ley McCoy*.

Minister Chamorro returned from Europe and similarly went to Washington to inquire as to his candidacy for president. The department informed him that if he ran and won, his government would not receive recognition.

In the months that followed the Peace of Tipitapa, McCoy did his best to arrange a successful election. A typical detail of McCoy's work was his effort to obtain a loan for the Nicaraguan government from the New York firm of J. and W. Seligman and Company. Contrary to appearances, this endeavor was not a sign of American imperialism; it was no attempt to fasten bankers' hands on the throat of Nicaragua so that regardless of who won in the election, the nation's policies, both foreign and domestic, might be made in New York. The problem was more complicated. Under American tutelage, the Nicaraguan treasury, emptied by Chamorro, was being refilled. The danger was that President Díaz's friends among the Conservatives, notably General Chamorro, might obtain loans from the surplus that would affect the election. As Munro put the case many years later, "We pointed out that at least $600,000 would thus be available for political purposes and that this would be enough to hire every registered voter in Nicaragua for one week at current wage rates." A loan from New York would establish financial control and prevent the government from using public funds for electoral purposes. Munro and his legation assistants also urged the department to persuade the Guaranty Trust Company, together with Seligman, to buy 51 percent of the national bank's stock, thereby removing the bank and the currency it controlled from Conservative temptation. Unfortunately, the department decided to await a survey of Nicaragua's economy by W. W. Cumberland, who had resigned as financial adviser to Haiti. This delayed McCoy's plan to ensure the fairness of *la ley McCoy.*[30]

McCoy took every precaution, including providing citizens of his own country with information about what he was trying to do. To his staff he added a public-relations counselor, a friend and former editor of the *Manila Times,* Walter Wilgus. McCoy wrote to his many influential friends, such as Walter Lippmann, Frank Knox of the *Chicago Daily News,* Felix Frankfurter of the Harvard Law School, and Chief Justice Taft. Frankfurter responded that he was glad the general was in charge of America's honor and good sense in Nicaragua. From President Wilson's secretary of war and a longtime progressive and likely critic, Newton D. Baker, McCoy received equal praise: "I do not know where the white man's burden begins and ends and I have no clear conviction as to whether we have a manifest destiny in the election you are supervising . . . but I dismiss all these questions because you are there."[31] The general received these replies in time to know that the issue of Nicaragua would not interfere with the U.S. presidential election of 1928.

Fortunately, the Nicaraguan election turned out well. McCoy divided the country into 351 small districts. Despite the fact that 72 percent of Nicaraguans were illiterate, 148,831 registered, 28 percent more than in 1924 and many more than in any earlier election. On election day, Moncada was the victor.

With the election out of the way, McCoy prepared to go home, but he received no comfort from two postelection aspects of his Nicaraguan experience. Both of them marked failures on the part of the United States.

First was the continued presence of self-styled Gen. Augusto Sandino, who operated with a few hundred men near the Honduran border. After Tipitapa, Sandino refused to come in. If the marines in Nicaragua, greatly reinforced by the time of Stimson's mission, had been better led, McCoy believed that they might have captured Sandino and ended the embarrassment of an alleged general fighting the American-supported government of Nicaragua and, according to Sandino, Yankee imperialism. One of McCoy's American opponents was a navy rear admiral, the bearer of two stars against McCoy's one; the other was a marine brigadier general who naturally considered himself McCoy's equal, even though McCoy was the personal representative of President Coolidge. In April 1928, McCoy finally told Brig. Gen. Logan Feland that if he did not show action within one month, McCoy would report his inaction. Thereafter there was a better result. McCoy arranged sub-rosa permission from the president of Honduras to let the marines attack Sandinistas in that country, which made Sandino's situation much more unpleasant. McCoy increased the size and training of the Guardia Nacional, which was not merely under American control but under McCoy's control. Such tactics paid off, and sixteen hundred guerrillas surrendered that summer. By autumn, Sandinista activity was down dramatically.[32]

But Sandino carried on, and in 1927–31 the Sandinistas killed forty-two marines and three thousand Nicaraguans. The marines' intelligence was poor, for local people hesitated to cooperate, and it was difficult to identify the renegade's supporters; after an attack, they blended into the population or the junglelike terrain. What should have been done was to double or triple the marine force under forceful commanders and, with Honduran cooperation, end the rebellion. Unfortunately, that would have been impossible during such an anti-imperialist era. American opinion would never have stood for it. To Americans, the vicious Sandino seemed a Robin Hood, and he obliged them by leaving certificates with individuals from whom he requisitioned what he needed, stating that "The Honorable Calvin Coolidge, President of the United States of North America, will pay the bearer $_____," inserting the amount at which he valued the levied goods.[33] By January 1931, the marine garrison was down to fourteen hundred. Two years later, the last troops left. In 1934, the American-trained guardia betrayed Sandino, who had come to Managua; they took him out to the capital's airstrip and machine-gunned him.

The other aspect of the intervention in which McCoy failed was securing what he would have described as a lasting solution. By this he did not mean an anti-Somoza solution, for he was advocating it at the end of the election, before the Somoza family rose to prominence. He had in mind the same sort of solution that Morrow desired for Mexico. Because of the primitive politics of Nicaragua, compared with the sensitivies of Mexican nationalism, he might have had better luck carrying out such a scheme. But even in Nicaragua it was a pipe dream; American public opinion was against imperial adventure, believing that because the United States had created an empire thirty years earlier, anything accomplished in foreign regions partook of imperialism. To be sure, the Great Depression that began in 1929 would have made American participation doubly impossible.

In the autumn of 1928, McCoy went to Washington to discuss what might be done after the election to ensure a stable, pro-American Nicaragua, and there he broached his Morrow-like scheme. He warned that there should not be "the unduly optimistic belief that a fair election is a panacea for Nicaragua's troubles." He considered the election a detail of the larger problem. He desired a program of internal reconstruction reminiscent of what the United States had begun in Cuba and the Philippines, "the preservation of order, the development of communications, . . . the elimination of widespread corruption of the government, the improvement of health conditions and the extension and modernization of schools."[34] This meant money, but it could be done under a plan drawn up by the former Haitian financial adviser Cumberland, who had completed his survey of the Nicaraguan economy. In return for a loan, an American commission would direct the economy.

McCoy's plan failed because Secretary Kellogg refused to go along. He would not associate the American government with a bankers' loan. He could not have done it if he had wished. And without association, the bankers would not make the loan.

In considering what happened with U.S. relations with Mexico and what occurred in the reoccupation of Nicaragua, it is clear that in the 1920s under President Coolidge, the nation was retreating from its imperial era under Presidents McKinley, Roosevelt, Taft, and Wilson. Popular feeling after World War I was that interventions abroad, even in Latin America, were foolish enterprises. The end of any threat to the Panama Canal made retreat strategically justifiable.

There were the occasional claims that the United States in the 1920s was still an imperial nation, that the diplomacy of the Coolidge administration with Mexico was sufficiently pressing that it amounted to undue influence, which the critics defined as imperialism. In Nicaragua, to be sure, U.S. marines were on the scene, and U.S. Navy ships were in or off the little nation's principal ports. A U.S. Army general supervised the election of 1928. Was that not imperialism? What was the difference between such actions and the heavy-handed behavior of the Theodore Roosevelt administration against any nations of Central America and the Caribbean that got out of line, that is, acted against the advice of the government in Washington?

In fact, the difference between imperial behavior and the sort of intervention the United States accomplished in Nicaragua was considerable. Those who believed that intervention and imperialism meant the same thing were wrong. Imperialism in the 1920s was out; it had been relegated to the dustbin of American foreign policy, but it did seem necessary to keep open the possibility of intervention.

The issue was raised at a meeting of the Sixth International Conference of American States in Havana in January–February 1928. The conference began auspiciously and then turned into real trouble. It opened with the appearance of President Coolidge, who arrived on the battleship *Texas*. There were no incidents during his address on 16 January, and he departed the next day. There was, however, tension during the conference sessions. The Washington government had imposed restrictions on Argentine beef to keep out hoof-and-mouth disease, and the Argentine delegation was unfriendly. Some of the other Latin American republics were willing to challenge the colossus of the North because of the intervention, still going on, in Nicaragua. The galleries were packed with anti-U.S. audiences, who cheered each remark against imperialism. Speech followed speech.

On the day before the conference's final session, the delegate from El Salvador, Dr. J. Gustavo Guerrero, agreed privately with former secretary of state Hughes, representing the United States, not to continue agitation against American intervention. The next day, 18 February, with the galleries packed and press representatives in full array, he lost his head and made a motion: "No state has the right to intervene in the internal affairs of another." The conference turned into a series of nasty speeches in which the United States' friends and enemies shouted at one another. A friendly delegate declared that opponents of the United States would take everyone back to life in the jungle, which was a strong phrase, an insulting phrase, in Latin America. Hughes murmured, "Save us from our friends." When Guerrero abused a Peruvian delegate, the latter called him a "cheap watch salesman." With the galleries in an uproar, Guerrero and his Peruvian antagonist were close to asking for pistols for two.

Hughes was forced to stand up and make what may have been the greatest speech of his life—defending American imperialism. He made the last American defense of what he had once described as "interposition of a temporary character." Hughes arose and held up his arms, fists clenched, beard bristling. Silence descended, necks craned, and he dominated the hall. Summoning the interpreter, he told him, "Interpret sentence by sentence." He did not want to trust a translator's summary. After explaining the situation in Nicaragua, he continued: "Now what is the real difficulty? Let us face the facts. The difficulty, if there is any, in any one of the American republics is not of any external aggression. It is an internal difficulty. . . . What are we to do when government breaks down and American citizens are in danger of their lives? Are we to stand by and see them butchered in the jungle?"[35]

The galleries rang with applause for the United States. Guerrero arose and in a weak, almost inaudible voice withdrew his resolution. He would not say who had proposed that he offer such a resolution. Hughes had won a momentary victory, for he was seeking time until the Nicaraguan intervention came to an end.

A special meeting after the Havana Conference, the International Conference of American States on Conciliation and Arbitration, was held in Washington from December 1928 into January 1929. It negotiated a multilateral treaty for the arbitration of all juridical questions and a multilateral treaty for conciliation. Hughes and Kellogg were the American delegates, and each of the Central and South American countries except for Argentina sent delegates. Sixteen of the twenty signatory nations ratified the arbitration treaty, eighteen ratified the conciliation treaty, and the pacts went into effect late in 1929.

Shortly before leaving the State Department, Secretary Kellogg on 28 February 1929 sent a long circular instruction, "strictly confidential," to American envoys in Latin American capitals, in which he stated that the United States had no right to use the Monroe Doctrine to enforce Latin American good behavior. He was disavowing the Roosevelt Corollary of 1905, which had claimed such a right. He explained that under the Monroe Doctrine, the rights and interests of the United States were "against Europe and not against the Latin Americas." The doctrine "is not a lance; it is a shield."

Confusion resulted in Kellogg's memorandum never being followed up, and another State Department official received credit for what Kellogg sought to do. In preparation for his circular, Kellogg had asked Undersecretary J. Reuben Clark to prepare a memorandum on the Monroe Doctrine and interposition. Clark passed the task to his assistant, Anna O'Neill, who put together a long exegesis from such sources as John Bassett Moore's *Digest of International Law and History* and *Digest of International Arbitration,* the *Encyclopaedia Britannica* (11th ed.), *Encyclopedia Americana,* and Carlton J. H. Hayes's *A Political and Social History of Modern Europe.* She quoted from those sources at length as to what the Monroe Doctrine meant when announced, what later presidents made or tried to make of it, what the law of nations said about intervention, and what was special about the intentions of the United States as opposed to those of the nations of Europe. O'Neill did not explicitly repudiate the Roosevelt Corollary, but Clark did so in a seventeen-page cover letter to Kellogg dated 17 December 1928. He said, in part, that "it is not believed that this corollary is justified by the terms of the Monroe Doctrine, however much it may be justified by the application of the doctrine of self-preservation." The O'Neill exegesis and its cover letter were lost in the changeover of Republican administrations in 1929. In some odd manner, the two items emerged as a publication of the Government Printing Office in 1930. President Hoover, consulted by Secretary of State Stimson, said that he did not wish any notice to be taken of the publication, as it might be momentarily inconvenient. He was probably referring to the London Naval Treaty, then before the Senate, which had inspired critics to accuse the president of a sellout to the Europeans. A statement about the Monroe Doctrine might have found the ready interpretation of a sellout to the Latin Americans. The document passed into a limbo in which it still resides. Upon being queried, department officials responded that the Clark memorandum, as it was called, was not part of the official policy of the United States. Years later, in 1965, I described the department's response as a repudiation of a repudiation. In 1974, Dana Munro published a memoir of his experiences of the 1920s and criticized my article by asking what other response the department could have made, given Hoover's prohibition of comment.[36]

Perhaps the Clark memorandum was meaningless, even if historians have cited it as marking the end of empire in the Western Hemisphere and elsewhere, such as the Philippines. But the Clark publication should have been credited to Secretary Kellogg and to Kellogg's chief, President Coolidge, who instructed him and Morrow and McCoy on what to do in Mexico and Nicaragua.

Election as lieutenant governor of Massachusetts, 1915. Grace Coolidge is perhaps about to congratulate her husband. Coolidge was an inveterate smoker of cigars. (Forbes Library)

Northampton, 1920. Accepting the nomination for the vice presidency. (Forbes Library)

At his desk in the Executive Offices, 15 August 1923. (National Archives)

Platform soup required a good cook. (*New York Herald Tribune*)

With running mate Charles G. Dawes, 1 July 1924. (Library of Congress)

The Coolidges with sons John and Calvin, 1924. The photograph was taken within days of Calvin's illness and death. (Library of Congress)

The cabinet, 14 October 1925. To the left of the president: Secretary Mellon, Attorney General Sargent, and Secretaries Wilbur, Jardine, and Davis. Front: Secretaries Kellogg, Weeks, New, Work, and Hoover. (Library of Congress)

The president, his wife, and their son John, 30 December 1925. (National Archives)

The Boss Cowboy of the U.S. Ranch....
PHOTO BY RISE

In the garb of the West at State Game Lodge, Black Hills,
South Dakota, 1927. (Calvin Coolidge Memorial Foundation)

President and Mrs. Coolidge leaving the homestead at the Notch, undated. In front is their Pierce Arrow. (Calvin Coolidge Memorial Foundation)

Retirement, 21 Massasoit Street, Northampton. When the former president sat on the porch in 1929–1930, tourists gaped. The card labeled "ice" asks the ice-man to replenish the household supply. (Forbes Library)

8

★ ★ ★ ★ ★

EUROPE AND THE FAR EAST

Early in his presidency, in November 1923, Coolidge wrote a revealing commentary to New York newspaper publisher Frank A. Munsey. "Of course I do not propose to implicate ourselves in Europe," he related. "I think you may feel safe in assuming that nothing of that kind is going to happen. We have interests there which I want to look after for our own sake, but we cannot attempt to shield them from the results of their own actions." On another occasion, also revealing, the president was conversing with Boone (while riding his mechanical horse, by which he took his exercise) and inquired as to how the doctor's young daughter Suzanne was doing in school. Boone told him that she had brought home her first French book to show her parents. The president inquired, "Does she know all the English ones?" Another instance of presidential testimony took place soon after Sir Esme Howard arrived in Washington as British ambassador. He and his wife, Isa, took dinner with the president and Mrs. Coolidge, and Coolidge told Lady Howard, who vigorously protested, that he would never visit Europe because he could learn everything he needed to know by remaining in America.[1]

Two issues with Europe and Europeans were responsible for such remarks. One was the war debts–reparations tangle. The European nations owed the United States for munitions and credits obtained during World War I and in the early postwar months. Having borrowed the money, they did not want to repay it. What the European debtors eventually chose to pay back was only such sums as they could collect from Germany in reparations. The debtors thereby forced U.S. officials into negotiating with Germany over reparations.

A second point of irritability for President Coolidge in regard to Europe was his desire to achieve greater limitation of naval arms, to pick up where the Washington Naval Conference of 1921–22 had stopped, which was limitation of battleships and aircraft carriers. Coolidge wished to extend limitation to the other categories of warships. Here he discovered that the nations that did not wish to pay their debts were the ones that maintained expensive navies and, in the instance of Great Britain, sought (he believed) to compete with the U.S. Navy.

In exchange for resolving debts and reparations and for limiting naval arms, the president was willing to help the Europeans with the organization of peace. This did not mean joining the League of Nations but accepting membership in the Permanent Court of International Justice, known as the World Court; U.S. membership would assist peaceful settlement of international difficulties, diminishing the possibility of another world war. In 1927–28, he went so far as to permit Secretary of State Kellogg to negotiate the Kellogg-Briand Pact, which undertook to outlaw war.

As for policy in the Far East—specifically, relations with China and Japan—the problem appeared to be that China was in turmoil during the 1920s. Fortunately, the several cabinets in Japan during that time were cooperative, assisting the Western powers in protecting citizens and investments in China.

The war debts had reached a total of $7 billion by the time of the armistice, and afterward the United States lent $3.2 billion. The interest was 5 percent, because the United States had raised the money with bonds paying 4.25 percent, and it seemed sensible to add .75 percent as a service charge.

In the 1920s, the government renegotiated the interest, determining rates roughly based on ability to pay. Congress in 1922 created the World War Foreign Debt Commission and instructed it to make 1947 the deadline for payment and to fix the minimum interest rate at 4.25 percent. There was an uproar, for the governments of France and Britain desired cancellation of their debts, not concessions over the interest. The French government flatly declared that it would not abide by the legislation. Britain in January 1923 agreed to pay its debt over sixty-two years at a rate of 3.3 percent. The Italians negotiated an interest rate of 0.3 percent. Congress had to accept these agreements, contrary to the 1922 legislation, and over the next few years it consented to other agreements, with all payments running sixty-two years.

But before the British government had agreed to pay its debt with a reduction in interest, the foreign secretary, Earl Balfour, addressed a note to six of Britain's debtors (the British government had also lent to its allies) stating the British view of what the London government should pay the

United States. He referred to the reparations the Allies had fastened on Germany at the end of the war—reparations for the hundreds of villages and towns destroyed by the German army in northern France, for farmland ruined, for ships sunk at sea with their cargoes, even for pensions to Allied veterans. Reparations, Balfour related, were the key to debt payments: "In no circumstances do we propose to ask more from our debtors than is necessary to pay to our creditors." President Wilson had begun a U.S. policy of denying any connection between debts and reparations, and his successors did the same thing, but Balfour made the connection. Over the next years, it became apparent that because of attractive interest rates private lenders in the United States, both individuals and banks, lent to German individuals and to German governmental bodies—national, state, and municipal—allowing the Berlin government to pay reparations. The United States itself had refused reparations, except for the cost of the small U.S. occupation force in Germany that returned in 1923. Reparations nonetheless passed to the United States as debt payments.

The issue of the debts rested on the collection of reparations. In 1921, an Allied commission set the total reparations figure at $33 billion, which the Germans claimed was impossibly high. With Germany in default, Secretary of State Hughes, in December 1922, proposed a committee of experts; two weeks later, he received the European response when France and Belgium sent troops into the industrial Ruhr to force Germany to meet its obligations under the Treaty of Versailles. The next months saw an impasse—the French and Belgian governments adamant, Germans sullenly resistant—until the German chancellor admitted in September that Germany could no longer carry on the struggle. Meanwhile, the mark fell to depths never reached by a currency, except that of Nationalist China after World War II. In October 1923, 4.2 trillion marks were worth one dollar.

In two conferences early in 1924, the American government took the lead in rearranging reparations. The French government weakened because of a run on the franc and consented to a conference in Paris from January to April 1924, under the leadership of General Dawes. The latter individual, it appeared, could handle the problem. Hughes saw him on 11 December, and a department official afterward wrote that the secretary "was reduced to a pulp by his interview with Dawes and was almost sorry for the French who have certainly never been up against such an astounding human dynamo. All the facts in the situation will be brought out or Dawes will know the reason why."[2] Dawes, it should be added, was an unofficial delegate; the United States government was not represented at this conference, which was technical, the State Department announced. In reality, however, another unofficial U.S. delegate, industrialist Owen Young, handled the work of bringing out the facts. The resultant agreement was ratified by the governments

147

involved at a second conference in London. This meeting set a reparations schedule, with payments to begin at a low level and Germany receiving a large international loan to stabilize its currency and pay initial reparations. Over a four-year period, payments would rise to $500 million annually and remain at that level. Collection was vested in an agent general, the former U.S. treasury official S. Parker Gilbert, who received considerable authority over German government finances.

In pushing through the reparations arrangement on which the payment of war debts would rest, President Coolidge did his part. At the conclusion of the first conference, he wrote to Dawes that "had you been representing the government you would have been hampered, and no doubt your proposed action would have become the object of political controversy here. I have said that you and your associates represented not the Government, but the American mind." A day or two before the end of the conference to ratify what Dawes had arranged, the U.S. ambassador in London, Kellogg, who was the American representative, received a cable from the president that if the conference was about to break up without adopting the plan, Kellogg should ask it to remain in session a day or two, as Coolidge had a proposition. Kellogg cabled back that there was no danger that the conference would break up. Coolidge said no more. After Kellogg became secretary of state, he became curious as to what Coolidge had had in mind. Years later he remembered that "I asked him about it. He smiled and said, 'The Conference did not break up, did it?' That is the only answer I ever got." Actually, at the time, the president had told a State Department official what he had in mind: he would propose that in case the signatories in some future contingency chose to accuse Germany of being in default, the chief justice of the Supreme Court would arbitrate. He based the idea on arbitration of the Costa Rican–Panamanian boundary by Chief Justice Edward White in 1914.[3]

At the beginning of the Dawes Plan, there was an augury of trouble, a sense that what seemed to be success was not unalloyed and that debts and reparations rested more on cupidity than comity. It was often remarked that the Dawes loan arranged at the London conference, a private loan to Germany of $200 million to enable the German government to get on its feet, was oversubscribed. This was taken as a sign of great things, but it was nothing of the sort. Kellogg obtained $110 million for American bankers, who took the bonds at 87 and sold them to the public at 92; the bonds were to be redeemed at 105. In New York and London, the bonds were nearly sold out the first day. In the United States, the issue was oversubscribed ten times; in Britain, thirteen. The London market took half the issue not taken by the Americans, and the remainder went to French buyers and nationals of half a dozen other European nations. To receive $200 million, Germany had to issue bonds worth $250 million.[4]

During subsequent years, reparations payments were in the hands of Agent General Gilbert, thirty-two years of age when he began his duties. The State Department had desired Young, but he was not available. J. P. Morgan and Company, closely involved in the Dawes loan, desired Morrow, but it was perhaps Coolidge who hesitated at the choice of so prominent a Morgan partner. The post went to Gilbert, who was bright, hardworking, and intense, spoke no German, and proved a master of many German and Allied economic issues.

What happened in outline during the years of Gilbert's supervision is easy to relate. Five years after the Dawes Plan, that is, in 1929, the Young Plan, again sponsored by governments involved with reparations and with the cooperation of the United States, sought to make reparations easier for the German government. It set the reparations total at $8 billion payable over fifty-eight and a half years at an interest rate of 5.5 percent—the total, principal and interest, being $26 billion. Curiously, annual installments exactly equaled the remaining number of war debt installments.

The coming of the Great Depression brought an end to the debts-reparations tangle. America's debtors met at Lausanne in 1932 and lowered the total reparations bill to $714 million, compared with the $33 billion originally asked for. In 1933, the debtors made token payments to the United States, their last. The exception was the Finnish government, which during the 1930s paid its debt in full.

But the debts and reparations issue was far more complex than the above recital shows. New analyses have become available, and it is possible to see the situation more clearly than did the people and the governments of the time. Adolf Hitler's rise to power in Germany in 1933 and the extraordinary war production he was able to obtain from the German economy displayed how much stronger that economy was than had been assumed. The chicanery of the president of the Reichsbank, Hjalmar Schacht, during the 1930s—arranging to depreciate German obligations held abroad and buy them back at bargain prices—showed that Schacht's financial expertise may well have been responsible for some of Germany's resistance to reparations payments during the 1920s. American historians and economists after World War II have looked closely into German behavior regarding reparations. In addition, when West Germany's economic revival beginning with the Marshall Plan, the *Wirtschaftswunder*, stalled in the 1970s, German historians and economists looked back to the 1920s to see whether what occurred then had meaning for their own time.

In examining events of the Coolidge era and later, consider the question of whether Germany could have paid reparations, which involved the transfer problem—the need to pass reparations payments over the national tariffs of the former Allies. A recent group of historians, of whom Stephen

A. Schuker is the most prominent, contends that Germany could have paid all reparations under the Dawes Plan and refused in 1929 because no German desired repayment. According to this way of thinking, the transfer problem was not really the obstacle. Had the German government cut spending and raised taxes to collect reparations in marks, it could have transferred the marks. According to Schuker, the government "had no intention of making the tangible sacrifice in the form of higher taxes that was necessary to promote effective transfer." Similarly, economist Fritz Machlup has written that "it is hard to understand why some economists in the late 1920s made such a fuss about the supposed severity of the German transfer problem."[5] In opposition, historian William C. McNeil has pointed out subtleties that Schuker and Machlup may have missed. One was failure of American and Allied experts to appreciate the size of the German public economy. States such as Prussia and Bavaria, and especially the cities, had budgets that if taken together consumed more than the government in Berlin; the national regime required only 30 percent of government expenditures. Government took fully one-third of the German gross national product. In the United States, government was no large consumer of national income. Britain and France had large government expenditures but preferred not to measure the German public economy in its full proportions. In addition, they did not sense how all three divisions of German government—national, state, and city—were capital starved, for capital had been scarce since 1914. When it became available with the Dawes Plan, they avidly competed for it.

More important than German government expenditures threatening to turn the Dawes Plan into insolvency were the social problems that brought another sort of competition for Dawes Plan funds. Every part of German society seemed to be organized and willing to trade political support for economic well-being. The conservatives had long been a force in German society, and leaders of the prewar empire pampered them. They were entrenched in agriculture, a hopelessly uneconomical portion of the economy, and demanded their payments. They were strong in such industries as steel and textiles and again were pleased to have government support, even though they had overdeveloped the steel industry and badly organized the textile industry. When conservative estate owners and industrialists received support, workers on farms and in factories sought their shares. Workers demanded unemployment benefits from an economy that, with unemployment as high as 12 to 15 percent, could not afford them. Workers asked for shorter hours and, when they retired, pensions. In the latter 1920s, the bureaucracies of industrial plants rapidly increased, filling offices with white-collar workers whose contribution to production was not notable.

Into this fiscally and socially awkward country poured not merely the government-sponsored Dawes and Young Plan loans of 1924 and 1929 but also a torrent of private money. Half was American, perhaps $2.5 billion. It is difficult to know, because more than half the American money was short term and was often covered by subterfuges such as intermediary borrowers. An American short-term loan might be made to a Canadian bank, which would pass the money to Amsterdam, from whence it might go to a German city that needed to cover interest on bond issues.

The German situation was extremely difficult to assess. It is little wonder that the Coolidge administration failed to confront it. The Harding administration had announced in 1922 that banking institutions sponsoring foreign loans sold to the public had to ascertain the attitude of the State Department in writing before concluding their transactions. Lenders were told either that "the Department, in the light of the information at hand, offers no objection to the proposed transaction" or that "the Department is unable to view the proposed financing with favor at this time." After the Dawes Plan went into effect, Secretary of State Hughes; the governor of the New York Federal Reserve Bank, Benjamin Strong; and Secretary of Commerce Hoover all thought that private loans were risky, but they differed as to what the policy should be. Hughes wanted simple State Department commentaries such as those of 1922. Strong opposed regulation and wanted to allow lenders to take their own risks, for if the United States government continued to be involved, it would have to take responsibility for default. Hoover argued that the government could work with bankers and gain support for good loans and cooperation in refusing bad ones. In the beginning, the Hughes policy became the rule, but as the decade advanced and after private money began to go out in indirect ways, the State Department gave up supervision and the Strong policy, which was no policy, prevailed. The Hoover policy might have worked but had little possibility because of the many lending institutions in the United States and the opportunities for commissions on bond sales and high interest on German government loans.[6]

At one juncture, in April 1925, Coolidge intervened, but his intervention failed. Secretary Kellogg told William Castle that the president in a cabinet meeting had insisted that the government keep some kind of supervision over German loans. Castle "agreed with this only if we really keep a supervision and really advise the bankers as the President evidently thinks we do." He told the secretary that he "thought it a dangerous business but that the danger could be reduced only by doing our duty to the limit." Unfortunately, this did not happen. As McNeil has written, "the primary motive for making the loans was surely the spectacular profits to be made and throughout the 1920s both bankers and public officials refused to accept the responsibility for a well-planned stabilization policy which America's monetary predominance demanded."[7]

Conclusion of the Locarno Pact in 1925 among Germany, France, Belgium, Britain, and Italy (a guarantee against the forceful change of Germany's western borders) and Germany's arrangement of arbitration treaties with the succession states of eastern Europe (which looked only to peaceful change of Germany's eastern borders and seemed a second-class arrangement, compared with the Locarno guarantee) commenced what was known as "fulfillment," Germany's acceptance of the Treaty of Versailles. The Locarno Pact and the arbitration treaties gave a European stamp of approval to what seemed to be stabilization.

When the Young Plan replaced the Dawes Plan, it ignored the political and social divisions within Germany, and not long afterward, everything collapsed. In 1928, American private money began going into the stock market rather than into German loans, and the market crash the next year confirmed the end of such loans. The coalition of political parties supporting the German government collapsed. The Social Democratic party destroyed the ruling coalition by refusing any cut in unemployment benefits. Chancellor Heinrich Bruening ruled by decree and imposed a deflationary fiscal policy, reducing expenditures of the federal, state, and city governments, to allow Young Plan payments. The Nazi party allied with the agriculturists and owners of the steel industry, and Hitler came to power.

In 1995, there was a strange denouement to the debts-reparations debacle. The newly unified German government created by the end of the cold war undertook to pay off the final obligations of the government-sponsored loans under the Dawes and Young Plans. In 1953, an international conference had decided that Germany would have to pay only after the divided nation was unified. West Germany paid the principal of the loans, which for American nationals meant $210 million, during the years ending in 1980. It did not pay back interest. In 1995, a German bank placed an advertisement in the *New York Times,* advising owners of Dawes and Young bonds, perhaps grandchildren of the original purchasers, that they would receive new German government bonds paying 3 percent interest and maturing in 2010. They would receive back interest to 1990, when Germany was unified. The total owed was $70 million.[8]

In the U.S. Navy's expensive ships and in the success of the Washington Conference lay the possibility of a new conference on the limitation of naval arms. The president kept that possibility in mind, and in 1927, an opportunity to pursue it seemed to arise.

Coolidge's attitude toward the navy was an interesting compound of prejudices. Although a son of rural New England, he was immensely fond of the presidential yacht *Mayflower*. He appreciated its beauty; often considered incapable of judging beauty, he knew a first-class steam yacht when he saw one. The ship's lines were perfect, he believed. One of the ship's captains obtained for him a handsome naval cap through the agency of Brooks Brothers in New York, and the president took to it with a passion, placing it on his head each time he came aboard. After he retired to Northampton, he hung in the Coolidge living room a full-sized oil painting of the *Mayflower*. He and his wife were dismayed by Hoover's decision to take the *Mayflower* out of service, and when it burned at its moorings not long afterward, they were distraught. But other aspects of the navy did not appeal to Coolidge. He flaunted his ignorance of naval terms, describing all ships as boats; in a letter to one of his former office secretaries in 1931, he wrote that "Mrs. Coolidge is going to Newport News to christen a boat for the Dollar Line." He disliked naval ceremonies. Theodore Roosevelt, Jr., went to the White House for a review of the marines, who made a splendid showing, but he noticed that Coolidge tired quickly of the rigmarole of having his photograph taken with the chairman of the Navy League, presenting medals. There also was his notorious inability as a sailor, such as when he reviewed ninety-eight ships of the Atlantic Fleet but suffered seasickness and sat on a sofa, clad in his hat, looking out glumly, saluting while sitting down. A photographer made his way to the scene and took a picture. Coolidge, incidentally, had his own remedy for seasickness—dropping cocaine into his ear with an eye-dropper.[9]

The president liked navy officers better than those of the army. He told Boone that he thought them more cultivated and wondered why that was so, when the education of both groups was basically the same. Boone explained that wardroom life was conducive to broad discussions, to more reading during long cruises, that navy officers were often linguists; there was a stress on social refinement and less distraction at sea than on army posts. But the president thought that they hid things from him. Moreover, he was annoyed with the way navy officers used Japan as an excuse to obtain appropriations. One evening, he told Boone that the navy started a war scare with "poor little Japan" every time it approached "naval appropriation season."[10]

Coolidge's problem with the navy was the competition among Britain, the United States, and Japan in the construction of ships other than those limited at the Washington Conference in 1921–22, especially cruisers. Before the Washington Conference, cruisers had been of indeterminate size, ranging in displacement from three thousand to twelve thousand tons. The naval treaty defined any ship over ten thousand tons as a battleship. Hence ten thousand tons, the maximum, became the ideal cruiser tonnage. The treaty defined the maximum size of guns for cruisers as eight inches in caliber. The ideal cruiser possessed eight-inch guns. Prior to the Washington Conference, no such cruisers had been launched. In 1922, Japan laid down five "heavy cruisers"; in 1924, five. In 1924, Britain laid down five. Congress authorized eight in 1924, and the navy laid the first keel in 1926.

Unhappily, as in the debts-reparations tangle, the president did not realize the complexity of the cruiser issue. Indeed, few political leaders did, and almost no navy officers. Consider the matter of eight-inch guns. A ship of a given displacement was always a compromise of the weight of propulsive machinery, guns, and armor. Any given "platform" had to have additions and subtractions—more for one, less for the others. The ten-thousand-ton platform with a high-speed propulsive mechanism could not take the weight of eight-inch guns and armor too; eight-inch guns meant no armor. This should have forced navy men to look closely at the advantage of eight-inch guns, but they noticed only that such guns could fire farther than the usual guns on cruisers, six-inchers. However, the latter could be hand-loaded because their shells weighed 100 pounds and could be tossed into the breech, whereas eight-inchers had to be machine-loaded because their shells weighed 250 pounds. This meant that six-inch guns could get ten or twelve shells in the air per minute, if loaded in the open where there was plenty of room, as opposed to three shells for the eight-inch guns. If a six-inch-gunned cruiser closed the range with an eight-inch-gunned antagonist, crossing the theoretically dreaded distance in which its guns could not reach, it could fill the air with shells. There were other subtleties not mentioned by eight-inch-gun enthusiasts. Everyone envisioned perfect weather for the cruiser duel, and there was little talk of the intervention of planes or of night battles or of good or bad luck.

Coolidge thought that it would be easy to hold a conference in Geneva in the summer of 1927, because a preparatory commission for a League of Nations–sponsored general disarmament conference was in session there. Perhaps for this reason he failed to make much preparation; there was little diplomatic exchange prior to the conference.

He appointed Rear Adm. Hilary Jones as the navy's principal specialist. It was said of Admiral Jones that he saw the world through a porthole. Whatever tonnage of cruisers the U.S. Navy achieved through negotiation, Jones insisted that except for the ten so-called light cruisers of the *Omaha* class (six thousand tons, six-inch guns) commissioned in 1923–25, it should all be allocated to heavy cruisers. Britain's technical delegates demanded a high total tonnage of cruisers to allow construction of exactly as many heavy cruisers as the U.S. Navy constructed. The Royal Navy already possessed a large tonnage of new light cruisers, unlike the U.S. Navy, which other than the Omahas had launched no cruisers since 1908.

Representatives of the third naval power at the conference, Japan (France and Italy refused to send delegations), watched impassively while the Americans and British fought each other on heavy cruisers. Japan's delegates knew that the U.S. Navy wanted heavy cruisers in part because they could carry more fuel and were thus longer-ranged, able to operate in the far Pacific, where the United States was forbidden by one of the agreements of the Washington Conference to increase fortifications or naval facilities in the Philippines or to fortify Guam and Midway.

When the conference came to an end, President Coolidge was angry about the British naval officers' failure to understand the American position, although he might have blamed Admiral Jones for British intransigence. He was irritated by newspaper speculation, reflecting official views in London, that he had called the conference without preparation; after all, the technicians should have been prepared, he thought. For the rest of his presidency he was willing to outbuild antagonists. He was even more willing when in the summer of 1928 the British and French governments announced a proposal acceptable to them that would have prevented the U.S. Navy from constructing heavy cruisers. The president allowed the navy to entertain a building plan for seventy-one ships, including twenty-five heavy cruisers, five carriers, and assorted destroyers and submarines, with a cost of $725 million, the largest building plan since the Naval Act of 1916. He settled for a smaller plan proposed by the chairman of the House Naval Affairs Committee—fifteen heavy cruisers and a carrier for $224 million. The latter program passed the House and Senate, and in one of his last presidential acts, Coolidge signed it. The way opened for a compromise with the British when Prime Minister J. Ramsay MacDonald came to the United States in 1929, spoke to a joint session of Congress, and offered parity. The London Naval Conference the next year produced a "yardstick" for calculating total national cruiser tonnages, which determined arbitrarily that one 10,000-ton heavy cruiser equaled 15,168 tons of light cruisers.

Much time and animosity went into the cruiser race of the 1920s, and in retrospect, it is regrettable, for other issues were more important. Unfortunately, American and British admirals represented national power, and Coolidge and MacDonald's predecessor Stanley Baldwin found it necessary to listen to them. The admirals had access to newspaper readers, who found technical calculations incomprehensible and accepted the admirals' assertions, even though the latter were simpleminded to a fault.

The Coolidge administration also considered the question that had troubled all public officials, American as well as European, since the beginning of the war in 1914—what people described as the organization of peace. Everyone believed that what was needed in 1914 was some sort of machinery, a mechanism that would have prevented the automatic working of the alliance system once the assassination of Archduke Francis Ferdinand at Sarajevo created a crisis between the governments of Serbia and Austria-Hungary.

For President Coolidge and the State Department, the initial American proposal for organizing peace, the League of Nations, was impossible. After the Senate refused to consent to the Treaty of Versailles in 1919–20, the league issue in the United States was dead. Harding had spoken of an "association of nations," but the idea was never firm in his mind, and after his election, he gave it up.[11] "There can be no question about the state of public opinion in America," said Coolidge's first secretary of state. "They want us to stay out of Europe. They are justified in wanting us to stay out. It would not have made any difference, and it would not have helped any, if we had joined the League of Nations. It merely would have turned the whole burden on our backs. They aren't making the use of the League of Nations over there themselves. . . . The League of Nations does not amount to much. All the things that are done in the way of hygiene and the like would have been done anyhow."[12]

When Coolidge became president, there was concern about his attitude toward the League of Nations, and a group of senators sought to discover it, with incomplete success. The group had been meeting for a year at the house of Representative Nicholas Longworth and his wife, seeking to oppose President Harding's infatuation, as they would have described it, with the World Court. Coolidge's succession roused them, and within days, Senators Curtis and then Brandegee spoke to him. Coolidge asked Brandegee if there was any way to work out an association of nations to fulfill Harding's pledge of 1920. Brandegee said that it was impossible. Characteristically, Coolidge did not commit himself beyond his question, did not show where his mind might proceed.[13] Gradually it became clear that he would not pursue the league question or any sort of organization that looked in that direction. He told a State Department official that some Americans feared entrance because of the commitments involved and the possibility that Americans would have to go abroad to fight again. "This argument does not concern me particularly," he said, "but there is one which I consider of paramount importance. Our great duty today is to unite the various racial groups in the United States into the large American group. If we were represented on the League of Nations each national group would feel that our representative should always strive to promote the interests of his fatherland. . . . The result would be that the country would be more divided into un-American nationalistic groups."[14] If nothing else, Coolidge was politically keen, and during his presidency he said little about the league. The fact that he sought to put an archenemy of the League of Nations, Senator Borah, on the ticket in 1924 said that he was not about to urge entrance into the league.

Coolidge did find himself with a singular commitment from his predecessor in regard to the World Court, in that Harding had submitted the court protocol to the Senate. The World Court was established by a treaty, known as a protocol, to which nations might adhere. It was not necessary to belong to the League of Nations to belong to the World Court. The American elder statesman Root had had much to do with drawing up the court's protocol, which received enough adherents to establish an organization in 1922. It did not seem to be a dangerous body, since cases could come before it only with the consent of both parties.

The purpose of the court was mainly to support and advance the rule of law not merely in Europe but in the world. This purpose was in accord with the long-held American belief that peace needed the support of law. In domestic issues, law kept order. International law, unfortunately, was much less formed than municipal law; it contained many weaknesses. The advancement of international law through bilateral or even multilateral treaties was a very slow process, because every single nation had to sign with every other nation. International law could also advance through the accumulation of precedent, the force of which might impress itself on the major nations and thereby pass down to the lesser powers. This was unfair to the lesser powers, however. In accumulating precedent, the World Court seemed a better solution than relying on agreements between the great powers. Moreover, the World Court, sitting in regular sessions, would be a far more important institution than the so-called Hague Court, instituted by the Hague Peace Conference of 1899, which was only a panel of jurists from which nations seeking arbitration might draw judges. In addition to the cases that disputing nations might take to the World Court, the new institution was charged with offering advisory opinions to the League of Nations, should league officials so request.

Because Coolidge in 1923–24 took the position that he had inherited the presidency, he had to stand for the World Court. This, however, did not present the dilemma it might have seemed. He told Ted Roosevelt, who raised the issue, that he would get together with party leaders to see what he should do. In October 1923, the president told Roosevelt what he had in mind. "Well, Colonel," he said, "practically the matter is this: The International Court cannot be mentioned without everything starting to discuss the League of Nations at once, and I have made up my mind to let it set. The Executive has acted, my predecessor submitted it to the Senate. No action is called for, therefore, by me as an Executive."[15]

Worry over the court diminished. There was a seeming crisis, ludicrous in its proportions, in which young Roosevelt managed late in November 1923 to acquire a copy of Coolidge's forthcoming state of the Union message to Congress. "We took the copy and went to the capitol and picked up Bill Borah, then we picked up Frank Brandegee, and then we went back to sister's house where we were joined by Medill McCormick." They read the message aloud, and the three senators thought "little or nothing of it." They thought that the president's stand on the World Court would "ruin" him, although the president merely reminded the Senate that Harding had submitted the protocol. On this score, Roosevelt saw more clearly than the senators, noticing that Coolidge's stand on the World Court was "sufficiently vague so as to leave loopholes for senate amendments."[16]

It became clear that the best procedure for the court's opponents was amendments, a procedure vastly assisted by international lawyer John Bassett Moore, who turned ultraconservative on the court issue, despite the fact that he was the American judge on the court. It was not necessary for the United States to be a member for the court to have an American judge; Moore served in a private capacity. The League Council had asked for an advisory opinion by the court on a dispute between Finland and Russia over Karelia. Russia was neither a league nor a court member and withheld consent, and the court ruled that it could not give an advisory opinion. That should have been enough, but because this ruling had been established by a vote of seven to four, Moore wanted an American reservation to the court protocol. Senator Pepper sponsored a resolution: "That the court shall not . . . without the consent of the United States, entertain any request for an advisory opinion touching any dispute or question in which the United States has or claims an interest."[17]

Coolidge initially did not think that a reservation to the court protocol was necessary, but he came to see it as a good idea. He asked Hughes for advice. "I have never been able exactly to determine," he wrote, "whether Judge Moore thinks we ought to go into the Court or stay out." In a second letter, written the next day, he asked "what possible authority there can be for the constant assertion that it [the court] has to declare the League law to be *the* law."[18] The secretary rested his judgment on the Treaty of Berlin that had ended the state of war between the United States and Germany in 1921: "The United States shall not be represented or participate in any body, agency or commission, nor shall any person represent the United States as a member of any body, agency or commission in which the United States is authorized to participate by this Treaty, unless and until an Act of Congress of the United States shall provide for such representation or participation." Coolidge in 1926 offered a supporting explanation for a Senate reservation to reporters attending his press conference:

As I understand the rights of members of the League who may be members of the Council, in order to have an advisory opinion it has to be by the unanimous action of the Council. That means that one nation in the Council can object to having an advisory opinion and the advisory opinion is then not called for. So I understand the . . . reservation is merely for the purpose of putting the United States in the same position as other countries, which I think when it is understood and studied by the other countries in interest will be regarded as entirely fair.[19]

With the Moore-Pepper reservation, the protocol passed the Senate on 27 January 1926 by a vote of seventy-six to seventeen. It was the last of five reservations, and the signatories accepted the first four: that by accepting the protocol the United States did not involve itself in any legal relation to the League of Nations or assume any obligations under the Treaty of Versailles; that it would have full participation in the choice of judges; that it would pay its fair share of expenses of the court; and that it could withdraw from the protocol if it wished and, if necessary, prevent amendment of the protocol. But the fifth reservation proved impossible for the court's members. In 1929, Root, aged eighty-four, journeyed to Europe to negotiate a formula acceptable to the Senate. The next year, President Hoover submitted the Root proposal. When it came up for a vote in 1935, it failed fifty-two to thirty-six—seven votes short.

A third possibility for organizing peace arose in 1927 and became the Kellogg-Briand Pact, named after the American secretary of state and his French opposite, Aristide Briand. This was the multilateral treaty for the renunciation of war.[20]

The antiwar treaty was the result of some exceedingly shrewd French diplomacy, some equally shrewd American diplomacy, and, bridging the two rather contradictory purposes, some exceedingly innocent American peace sentiment, which was so typical of the 1920s. French diplomacy was marked by an effort of Foreign Minister Briand to bring the United States into his European calculations in what, diplomatically speaking, was a negative military alliance—a pledge that the United States and France would never go to war with each other. For Briand, such a bilateral treaty would read well when made known to German statesmen, about whose outlook on peace and war he was incessantly worried. A bilateral treaty might mean that in any future war in Europe, with Germany aligned against France, the French government could push American neutrality as far as it wished, as it and Britain had done during the period of U.S. neutrality during World War I, and no French excesses against American shipping would suffice to bring the United States into war with France. The French government had already concluded alliances with such European nations as were willing to stand against any future German desire for revenge, and because France's prewar ally Britain was wary of joining a specifically anti-German combine and Russia was militarily weak, there were no more nations to enlist in what critics described as France's "pactomania," or willingness to sign up allies. Briand heard suggestions from visiting Americans that he propose such a pact to the United States, and an opportunity presented itself on 6 April 1927, the tenth anniversary of American entrance into World War I.

Several factors, or forces, initially supported Briand's proposal. One was Lindbergh's flight from New York to Paris, which took place shortly thereafter and produced a surge of Franco-American amity. Another was the imminent opening of the naval conference at Geneva, at which France would be absent because Italy had been invited; Italy refused, but the double invitations seemed to say that Italy was the naval equal of France. Briand needed something to take the place of the declined conference. Third and last in support of Briand's proposal was the almost instant enthusiasm it generated among private American peace groups, which ranged from such conservative organizations as the World Peace Foundation and the Carnegie Endowment for International Peace, advocating membership in the League of Nations and the World Court, to radical groups that believed that world peace might be inaugurated by a single treaty signed by two nations and extended to or imitated by others. Members of these radical organizations believed that it would be possible to "outlaw" war, that a legal solution was possible for world peace, just as law had proved helpful within the borders of nations.

In December 1927, the Coolidge administration feared that it could hold out no longer against the pressure to do something for world peace. Upon learning that the French embassy in Washington was decoding a proposal from Briand that State Department officials believed would be embarrassing in its specificity, Secretary Kellogg "turned the tables" on the French government with a counterproposal that France and the United States invite all nations of the world to sign a multilateral peace pact.

Negotiations having taken this turn, the French government sought to delay the American démarche by bringing in legal experts to examine the idea of a multilateral treaty, turn it into a proposal that France and the United States sign such a treaty first, or encapsulate it in the preface of a bilateral arbitration treaty. But the State Department, led by Kellogg, who began to see merit in the proposal, pursued it. Briand gave in and invited fifteen nations, including his own, to sign the pact in Paris on 27 August 1928: Germany, the United States, Belgium, France, Great Britain, Canada, Australia, New Zealand, South Africa, Ireland, India, Italy, Japan, Poland, and Czechoslovakia. Meanwhile, the nations made a series of reservations, the largest being by Britain, which observed that the pact did not cover "certain regions" of the world, presumably India and Ireland, both imperial possessions in near revolutionary turmoil. The United States reserved self-defense and domestic issues. Kellogg arranged to include the reservations as accompanying correspondence rather than group them with the text, which consisted of two substantive articles and a third concerning ratification:

> 1. The High Contracting Parties solemnly declare in the names of their respective peoples that they condemn recourse to war for the solution of international controversies, and renounce it as an instrument of national policy in their relations with one another.
> 2. The High Contracting Parties agree that the settlement or solution of all disputes or conflicts of whatever nature or of whatever origin they may be, which may arise among them, shall never be sought except by pacific means.

Senate consent to the treaty proved easy. After several days of debate, not so much substantial as playful, in which senators set out their views about war and peace and how the treaty might affect those phenomena of international relations, the Senate approved the treaty on 15 January 1929 by a vote of eighty-five to one. The dissenter, John J. Blaine of Wisconsin, voted against the treaty because he did not believe in the British "certain regions" doctrine, as he described it; he believed that a vote for the treaty was a vote for the empire.

Upon ratification by the original signatories and by adherents, President Hoover proclaimed the treaty in July 1929. Nearly every nation signed, save Argentina, Bolivia, El Salvador, Uruguay, and five uninvited countries: Andorra, Monaco, Morocco, Liechtenstein, and San Marino.

The only effect of this signal American contribution to the organization of peace was to make wars in the 1930s undeclared. Somewhat strangely, the pact became one of the bases of the war crimes trials after World War II, when American international lawyers construed it in a way that Kellogg and Briand could never have imagined, as applying not merely to nations but to individuals as well.

The problem in the Far East in the 1920s was the turmoil in China, which lasted through the Coolidge years. The Manchu dynasty had collapsed in the era just before World War I and gave way to a multiplicity of governments. No single regime had the capability of becoming the government of the entire nation until the rise of Dr. Sun Yat-sen and his military assistant, Gen. Chiang Kai-shek, who took over when Sun died in 1925. General

Chiang balanced and bought off his warlord competitors and gradually extended his government first to Nanking in 1927 and the next year to Peking. Keeping his regime in Nanking, he announced the formation of an all-China government when his power extended to the one-time capital of the Manchu dynasty.

The concern of the United States was partly the hope that China, after its government reorganized, could take a seat among the major powers of the world, or at least occupy a position of respect among the lesser powers. A second concern of Americans was the longtime missionary effort to convert the Chinese people or some considerable portion of them to Christianity. It was a Protestant and Catholic concern, and at the turn of the century and later, many missionaries took their churches' causes to China. Those of the Protestant faith often adhered to the slogan announced by YMCA leader John R. Mott: "The evangelization of the world is this generation." Third and distinctly last among American concerns about China was the possibility of trade. A generation or two before the Coolidge era, economics had seemed the principal American concern, but it had lost much of its attraction by the 1920s. The American economic stake in China was small; exports in the 1920s never exceeded $138 million, 2.3 percent of U.S. trade. In every year save 1921, the United States had an unfavorable trade balance. Investments in China ranked behind those by Britain, Japan, and Russia—$200 million in 1930, or 1 percent of American foreign investments.

Two efforts to assist China—one financial, the other diplomatic—failed ·in the early 1920s. The Washington Conference arranged for a consortium of American, British, French, and Japanese businessmen and investors to assist in China's modernization. This involved financing railroads and other enterprises. The purpose was to avoid the national rivalries of preceding years that had divided China into spheres of influence. But in the 1920s, civil strife made the work of the consortium impossible. Until 1928, when the Nationalists led by Chiang announced a government under "tutelage" of their party the Kuomintang, China had two governments, and for a while three. Within the American arm of the consortium led by Thomas Lamont, there was little enthusiasm for loans without U.S. government guarantees, and Lamont's own firm, J. P. Morgan, took far more interest in loans to Japan. The Morgan firm was interested in the South Manchuria Railway, although that imperial project, nominally independent of the Japanese government, enjoyed a poor press in the United States. American capital found its way to Manchuria by way of loans to other Japanese businesses, where it was laundered.[21]

Meanwhile, another effort to assist China had come out of the Washington Conference. Conferences were assembled in Peking to reorder China's tariff, which was then under foreign control, and to lessen and eventually eliminate the treaties of extraterritoriality. Conferences met in 1925 and 1926, but to no avail because of China's chaotic politics. Seven of ten Chinese delegates to the tariff conference fled to foreign concessions, making it impossible to carry on. The conference on extraterritoriality signed its report and disbanded, recommending no relinquishment of extraterritoriality until the Chinese judiciary had protection against interference by executive or military authorities.

Outbreaks against foreigners in 1925 and 1927 encouraged the treaty powers to avoid any relinquishment of extraterritoriality. The first occurred on 30 May 1925, after a strike against Japanese textile mills in Shanghai. Two thousand demonstrators in the international settlement attempted to overwhelm a police station, and a British officer commanding Indian troops gave an order to fire, killing twelve Chinese and wounding seventeen. Throughout China, which was unified in spirit if not in government, antiforeign demonstrations, strikes, and boycotts erupted. Two years later, on 24 March 1927, when Nationalist troops entered Nanking on their northward march from Canton, they killed an American, three Britons, a Frenchman, and an Italian priest. They sacked the American, British, and Japanese consulates and foreign businesses, burned ten mission buildings, pillaged missionary residences, and took hospital equipment and robbed patients. When a group of Americans retreated to the Standard Oil Company compound on Socony Hill and soldiers surrounded their refuge, American and British destroyers in the river threw up a barrage that held the attackers off until the refugees could get out to the ships. The well-known author Pearl Buck, then a missionary, was in the group.[22]

A confusion of policy momentarily appeared after the Nanking outbreak in 1927, because the American minister in China, MacMurray, desired a more forceful policy than did Secretary Kellogg and his assistant secretary for the Far East, Nelson T. Johnson, an "old China hand."[23] The Nanking incident carried a threat of war. Foreign naval forces in Chinese waters included 171 warships commanded by eight admirals. Thirty of the ships and three of the admirals were American. For a moment, Kellogg sided with MacMurray, and in identical notes of 11 April, the envoys of the United States, Britain, France, Italy, and Japan demanded reparation and apology from the Nationalists. MacMurray wanted to go further. He saw the Chinese situation in terms of the Western, European-centered powers attempting to force respect for the rights of foreigners. But Coolidge and Kellogg refused to go beyond the note of 11 April. They had been reluctant to intervene in Nicaragua and were even more reluctant to do so in China. On 2 May, Kellogg wrote to the American ambassador in London that "our main object is to protect American citizens, evacuate them from such places where they cannot be protected by our forces and to be patient and to work out in the end a system which may stabilize China. It is impossible to make war on four hundred million people and, in my judgment, you cannot longer parcel out China in concessions or by spheres of commercial influence by armed force."[24]

In the later 1920s, the issues of tariff autonomy and relinquishment of extraterritoriality began to wind down in favor of China. Even before the Nanking outbreak, the British government led the way. In a note of December 1926, known facetiously within the State Department as "the Christmas present," Britain proposed reduction of Western treaty rights. The cause of the outbreak in Shanghai in 1925 had been Japanese exploitation of workers in the cotton mills, and the Japanese thereafter distanced themselves from Western démarches, perhaps hoping that the antiforeign sentiment would turn anti-Western. The deaths in the international settlement had directed antiforeign sentiment against Britain, and the British wanted out. Secretary Kellogg decided to make his own statement and on 27 January 1927 related his government's willingness to negotiate over the tariff and extraterritoriality. He was willing to meet delegates "representing the authorities of the people of the country," not necessarily representatives of a responsible Chinese government. The House of Representatives in February 1927, a few weeks after the unanimous Senate resolution urging arbitration of U.S.-Mexican differences, passed the Porter Resolution (named for the chairman of the House Committee on Foreign Affairs, Stephen G. Porter), calling for negotiation to give the Chinese the treaty revisions they desired.

Once on course, the change seemed less difficult than Western representatives in China had anticipated, although it took more time than anyone expected. The Chinese governments in Canton and Peking began a competition to see how many foreign rights each could abridge, however illegally. Already, during World War I, the Germans and Austro-Hungarians had lost their rights. At the end of the war, Russian citizens lost theirs. The Chinese governments moved against the weaker Western governments, such as the Belgians and Spanish. The disgusted MacMurray advised Kellogg to bend like bamboo, to swim with the current, and MacMurray signed a tariff treaty with the Nationalist government on 25 July 1928. The treaty constituted recognition of that government. Perhaps out of irritation with the British Christmas present of 1926, he did not tell his colleagues in Nanking what he had done. The treaty represented an American enterprise, in the tradition of the open door of thirty years before. It allowed tariff autonomy only on a most-favored-nation basis, if other tariff-treaty nations did likewise, and marked no immediate change; the proviso delayed tariff autonomy until 1933. As for extraterritoriality, it proved less of an issue when the Nationalists in the 1930s became involved in an undeclared war with Japan. The United States did not give up extraterritoriality until 1943.

In the several démarches by the United States and the other nations toward China during the 1920s, the government of Japan was for the most part cooperative. Japan had been on the Allied side during World War I, and after that conflict, many Japanese believed that democracy was the forthcoming order of governments, including their own—that war and autocracy had lost out. Baron Shidehara served as foreign minister in six of the seven cabinets from 1924 to 1931 and stressed economic diplomacy and the search for markets. Giving up the older "force diplomacy," stressing control over strategic places in China, he went back to the diplomacy that Japan had followed for a generation prior to 1914. Shidehara was the brother-in-law of the president of the Mitsubishi combine, which was considered the principal financial backer of the Kenseikei and Minseito parties.

In 1923, Japan suffered a terrible earthquake that destroyed much of Tokyo and other cities. The commander of the Asiatic Fleet took his small squadron to Yokohama, where he engaged in all manner of humanitarian endeavors. Private citizens in the United States subscribed to funds for the destitute. J. P. Morgan and Company floated a $150 million loan for Japanese relief. All in all, the occasion of the earthquake gave the appearance of excellent relations between the countries, hope that Japan and the United States would continue to respect each other, that their national policies would not drift apart.

Beginning in 1924, exclusion of Japanese immigrants did not help matters. Shidehara sought to paper it over, remarking that trade with the United States was flourishing. "America is Japan's best customer," he observed. "One does not fight with his best customer."[25] As years passed and other reasons to dislike Americans—notably, American support for Chinese nationalism—intruded into Japanese-American relations, exclusion took on more importance.

All the while, social troubles were increasing within Japan, as they were within Germany. Many Japanese were not living well, and they resented the opportunities of the upper classes, who mingled with the privileged members of Japan's aristocracy and with the privileged foreigners who flocked to Japan's ports on their cruises or business visits. The peasants who worked in the rice fields lived on the edge of subsistence. Peasant sons entered the enlisted ranks of the Japanese Army and began to rise in the officer corps.

Even before the Japanese Army received its infusion of peasant officers, the army's younger officers were unhappy that Shidehara economic diplomacy had replaced force diplomacy, and they let their dissatisfaction become known in a disturbing way. A little-noticed "incident," as such occasions would be described in later years (in contrast to the more serious "affair"), occurred in China, in Tsinan on the Shantung peninsula, in May 1928. Japanese troops were brought into the peninsula to protect Japanese merchants and traders, in accord with arrangements made with China at the end of World War I. At Tsinan they attacked Chinese Nationalist forces, undermining Shidehara's efforts to negotiate with General Chiang, who appeared to be a moderate nationalist and hence could protect Japanese businessmen. Shortly thereafter, the Tokyo government sought to help Chiang, whose forces had not yet occupied Peking, and ordered the Manchurian warlord Chang Tso-lin, whom it had permitted to take over the Peking government with its rich customs revenue, to retire back to Manchuria. As his train passed under a bridge of the South Manchuria Railway, there was an explosion in which General Chang was killed, assassinated by young officers of the Japanese Army. The officers hoped that his death would allow them to take over Manchuria. This meant that three years before the Mukden Incident of 1931, which allowed the Manchurian takeover, right-wing elements of the Japanese Army were defying the Tokyo government in a duel for power that during the 1930s turned Japan in a new and dangerous direction.

9

★ ★ ★ ★ ★

COOLIDGE PROSPERITY

If Calvin Coolidge prided himself on one single aspect of his presidential years, it was his policy of fiscal economy. "I favor the policy of economy," he declared, "not because I wish to save money, but because I wish to save people." The "people" part of the equation was perhaps a rhetorical flourish, yet people were involved; he may have been speaking of their labor, which he would save by not spending it. In any case, he saw absolute, positive good in fiscal economy, and therefore he not merely balanced the budget but obtained a surplus during every one of his presidential years (as had Harding before him).

Coolidge liked the idea of living within one's means. Perhaps ever since his father in 1880 refused to advance him a penny until the election of Garfield, he had thought about debt. As soon as he finished reading law in Northampton, he balanced income with outgo. After marriage in 1905 the Coolidge family always came up with a surplus. As president he watched over the national debt, bringing it down from $22.3 billion in 1923 to $16.9 billion in 1929, a major achievement of economy. Coolidge considered the national debt to be the same as a private debt. In his day, there was none of the intricate calculation that would later grace—or disgrace, depending on the observer and his or her political party—government account keeping, whereby the government debt became subject to management and became a positive good, a vital necessity for the nation's economic well-being. No one ventured that a rising gross national product would shrink the debt in a relative sense, or that what shrinkage did not occur relatively could occur through inflation. To Coolidge, the debt was an unadulterated

debit, an evil, something to be rid of. Retiring the debt was "the predomi-
nant necessity of the country." Retiring the debt was "the very largest internal improvement . . . possible to conceive."[1]

In holding down government expenditures and saving enough money
to retire the debt, Coolidge employed several devices, one of which was
the Bureau of the Budget. The very fact that the bureau's statisticians and
accountants were screening the proposed expenses of cabinet departments and the independent agencies gave comfort to the parsimonious
president. The bureau's experts also could watch for special proposals by
those well-known spendthrifts, the members of Congress. When the president presented his annual budget he could feel fairly sure that it was as
low as he properly should go, and not a crazy quilt of special-interest
propositions.

To estimates obtained by the Budget Bureau, the president applied his
own talents for economy, which were formidable. He told a press conference that he did not wish to resort to cheeseparing but desired to speak
about pencils. The government, he informed the reporters, possessed a
great many departments, "and a little saved in each one, each division, in
the aggregate amounts to a very large sum. I don't know whether I ever
indicated to the conference that the cost of lead pencils to the Government
per year is about $125,000."[2]

Lastly, the president resorted to the calculations of his secretary of the
treasury. Secretary Mellon had been appointed by Coolidge's predecessor,
but the small, quiet, almost bashful Mellon had not been Harding's first
choice. Harding initially asked Dawes, who thought about the appointment for several weeks and turned it down. At that juncture, a political
equation entered. Eastern bankers had not admired Dawes's selection and
came forward with candidates from their part of the country, such as the
Bostonian John Weeks, whom Harding appointed secretary of war; former
New York senator Charles Hilles; and New York financier Frank Vander-
lip. Sens. Philander C. Knox and Boies Penrose of Pennsylvania suggested
the Pittsburgh capitalist Mellon. Harding was having difficulty bringing
Hoover into the cabinet because of Hoover's participation in the Wilson
administration, and he struck a deal with the Pennsylvania senators whereby they would obtain Mellon and drop their opposition to Hoover for the
Commerce Department.[3]

Secretary Mellon quickly gained a great reputation, in part by accident.
After the Harding administration took office, the depression that had
begun in 1920 came to an end, and Mellon received credit. The secretary
benefited from the return to peacetime financing, as the budget dropped
rapidly because of reduced military expenses. Almost without effort on his
part, the rise in revenues and drop in expenses drew the secretary as a mas-

ter of budgets. The *Saturday Evening Post* recalled great secretaries, including Hamilton, and opined that none was "so completely the master of finance as Mellon." According to Senator Norris, he became the "wizard of finance" under whom three presidents served.

Mellon may have wondered how he would make out under Harding's successor, but he soon discovered that he had nothing to fear. After Secretary of State Hughes left in 1925, Mellon became virtually the first member of the cabinet, for Hughes's successor, although able, never cut the figure Hughes did. Mellon told Senator Pepper of his first encounter with his new chief, and it demonstrated the trust Coolidge placed in Mellon's judgment. The secretary of the treasury had called on Coolidge, bearing in his pocket a written resignation, as was customary when a new chief executive took office. After greeting the secretary, the president plunged into a discussion of the nation's fiscal system, the two men became engrossed, and only after Mellon had left the presidential office did he realize that he had not offered his resignation. Reentering, he said, "Mr. President, I neglected to tell you that I had come to resign." "Forget it," said the president.[4]

One might wonder whether Mellon chafed under the Budget and Accounting Act of 1921, with General Dawes as the first director of the budget. Dawes was no wallflower, and working with him would have been difficult—on occasion, impossible. There is no evidence that Mellon was ever troubled by interventions by Dawes or his successor in the bureau, General Lord. Admittedly, Mellon was not the sort of man to rise in choler over an intervention. He would finesse it and make his point later. There is no evidence that this ever happened.

The main contours of the budget, the object of cooperation between Mellon and Coolidge, are not difficult to relate. In the 1920s, the size of the budget remained virtually the same, after it decreased from the wartime era. In fiscal year 1921 (July 1920 through June 1921), federal expenditures were $5.1 billion; in fiscal year 1922, $3.3 billion. They stayed there during the Coolidge presidency, amounting in 1923 to $3.294 billion and in 1929 to $3.298 billion. Sources of revenue changed a great deal from prewar years. In 1913, one-third of the federal budget was from excise taxes on liquor, two-thirds from the tobacco tax and the tariff. In 1930, with no liquor tax, one-third came from tobacco and the tariff, one-third from personal income tax, and one-third from corporate income tax. The income tax, permitted by the Sixteenth Amendment, had gone into effect during the war.

It was in the budget's surtaxes on personal income that Mellon sought major changes. He believed that surtaxes on high incomes needed drastic reduction, that they stifled initiative on the part of wealthy investors. Such individuals, he held, needed to place their money in high-risk investments. Low risks were for institutions and individuals with few resources.

The rich were not doing their part because of high surtaxes, a result of both the need for tax revenue during the war and its aftermath and the progressive era's philosophy that great wealth was wrong and ought to be taxed. Mellon's favorite proof of erroneous investment by the rich was the estate of William Rockefeller, who died in 1922. It was discovered that he had $44 million in tax-free bonds, the most low-risk investment anyone could imagine.

The result of Mellon's philosophy of investment was a series of tax cuts on personal income. The first Mellon cut, passed in 1921, was distinctly a compromise, for the secretary wanted the maximum surtax reduced from 65 to 33 percent, and Congress cut it to 50 percent. In 1924, the secretary desired a cut to 25 percent (each time he asked for a reduction by half), but Congress would only cut the maximum surtax down to 40 percent. In 1924, Congress defied Mellon's proposal to repeal the estate tax, which stood at 25 percent, and instead raised it to 40 percent. Congress also made two other additions—a gift tax with a $50,000 exemption, and a requirement that all income tax payments be made public.

Personal income tax rates were highly political propositions, both in recommendation and in passage through Congress, and it is noteworthy that Coolidge proposed the Mellon tax cut of 1924 in March of that year, in time for the Republican convention and the subsequent election. It immediately placed the president in the public eye. Reporter Mark Sullivan discovered the president's pleasure over the publicity from a fellow reporter, Henry L. Stoddard, who had just seen Coolidge: "Stoddard spoke of Coolidge being pleased, and acting almost like T.R. [Theodore Roosevelt] as he said 'I had the front page this morning.' "⁵

The tax cut of 1926 marked the apogee of Mellon's program, for it reduced the surtax on personal income from 40 percent to 20 percent, halved the estate tax to 20 percent, and abolished the gift tax and the publicity requirement of the act of 1924. In 1928, the Mellon program again reduced income taxes.

Of course, the subtleties involved in these reductions often made large differences in the savings of individual taxpayers. In 1921, the highest personal tax rate was for incomes beginning at $200,000, down from the previous beginning point of $1 million. In 1924, the beginning point was $500,000; in 1926, $100,000. These categories were so far removed from the incomes of most Americans that they meant little. More important was the exemption for married taxpayers, which the act of 1921 raised from $2,000 to $2,500 and the act of 1926 raised to $3,500. The latter raise exempted 40 percent of all individuals who had paid taxes in 1924, leaving only 2.5 million taxpayers. Between 1921 and 1929, the number of taxpayers declined by 1 million. By 1927, 98 percent of the population paid no income tax.

Three-tenths of 1 percent paid 94 percent of income taxes. As Mellon explained that year, "The income tax has gradually become so restricted in its application that it is a class rather than a national tax."[6]

One might suspect that all the encouragement to the rich to put their money in high-risk investments would have resulted in a remarkable increase in personal wealth, a reward for all the risk taking. It is true that rich Americans of the 1920s were becoming richer. In 1923, the top 5 percent of the population received 22.89 percent of the national income. In 1929, the top 5 percent received 26.09 percent. But the average percentage of income for the top 5 percent in 1923–29 was 25.21—not much of a jump. Moreover, the Mellon tax cuts favored "small Americans." Seventy percent of the lost revenue under one Mellon proposal would have gone to taxpayers with incomes under $10,000—the latter figure admittedly a handsome income in those days. Under the same proposal, the percentage going to taxpayers with incomes over $100,000 would have been 2.5.

As for corporate profits under the Mellon cuts, they averaged 8.2 percent of the national income. Compared with the decade 1910–19, they were anemic, for profits then had been 9.7 percent. For the decade 1900–09, profits were 6.9 percent. During the thirty years from 1900 to 1929, corporate profits averaged 8.2 percent, the same as in the 1920s.

Compensation in salaries and wages in the 1920s rose by 5 percent, from 55 percent of national income to 60 percent. The 1920s marked the high point of employee and worker income during the first thirty years of the century. Clerks in manufacturing averaged $2,428 per year in 1926 (in real earnings, 106 percent of 1914 wages); postal workers, $2,128 (106 percent); federal government employees in executive departments, $1,809 (91 percent); railway clerks, $1,604 (112 percent); teachers, $1,277 (130 percent); telephone employees, $1,117 (135 percent); book and job printers, $1,730 (144 percent); anthracite coal miners, $1,691 (70 percent); and iron and steel workers, $1,687 (128 percent).

Contemporary and later critics of the Mellon tax proposals abounded, and one historian wrote that individuals making $5,000 a year (a good income for the 1920s) received 1 percent gain in income after taxes; people with higher incomes gained more, until those making $1 million saved 31 percent.[7] Congressman LaGuardia told his constituents in the Star Casino on 107th Street in New York that Secretary Mellon took as his guide the twenty-fifth verse of the fourth chapter of St. Mark: "For he that hath, to him shall be given: and he that hath not, from him shall be taken even that which he hath." The congressman compared the financial genius of Mellon, as well as that of Ford, Morgan, and Schwab, to "the financial genius of Mrs. Maria Esposito or Mrs. Rebecca Epstein or Mrs. Maggie Flynn who is keeping house in a New York tenement raising five or six children on a weekly envelope of thirty dollars a week, paying thirty and thirty-five dollars a month rent, trying to send the children to school warmly clad and properly nourished, paying exorbitant gas and electric bills and trying to provide meat at least once a day for the family."[8]

There was an accusation that the federal government not merely arranged lower surtaxes for wealthy Americans but surreptitiously (until Senator Couzens pointed it out) engaged in refunds, credits, and abatements to favored businesses totaling $3.4 billion beginning in 1921. The Couzens contentions were a peculiar mixture of public and private concern. Couzens accused Mellon of attempting to impose his ideas of wealth and investment on the nation.[9] That may have been true; in any event, Couzens had a right to argue the point. Almost immediately, however, he became personal. He listened to Governor Pinchot—another disgruntled Republican, as well as a prohibitionist—who told him that there was a scandalous situation in the Bureau of Internal Revenue, that is, in Mellon's Treasury Department, in regard to the enforcement of Prohibition. Couzens arranged a Senate investigation. It turned out that because of an oversight, there was no money for an investigator, and Couzens offered a solution in favor of engaging Pinchot's candidate for the post, an old-time Roosevelt progressive, Francis J. Heney: "I will pay Heney out of my own pocket!" This was not much of a public-spirited sacrifice on Couzens's part, for the senator was a multimillionaire. The Senate committee members, knowing a bargain when they saw one, accepted Heney. The prospect loomed of another Teapot Dome investigation, this time into bootlegging, all because Couzens did not admire the Mellon tax cuts. In the midst of these contentions, Couzens claimed that the administration had sought to buy him off by offering appointment to the Court of St. James's in London, an emolument he refused by telling President Coolidge, "I won't be kicked upstairs."

The Coolidge administration seemingly had to suffer more slings and arrows from its friends than from its enemies, and Senator Couzens was nearly as bad a renegade Republican as were the GOP members of the farm bloc. When Couzens turned the tax-cut issue into a prohibitionist investigation of Mellon, it was too much. The scene shifted to the White House, where Senator Watson, outraged by Couzens's disloyalty to the party, demanded action. Watson was chairman of the committee that Couzens was about to use to investigate Prohibition enforcement. Watson did not need to say very much at the White House, for Mellon and Coolidge were both furious. Mellon was outraged over Couzens's accusation that he was handing out money to big corporations, including some of his own, and he wrote a letter to Coolidge, who enclosed it with a stentorian message to the Senate: "It seems incredible that the Senate of the United States would knowingly approve the past and proposed conduct of one of its committees which this letter reveals. . . . Against the continuance of such conditions, I enter my solemn protests and give notice that in my opinion the departments ought not to be required to participate in it. . . . It is time that we return to a Government under and in accord with the usual forms of law of the land."

Coolidge's message allowed the Senate to stand on its privileges and honor. Words flew, mostly Democratic words. Senator Walsh of Montana described the Coolidge message as "the most arrogant sent by any executive to a parliamentary body since the days of the Stuarts and Tudors." Reed of Missouri certified it as "such an insult as one branch of the government could not accept from another." Senator Reed—who had not hesitated to oppose the League of Nations and Treaty of Versailles because, it was said, President Wilson had refused to appoint his candidate to the postmastership of Kansas City, Missouri—asked that the presidential message be expunged from the record. Carter Glass, a Democratic senator from Virginia and formerly one of President Wilson's secretaries of the treasury, announced that the letters of Mellon and the president "constitute the most extraordinary breach of official etiquette that has ever occurred in the history of the Republic."

The truth about the refunds was nearly lost in the larger arguments, but gradually it emerged. The refunds had run into many millions, with $4.5 million to Gulf Oil (a Mellon company), $3.3 million to Standard of California, and $5 million to Sinclair. Couzens also reported "improper amortizations" on war plants amounting to $460 million, including $15.5 million to the Aluminum Corporation of America (Mellon), $55 million to U.S. Steel, $22 million to Bethlehem, and $15 million to DuPont. But there was a good deal less fire than smoke in what the Michigan senator was viewing with alarm. He said that Mellon money invested in the Overholt distillery, which made industrial alcohol, ended up as bootleg whiskey. He discovered a notation by a treasury employee on a file of the Standard Steel Car Company, "This is a Mellon company." All this was interesting but unprovable or unimportant. It became evident that treasury refunds to big corporations had been made mostly for two reasons: Supreme Court decisions, such as one making stock dividends nontaxable, which required a refund of $70 million; and clerical error. Rep. William C. Hawley of Oregon, a congressional expert, said that Court decisions accounted for 28 percent of refunds, administrative and clerical errors for 57 percent. The total of government refunds, credits, and abatements for the decade 1921–29 was $3.4 billion, and the total of additional assessments, necessary to balance against disbursements, was $5.3 billion.[10]

Behind Couzens's virtual vendetta against Mellon was a complicated tax suit by the government against several former Ford Motor Company executives, including Couzens. The suit claimed that by selling their Ford stock back to Henry Ford, the executives had cheated the government of $30 million. The Bureau of Internal Revenue claimed that Couzens and the other executives were asking for a very high cost basis of the stock, so as to avoid paying a large excess profits tax. The whole business was a tangle. For years the case remained unsettled, with arguments and counterarguments, until the Board of Tax Appeals decided that instead of paying the treasury the executives should receive a refund of $3.6 million.[11] Couzens chose to take this decision as a victory against his enemies such as Secretary Mellon, and perhaps it was. It was, however, a bipartisan victory. Democratic lawyer Joseph E. Davies, later ambassador to the Soviet Union, accepted a $2 million fee for assisting Couzens, the largest up to that time in the history of the Washington bar.[12]

One possibly negative aspect of Mellon-Coolidge economy was a decision made in 1925 as a result of a letter in which Mellon pointed out to the president how the government in Washington and elsewhere had been housing its bureaus in privately owned buildings. That letter and Coolidge's approval started a $250 million program for constructing federal office buildings, which, among other accomplishments, produced the row of classical behemoths in Washington between Pennsylvania and Constitution Avenues known as the Federal Triangle. The first to be erected was the new Commerce Department building, completed when Hoover was inaugurated. One could argue that their marble facades and innards betokened the reign of big business in an industrial age, that their excesses of ornament, including ceilings twice as high as necessary, showed pink trying to be purple. Architecturally, the Mellon-Coolidge buildings did nothing to illustrate the triumph of democracy, and their upkeep, including heating, air-conditioning (in a later era), and the replacement of tiled roofs and mortared joints, promised to afflict untold generations of taxpayers.

Finally, in examining budgets for the Coolidge administration, one should notice not merely the achievement of paying one-fourth of the national debt and maintaining the same-sized budget year after year, when 98 percent of Americans paid no income tax, but also the large growth of state and local expenditures. In current dollars, the national budget increased ten times between 1902 and 1921, from $500 million to $5 billion (the latter figure exaggerates, as fiscal year 1922 brought the budget down to Coolidge-sized totals). State and local costs increased five times, from $1.1 billion in 1902 to $5.6 billion by 1922. But during the 1920s, state and local budgets passed well ahead of the federal budget, reaching $7.8 billion in 1927. There may have been an assumption outside Washington that if Coolidge was practicing economy, it was a good time to do the opposite. State and local budgets also picked up the costs of road building, other than the federal matching grants, and the entire cost of road maintenance. Then there were the increasing social services for the elderly, the ill, and orphaned or abandoned children—individuals who did not fit into the dividends-interest-salaries-wages system.

During the 1920s, the Coolidge administration reduced the debt, kept the budget flat, and brought in sufficient revenues through markedly reduced tax rates, both personal and corporate. This was the fiscal side of the government. The institution by which the federal government managed bank credit was the Federal Reserve System. Established by Congress in December 1913, its purpose was to prevent credit crunches, such as those that had convulsed the economy in 1873, 1884, 1893, 1903, and 1907. Just as Secretary Mellon was pleased with his handiwork in regard to tax cuts, the budget, and the debt, so he was pleased with the work of the Federal Reserve, declaring in 1928 that because of the system there was no longer "any fear on the part of the banks or the business community that some sudden and temporary business crisis may develop and precipitate a financial panic such as visited the country in former years. . . . We are no longer the victims of the vagaries of business cycles. The Federal Reserve System is the antidote for money contraction and credit shortage."[13]

When Coolidge became president, the Federal Reserve was barely a decade old and was gradually learning how to manage bank credit through two devices. The first had been foreseen when the act of 1913 created a national reserve, drawn from the system's commercial bank members. The Federal Reserve's board of governors was to use the reserve to extend credit by lowering the rediscount rate for commercial paper purchased by the reserve banks and, if necessary, tighten credit by raising the rate. The second device for dealing with bank credit was unanticipated and came to the attention of the board only after the war. This was the ability of the reserve banks to engage in open-market purchases or sales of government bonds. The war had injected $25.3 billion worth of bonds into the economy, and this massive infusion gave the reserve banks the opportunity to buy bonds to ease credit, or sell bonds to tighten it. In the middle and later parts of the postwar decade, open-market operations by the Federal Reserve became at least as important to controlling bank credit as lowering or raising the rediscount rate for commercial paper.

Meanwhile, the war and its aftermath had given the Federal Reserve several experiences that it was unprepared for and did not always deal with well, despite Secretary Mellon's words of a decade later. The beginning of the war in Europe brought first an outflow of gold; then, as the Allies purchased American munitions, an inflow. The board of governors perhaps should have been more alert to the deflationary and inflationary aspects of these gold movements. During U.S. participation in the war, the Federal Reserve became the bond-selling affiliate of the treasury and found itself manipulating credit to keep up the market for liberty bonds. The legislation of 1913 never anticipated such a possibility, and the system probably did as well as it could, but the war produced a serious inflation that turned into a horrendous inflation after the armistice, when the Federal Reserve received the task of floating the victory bonds to permit postwar extension of credits to the Allies and to some of the former enemy nations. Finally came the sharp deflation of 1920–21, for which the Federal Reserve was responsible. Something had to be done to bring postwar prices back to reality, and the board of governors decided that there had been overextension of credit, which was doubtless true. But raising the rediscount rate precipitated a too-rapid deflation, and the fall in prices brought unemployment and bankruptcies. In faraway Kansas City, Missouri, it forced the closing of a small haberdashery by the name of Truman and Jacobson, and a future president of the United States and his partner were in financial straits for years. Edward Jacobson took bankruptcy in 1925, and Truman was protected only because he was a county official and could not be forced. The *Federal Reserve Bulletin* described the board's actions as "necessarily more or less gradual," but the board of governors hardly followed this prescription.[14] By June 1921, wholesale prices had fallen 56 percent from the level attained in May 1920, and the money supply declined 9 percent. Unemployment at its peak exceeded 10 percent.

In the postwar years, the Federal Reserve arrived at an understanding of how it could use open-market operations, but not before it came up against a fallacious theory or two. One was that government bonds should not be considered part of the assets of member banks. Another was that bonds in the hands of banks were bad, and bonds in the hands of individual investors were good; for a while, the Federal Reserve sought valiantly to get bonds out of bank vaults, and this exercise had something to do with the system's adding to the intensity of the price readjustment in 1920–21. After everything settled down, the system in April 1923 formed an open-market investment committee, by which it coordinated bond purchases and sales.

Subsequent years saw two recessions, in 1924 and 1927, and the board did its best to control them. The index of production in basic industries finally turned up in September 1924, after being in the doldrums throughout the summer. Recovery proved unusually rapid; the index was up 35 percent in January 1925 from where it had been in August, equaling the peak level previously attained in May 1923. Wholesale prices rose 7 percent, regaining ground lost during the recession. Open-market rates for loans paralleled movements in the production index, and the spread between the 3 percent rediscount rate in New York and the open-market rates disappeared.

The Federal Reserve obtained better statistics in the 1920s and thus could make its calculations more precise and avoid what it had previously been forced to do—watch commercial rates and presume that they reflected real movements in production and the need for credit. In May 1926, the board had available for its own use, although it was not made public for another year, a revised index of production with sixty individual series for thirty-five industries, including both manufacturing and mining. The new index contained measures, hitherto lacking, of output in automobiles, petroleum, tires, plate glass, and boots and shoes.

After recovery from the recession of 1924, there followed two quiet years in which monetary policy was not put to any remarkable test. Gross national income in constant dollars increased 4.5 percent in 1925 and 5.5 percent in 1926. Unemployment in 1925 has been estimated at 4 percent and in 1926 at 1.9 percent, compared with 3.2 in 1923 and 5.5 during the recession year.

The year 1927 brought another recession, and its effect on Federal Reserve policy was a matter of concern. Recession meant lowering the rediscount rate, which was done, but the reasoning behind it was a combination of the domestic recession and Great Britain's need for low interest rates so that pounds would not be drawn to the United States (Britain had returned to the gold standard in 1925). In July 1927, the governor of the Bank of England, Montagu Norman; the head of the Reichsbank, Schacht; and Charles Rist of the Bank of France held a meeting on Long Island with the governor of the New York Federal Reserve Bank, Benjamin Strong, who was generally considered the most important official in the Federal Reserve System. After debate, Strong supported Norman in an easy money policy. Between the middle and end of 1927, reserve banks bought $435 million of government securities. In the last half of the year, loans and investments of member banks rose by $1.764 billion. Only 7 percent of the increase went into business loans. The rest went into speculative building and the stock market. Brokers' loans, for buying stocks on margin, rose by 24 percent.

Curiously, the collapse of the Florida land boom in 1925 had little effect on the nation's economy. The assumption—which doubtless partook of the euphoria of 1925–26, when everything was going well—was that the Florida speculation (in which real estate assessments of $250 million in 1920 went to $475 million in 1925) was insulated from real business, a sort of local absurdity, not a sign of national speculative mania. People recalled the talk of the perennial Democratic standard-bearer, William Jennings Bryan, who had moved to Florida in 1921, giving up his Nebraska voting residence. In his enthusiasm, he had invested in Florida real estate and by his own account had made a lot of money, contrary to his earlier belief that no one could earn a million dollars honestly. Florida seemed a special case.

Collapse of the Florida land boom provided no warning, and the need for low interest rates to end the 1927 recession, combined with the need to accommodate the Bank of England, might have produced what became in 1928 an increasing speculative surge. When Governor Strong attended a central bank governors' meeting early in July 1927, he was overheard to say that his credit policy would provide the stock market with "a little *coup de whiskey.*" As a recent writer put it, "Light in the head, the market rose."[15] When a return to prosperity persuaded the Federal Reserve to raise the rediscount rate and sell government securities, brokers' loans continued to grow, increasing by $2 billion in 1928 and another $2 billion up to October 1929. Deflationary moves by the Federal Reserve did not discourage speculators, because profits in the market were far greater than the increasing cost of bank loans.

At this juncture, which was Coolidge's last presidential year (1928), there was a discouraging complacency in Federal Reserve policy. This was epitomized by the calculation of a system economist, E. A. Goldenweiser, who wrote on March 16 that "it is impossible to expect instantaneous results from open-market or discount policies of the reserve banks. It takes time for the mechanism to become effective. The first effect is a passing around of the loans between different banks and different groups of lenders and it is only after a while that the pressure of higher rates and scarcer money begins to be reflected in some reduction in the volume of credit outstanding."[16]

That undoubtedly was true. But the fact was that the system was beset by some sort of inertia; call loans were rising rapidly, and the basic encouragement for those loans, rising stock prices, was clearly out of order—one might even say out of control. Share prices rose 38 percent in 1928, and four-fifths of the increase occurred between July and December, when the Fed's deflationary moves should have had enough time to take effect. Brokers' loans reached an unprecedented $6.4 billion by the end of 1928, an increase of 45 percent for the year; this roughly paralleled the rise in stock prices, evidence that the more stocks rose, the more money chased them.

There were other bad signs in 1928. One was the virtual cessation of foreign security offerings in the American market. Foreign money was coming into the stock market. The gold inflows forced foreign banks to sell dollar balances or embark on restrictive policies, for the gold covers of foreign currencies were not large. One good sign was that business activity in the United States was high and rising, but there was less mortgage money available, there was a downturn in construction, and long-term bond issues were not selling. A highly disturbing factor in 1928 was that corporations and individuals were lending money to the call market, making end runs around the banks and the Federal Reserve.

An interesting theory might be that the Federal Reserve's inactivity in 1928 occurred because it was an election year. It is also possible to contend that Coolidge let the economy go, refused to allow the Federal Reserve System to do anything, because he was willing to see the GOP candidate that year, Hoover, take responsibility. The only difficulty with this latter theory—that Coolidge "set up" Hoover, who by this time he clearly was not fond of—is that it is unprovable.[17]

It is possible that the illness and death in October 1928 of Governor Strong—an incisive, powerful official, with a great understanding of finance—produced indecision on the part of officials in other banks and particularly in Washington. Strong's able successor, George L. Harrison, was elected in November and might have hesitated to suggest the drastic restriction of credit and other measures—such as a congressional enactment granting the system the right to set margin requirements and the setting of a very high margin figure, such as 75 percent—that would have broken the bubble.

There followed a chapter in the history of the Federal Reserve that, in retrospect, appears almost incredible. Early in 1929, it became apparent that money was going into the stock market in far larger amounts than were advantageous for both the economy in general and the Federal Reserve System in particular. The spread in interest between time funds and call funds was all in favor of brokers' loans, and people in the market did not care how high that spread went, for they believed that stock market prices, known as values, would go higher. Money clearly was going to brokers' loans. The annual spring need for commercial and agricultural loans was upon bankers, and this meant use of the Federal Reserve System. If the latter's money went to the brokers, the result could be calamitous. On 2 February, the Federal Reserve Board sent out an instruction to member banks that was sharply critical of what was happening, relating that "the Federal Reserve Act does not, in the opinion of the Federal Reserve Board, contemplate the use of the resources of the Federal Reserve banks for the creation or extension of speculative credit. A member bank is not within its reasonable claims for rediscount facilities at the Federal Reserve bank when it borrows either for the purpose of making speculative loans or for the purpose of maintaining speculative loans."[18] A few days later, on 6 February, the board made this announcement public, but it did so carefully. Early in the day, officials announced that a statement on the credit situation would be released later. Speculators guessed the nature of the statement and anticipated it by selling, so the market was unsettled well before release of the statement after the New York Stock Exchange closed. Simultaneously that evening came an announcement that the Bank of England was raising its rediscount rate from 4.5 to 5.5 percent. Governor Norman had been in Washington conferring with Secretary Mellon, and the British announcement seemed to have been made at least with U.S. concurrence, if not encouragement.

By this time, the market needed depressing through the restriction of brokers' loans. It was a fine time to move. Figures for call loans obtained from member banks of the Federal Reserve had reached $5.5 billion and were moving up. They comprised loans within the New York Federal Reserve Bank's district, those of the other reserve banks, and loans by corporations. The New York Stock Exchange reported brokers' loans from members and was employing a larger figure, by $1.2 billion. Loans from banks using the New York Federal Reserve Bank were down, but the total nationally was up. "As we look over the past year," Governor Harrison wrote, "we feel that an expansion of 4½ billions of dollars, representing an expansion of about 8 percent in the total volume of credit in the country contrasted with an expansion of 3 percent in business, was an exorbitant use of credit."[19]

The result of the Federal Reserve warning and Norman's raising of the discount rate—to keep British speculators from putting money in the New York market—was a plummeting of stock prices the next day, 7 February. A front-page story in the *New York Times* for 8 February reported, "Reserve Board Warning Sends Stocks Tumbling; London Raises Bank Rate."

Here was a lesson to Federal Reserve authorities on how to handle speculation, but they failed to give attention to what followed over the next weeks, until the final week of March 1929, when the incredible chapter in Federal Reserve history took place. After the February scare, speculators milled around, but once they thought they were safe, they began to move stocks up again. In late March, the interest rate on call loans moved rapidly upward, resulting in a pronounced tightness in the call money market on 25–26 March. On Tuesday the twenty-sixth, it jumped from 12 to 20 percent. The Federal Reserve Board was in session and did nothing to loosen credit in call money. Then on Wednesday, Charles E. Mitchell, the president of the largest bank in the country, the National City Bank of New York, announced that he stood ready to employ the resources of his bank by lending $25 million in the call money market, in increments of $5 million; if the market were at 16 percent, he would lend $5 million, and similarly for each percentage point until it reached 20 percent. The announcement broke call money rates to 15 percent, and they ended the week at 8 percent.

What Mitchell did was defy the Federal Reserve Board. Although a director of the New York Federal Reserve Bank, he had contacted no reserve official in either New York or Washington; he acted solely on his own authority and that of his commercial bank. He knew that the Federal Reserve System was attempting to restrain credit. "We feel," he said, employing a careful plural, "that we have an obligation which is paramount to any Federal Reserve warning, or anything else, to avert any dangerous crisis in the money market."[20]

About this challenge to its own authority—perpetrated by a man who would be revealed, in the subsequent Great Depression, as a stock plunger and an incurable bull in the market—the Federal Reserve System did absolutely nothing. The Reserve Board continued to meet in daily session until 28 March and did not do a thing. A public debate opened, led by Senator Glass, who charged that Mitchell had slapped the Federal Reserve Board "squarely on the face" and treated its policies with "contempt and contumely." Mitchell, who knew when to keep quiet, responded, "That's very interesting, but I have no comment to make." On Saturday, 30 March, former senator Robert L. Owen of Oklahoma came out on Mitchell's side, relating unctuously that low call money rates were necessary to keep credit charges down. He said that the New York Stock Exchange community should correct high rates. Senator Glass in 1913 had been the sponsor of the Federal Reserve Act in the House of Representatives. Former senator Owen had sponsored it in the Senate. With this stalemate by sponsors of the Owen-Glass Act, public debate on Mitchell's outrageous behavior closed.

The wellsprings of Mitchell's public contradiction of his own government are difficult to understand, apart from his market involvement and bullish outlook. He may have acted out of a sense of the increased power of the large New York banks that, despite what the American public believed, had come with passage of the act of 1913, which transformed their operations. As often happens, under the new legislation, the regulated obtained more than they had under the old. Large banks around the country found themselves with lower reserve requirements for deposits than under the National Banking Act of 1864. They lost their correspondent business, as the act intended. No longer having to cultivate the little banks for deposit balances, they were free to compete with them, and they did. National City Bank sent officers around the country seeking business borrowers and doubled its corporate accounts. Moreover, the McFadden Act of 1927, which confined branches of national banks to their local cities, led to a large increase in branches, from 480 in 1920 to 3,350 in 1929. For such reasons, Mitchell may have thought himself more important than the Federal Reserve System.

As for the Federal Reserve Board, it did not have enough spine to stand up to Mitchell. The chairman of the board of governors, Roy A. Young, was an experienced official who, before joining the board in 1927, had spent eight years as governor of the Minneapolis Federal Reserve Bank. In a private talk with Goldenweiser on 6 March, he said that Strong's successor in New York, Harrison, had been proposing a course that had come from

Norman of the Bank of England, who wanted a radical increase in the reserve system's rediscount rate for a short time (Norman did not want a long-term increase, for it would affect his own need for easy credit). The idea was to break the stock market. Young had refused to raise the rate, because he saw Norman's hand in the proposal. Young told Goldenweiser that there were three ways to go. One was to continue pressure against speculation without raising rates, and to raise them only when commercial paper rose above 6 percent. A second was to start advancing rates radically, to break the speculation, but this was the Harrison-Norman proposal. He hoped for a third alternative, "which is in substance to do nothing, with the hope that the market would break itself and that then further rate advances would not be necessary."[21]

The theory under which the Federal Reserve Act had been conceived and passed was that extension of credit to banks, under government supervision, should not have a connection with politics. This was also Coolidge's point of view, for there is no evidence that he ever sought out any reserve official with the purpose of influencing him. Nor, unfortunately, is there any evidence that the president talked with officials of the system for the purpose of understanding what it was or was not doing and whether it needed better officials or legislation. In his customary way, which was almost military, he envisioned himself as the nation's chief executive, with a careful ordering of responsibilities among subordinates that he did not interfere with unless some crisis arose.

Because a crisis was arising, one must ask whether Coolidge, seeing signs of trouble, displayed any reaction. The question here is whether he watched the economy carefully. There would have been several things to watch. One was underconsumption, which now stands out as a general failure of the economy during the Coolidge years. About this failure of Americans to buy enough of the output of American industry, the president seems to have been blind as a bat. He did not understand that production is one thing, consumption another, and that the one had better match the other.

There were all sorts of signs of underconsumption. The Brookings Institution in a 1928 report that received little attention, found that six out of ten families had less than the $2,000 annual income necessary to supply the basic needs of life. Between 1923 and 1929, it was discovered, dividends rose 65 percent while wages and salaries advanced 20 percent. Cases in point were U.S. Steel and Toledo-Edison. Hourly earnings at U.S. Steel rose modestly, and weekly earnings fell because of a shorter workweek, but profits doubled. Toledo-Edison had no general wage increase during the period, but earnings rose 60 percent. Coolidge knew what this meant. In August 1923, he told Gompers that "I was brought up to think that a man has a right to make as much money as he can, and that the more money a man makes the more he can pay to his workmen."[22] He made no effort to discover cases in which his own rule was not being observed.

The best sign of underconsumption, and one that was fairly well known and should have come to the president's attention, was what was happening in the automobile industry. But not owning a car, Coolidge showed no interest. In the later 1920s, the automobile industry began to mature: sales of replacement vehicles matched and thereafter outnumbered sales to first-time owners. The automobile boom displayed unmistakable signs of coming to an end in 1927, the year of the industry's maturity. Between 1926 and 1929, the automobile industry operated at less than four-fifths of capacity, prompting Walter Chrysler to remark privately that he could "feel the winds of disaster blowing." Production had outrun consumption. By the end of the 1920s, half the families in the nation still did not own an automobile. The bottom two-fifths of salary recipients and wage earners in the United States received 15.5 percent of national personal income. They could not afford to own, operate, and maintain a car.

It was in 1927 that Henry Ford changed over from the Model T to the Model A, a fact that all admirers of automobiles note as a turning point in styling, seldom realizing its larger import. The purpose of styling was to encourage lagging sales. By that time, closed cars were rapidly replacing open cars—in 1923, for the first time, sales of closed cars equaled those of open models. There was good reason for such a change, but subsequent changes in styling were mostly sales gimmicks. General Motors emphasized bright colors and model changes. When GM surpassed Ford in sales, Ford had to meet GM on its own terms. In later years, after World War II, one-fourth of the purchase price of American automobiles went into annual styling modifications that had little or nothing to do with technological improvement.

The immediate solution to underconsumption in the 1920s was installment sales, and for a while, this basically uneconomical device helped a great deal. Consumer debt rose from $3.1 billion in 1922 to $6.9 billion in 1929. Installment selling had been introduced in the automobile industry in 1915. "Take Off Your Hat to the Man Who Buys on Time," the magazine *Motor* urged dealers. Installment sales amounted to a great personal reform, *Motor* said. "Time-buying has caused more intensive work than any scheme of mere money-saving ever devised—meritorious though such plans may be."[23] Dispensers of credit pushed hard in the automobile industry when sales for cash began to lag. By 1927, however, creditors were backing away, advising customers to purchase refrigerators and stoves, the principal of which could be paid off sooner. In 1925, 68 percent of new cars were sold on time payments; by 1927, the percentage was down to 58. In the 1920s, after success for a while with cars, installments were offered for almost everything else, from vacuum cleaners to, literally, the kitchen sink. By 1927, 85 percent of furniture sales were by installment, 80 percent of phonographs, 75 percent of washing machines, and 50 percent of radios, pianos, and sewing machines. By 1929, billions worth of consumer goods had been bought on time. In 1926, Merriam-Webster admitted "down payment" into the language.[24]

Speaking of underconsumption, it is of interest that in 1928, although a large percentage of houses wired for electricity had electric flat irons, less than one-third had washing machines, slightly more than one-third had vacuum cleaners, and less than 5 percent had electric refrigerators. For years after the 1920s, people of that era referred to electric refrigerators as "iceboxes," in memory of what they knew in Coolidge's time. They also remembered the metal containers with sliding doors they used in winter, placed in the open kitchen window above the sink, in which they stored milk and other perishables.

To all this the president was impervious, unable to see danger. He believed that installment buying was not a danger sign but a positive good, and so he told a press conference, adding a convincing bit of Vermont imagery:

> Here is an inquiry about the purchase of commodities on the installment plan. I don't know as I can very well discuss that in a newspaper conference in a way that might not be misunderstood on one side or the other. The basis of installment buying is, I think, entirely sound. It is a provision of credit for those that otherwise wouldn't be able to secure credit. So far as the installment buying goes, I think it is a little better than the old way that was customary around my neighborhood when I was young—of going to the store, getting a bill and having no plan or purpose as to when it was to be paid. When a commodity is bought on installments, it means that there is then laid out a plan on which it is to be paid, and installment buying is really a plan of financing and extending credit to people who otherwise wouldn't be able to secure credit. . . . So far as I can ascertain, it has not been overdone at the present time.[25]

In an effort to push up sales, advertising played its part. It gave the impression that everyone was buying the wares that the advertisements were sponsoring. Advertising had become a serious proposition during World War I, when liberty bonds and then the postwar victory bonds received much attention through billboards and campaigning in public places. Once the possibilities of advertising became known, the practice was pushed hard by the new advertising agencies of the 1920s and became an acceptable business expense. Edward L. Bernays was one of the first masters of advertising and went from triumph to triumph, becoming a rich man in the process. The question remained as to the usefulness of such salesmanship. It did nothing substantial, which in the 1920s would have meant giving working men and women higher wages and salaries with which to purchase the output of the economy. It may well have pushed consumers into the wrong purchases and too many purchases for their thin pocketbooks.

It was possible to look at the consumption problem and yet not see it. Secretary Hoover had more reason than Coolidge to understand consumption. After all, he was secretary of commerce. But his understanding was not much better than Coolidge's. For a man with a factual bent, Hoover's view was surprising. During a dinner, he told one of his guests, Mark Sullivan, that there should be more consumption of goods of the better kind, by which he meant more expensive items. There had been a "Better Homes Week," and the celebration appeared to stimulate expenditure, which was good. Coolidge, he said, would have been a better citizen if he had lived in a house that cost $60 a month rather than $32. Sullivan speculated to his diary on Hoover's "curious notions about political economy." He thought Hoover unsympathetic to "the old-fashioned political economy which lays emphasis on thrift," that Hoover believed in "the maximum of consumption so long as that consumption is in proportion to the earning capacity of the consumer." Hoover thought that this was "what makes for the higher stage of civilization."[26] Altogether lacking in this analysis was what would happen if the consumer did not have the capacity to consume. Hoover had been a millionaire too long. He was not a man of great wealth, like Ford, Rockefeller, and Mellon or (to come down a bit) Morgan and Schwab. He possessed $4 million. It was enough to forget what life could be like on $2,000 a year.

To economists of the time, underconsumption did not appear to be a problem. *Recent Economic Changes in the United States* (1929) had a point of view that was as forgetful of consumption as were Hoover's speculations. Its prefatory remarks announced an unseen hand guiding production and consumption. That hand was guided not merely by "scientific fact finding, by a carefully predeveloped consumption, a measurable pull on production . . . which releases capital otherwise tied up in immobile goods and furthers the organic balance of economic forces," but also by advertising. The companion study to *Recent Economic Changes,* entitled *Recent Social Trends in the United States* (1933), was released when the unseen hand had failed; its preface stated that "capacity to produce goods changes faster than our capacity to purchase."[27]

Underconsumption was the most ominous economic sign of the 1920s, but there were others—notably, the increase in holding companies and the development of investment trusts in 1927 and thereafter. It was a time when demand for investments of any sort threatened to outrun availability, and many rascals made sure that supply would equal demand. The decay of credit quality in investments was marked. Caldwell and Company, headquartered in Nashville, moved from municipal bonds to real-estate mortgage bonds to "high-yield" corporates, becoming speculative as the country became bullish. After 1924, S. W. Straus and Company, which advertised its existence as "forty-three years without loss to any investor," relaxed its opposition to junior liens; in addition to first mortgage bonds, it began offering seconds and thirds and what its marketing staff described as "general mortgages." A later writer remarked that without saying anything to his customers, Straus "entered the junk-bond business."[28] Stocks hitherto had been regarded as speculative, as opposed to bonds, but a treatise by Edgar Lawrence Smith entitled *Common Stocks as Long Term Investments* appeared in 1924 and became the bible of new thought on investing.[29]

Holding companies flourished for the benefit of investors who had learned about securities through the wartime bond drives but in the 1920s still hardly knew the difference between stocks and bonds. Such companies were common in the electrical industry, where there was a need for expansion; these holding companies were under state regulation, which removed their shenanigans from public visibility. *Recent Social Trends* did not have the opportunity to see the collapse of the utility empire of Samuel Insull of Chicago, one of the worst cases of holding company excesses. The book related gullibly that the "largest, most rapid and most perfect development of the holding company has taken place in public utilities, especially in the electric light and power and gas business."[30] It was correct in relating that ten groups of systems did three-fourths of the electric light and power business in the country, and sixteen systems controlled half the country's gas. What it did not relate was that Insull had taken his first step into temptation in 1912 and by 1929 was the chairman of sixty-five concerns and the president of eleven others. Relations between the pyramid's layers were so complex that even Owen Young, when he took it over for its creditors in 1932, could not understand them. Insull had been secretary to Thomas Edison and had gotten his start that way, eventually accumulating several millions for himself, which he lost in the debacle. He also took down with him $750 million of other people's money. As mentioned earlier, the Van Sweringens did likewise. So did the Swedish adventurer Ivar Kreuger, "the match king," who bilked American investors of $250 million. Insull and the Van Sweringens at least had operating companies. Kreuger left only a few matches.

President Coolidge learned about holding companies from an article in the January 1926 issue of *Atlantic Monthly* and invited the author, William Z. Ripley of Harvard, to the White House on 15 February. Ripley earlier had drawn up a plan of reorganization for the country's railroad lines, because the ICC was having trouble estimating rates; weak lines had higher costs, and it was difficult to estimate charges that included bad management. During this experience, he learned about holding companies, and his *Atlantic* article anticipated a book published the next year, *Main Street and Wall Street*. In both article and book, Ripley related how the corporate buccaneers were selling preferred, that is, nonvoting, stock to investors, spreading the common stock, and buying control through layers of holding companies. As an example, he took the fate of the Pine Bluff, Arkansas, electric company.

> This is controlled by the Arkansas Light and Power Company, which is a part of the Southern Light and Power Company of Delaware, also controlling the Mississippi Power and Light Company, the Louisiana Power Company, and the Louisiana Power and Light Company. And the whole congeries of them has been in turn acquired by the Southern Power and Light Company, this time incorporated in Maryland, which seems to be a part of the Electric Bond and Share Company of New York. Being the proud and happy possessor of some shares in this last-named corporation, I am thrilled with the sense of immediate participation in the local concerns of Pine Bluff, Arkansas![31]

Coolidge reported to a press conference what Ripley had said. "The class," as he referred to the little group, was interested. On 27 August 1926, the president again mentioned Ripley, saying that the nation had 20 million stockholders who needed protection.[32]

The result of presidential exposure to what was nothing less than fraud in holding companies was absolutely nothing. On 27 August, the president said that he supposed the Federal Trade Commission might look into holding companies if they entered interstate commerce, but until then, it was all the business of the states. Government could not tell private individuals where to put their money.

For investors, there were also investment trusts, seven hundred of which were formed in 1927–30. They invested in anything; the more interest the investments paid, the better, for that brought in more investors. John K. Galbraith described them wittily, saying that they "brought about an almost complete divorce of the volume of corporate securities outstanding from the volume of corporate assets in existence."[33] One of them, American Founders, put $23.6 million in the call money market. Stock purchases in American Founders were made with money lent by American Founders, presenting the picture of a dog chasing its tail. Trusts sold $400 million in securities in 1927, $3 billion in 1929; by autumn of the latter year, their so-called assets were $8 billion, an elevenfold increase from 1927.

A third problem that the president might have seen, in addition to underconsumption and the increase in holding companies and investment trusts, was the new morality operating on Wall Street. A recent writer ascribed what happened to two groups: the Establishment, represented by the Morgan house and others that stood not merely for old values but for solid investments; and the Outsiders, who came primarily from the Midwest and brought their morals with them and were represented by the founder of General Motors, William C. Durant, a talented plunger. Years before, according to this writer, Baruch had proposed a scheme to the elder J. P. Morgan and inadvertently used the word "gamble." Morgan brought him up short, telling him, "I never gamble" as he terminated the meeting. Even if this was not quite true, it was a good story and showed Morgan's feeling for propriety. But during the 1920s, opportunities were large, the midwesterners speculated, and the younger Morgan, who would not sell German bonds other than the Dawes issue because he was anti-German, put $110 million in call loans.[34]

Coolidge could not have heard of the Establishment-Outsiders dichotomy, but after he retired from the presidency, he engaged personally in a dichotomy about which he felt no qualms. A flotation in 1929 included, as did many of the time, a preferred list; under a two-price system, insiders purchased stock at one price, and the public purchased it at another, higher, price. The stock was Standard Brands, and the preoffering distribution included Coolidge at three thousand shares, Baruch at four thousand, former senator Hilles at two thousand, and so forth; the list was bipartisan, Democrats as well as Republicans. For members of the Establishment, it was a questionable arrangement.

Lastly, there was a notable occasion when Coolidge confronted an economic problem and spoke out about it, instead of following his usual custom, which was to say nothing. Coolidge's biographer McCoy has criticized him for what he said. His earlier biographer Fuess averred that it was "the one important occasion when Coolidge did not keep his mouth shut, and his untimely utterance proved to be the most unfortunate blunder he ever made."[35] At a press conference on 6 January 1928, Coolidge responded to a written question from one of the reporters inquiring whether brokers' loans were too high. They had jumped $100 million in a week; the increase since October had been $450 million; and the total, including loans from non-Reserve banks, stood at $4.4 billion. His answer was on the tentative side:

I am not familiar enough with the exact workings and practice of the Federal Reserve System so that comments that I might make relative to the amount of brokers' loans and so on would be of very much value. I do know in a general way that the amount of securities in this country has increased very largely in recent years. The number of different securities that are dealt in on the stock exchange are very much larger than they were previously. The deposits in banks also are larger. And those two things together would necessarily be a reason for doing more business of that kind that is transacted by brokers and would naturally result in a larger sum of money being used for that purpose. Now, whether the amount at the present time is disproportionate to the resources of the country I am not in a position to judge accurately, but so far as indicated by an inquiry that I have made of the Treasury Department and so on I haven't had any indications that the amount was large enough to cause particularly unfavorable comment.[36]

Offered on a Friday afternoon, this judgment received indirect quotation in newspapers the next morning to the effect that everything was all right. The exchange was open on Saturdays, and that day stocks enjoyed their second highest Saturday turnover in history, 1.6 million shares. "Coolidge's Optimism Gives Stocks a Lift," announced the front-page story in the 8 January *New York Times*. Durant helped matters along by asking if brokers' loans were too high and answering his own question, saying that the function of a bank was to receive and lend money. At the close that day, the ticker was sixteen minutes behind.

The president had not said that everything was all right with the market. His remarks had been misinterpreted, but he did not correct the reporters' accounts.

10

★ ★ ★ ★ ★

RETIREMENT

The end of a long political career is always difficult for the political leader himself, especially for those who make it to the very top of American politics. There necessarily was some awkwardness, and perhaps bitterness, in Coolidge's decision to step down, made well before the Republican national convention in 1928.

Lurking behind the decision to leave politics was the question of what the president, after all the years of striving, would do with his sudden leisure when he became a common citizen. He had had little time to think about it. So many things had happened. His movement upward in politics had been an almost daily proposition—"Do the day's work." He hardly had time to meditate over the prizes he had received along the way, including the greatest, the presidency. He probably also knew the lesson that all holders of prizes eventually learn—that the pleasure is in the striving and the anticipation; the prize itself, in almost ineluctable ways, never seems to live up to its promise. In 1924, with Teapot Dome behind him, he had managed to defeat his rivals within the party and obtain the nomination, and the dissensions of the Democrats were demonstrating that he could easily take the election. That year, however, he suffered the greatest tragedy of his life, the loss of Calvin, Jr. The passing of that slender youth who was so much like him, both in looks and in quiet earnestness, undoubtedly drove him back to work, taking refuge in the day-to-day routine rather than contemplating his triumphs or looking ahead to others. All his life, there had always been tasks, one after the other, that had accompanied the opportunities as he worked at his courses at Amherst, studied law in Northampton, and began the long upward climb politically. Now, having reached the top of politics, what could be the next task? Retirement was necessary, but from the outset, he was unsure where it would lead. As it turned out, there was little time to go in any direction—his life itself was running out.

The great political bombshell of 1927, the effects of which lasted until Coolidge left the presidency in March 1929, was the president's announcement on 2 August 1927, the anniversary of President Harding's death four years earlier, that "I do not choose to run for president in nineteen twenty-eight." On this score, Coolidge did not consult anyone, least of all his wife. Senator Capper, who was a guest at the presidential hunting lodge in South Dakota, accompanied Coolidge to his summer executive offices in Rapid City and after the routine morning press conference heard Coolidge dictate to a stenographer the soon-to-be-famous words. The stenographer typed up the same sentence over and over. When the reporters returned for what the president had described as an announcement, he gave each one a little strip of paper containing his decision, and each reporter was free to write his story, making whatever speculations he wished. Coolidge and Capper rode back to the game lodge in virtual silence and then had lunch with the president's wife. Only after the president had excused himself for an afternoon nap did the senator tell Mrs. Coolidge what her husband had done.

In faraway New England, Dr. Boone was staying with Frank Stearns, who had no warning—which might be considered a typical way of informing Stearns. Stearns was not a maker of policies but a sounding board, only in this case, Stearns had no use as a board.

As for the rest of the country, it was astonished. Most of the presidential pundits had presumed that the New Englander would run in 1928. For a short while, there seemed to be nothing to do but resort to humor. The Democrats laughed over the joke related by New York newspaper editor Claude Bowers, who predicted that pancake eaters would have to do without maple syrup in 1928. Asked why, Bowers responded, "Because the Vermont sap chooses not to run in 1928." Another joke of the time, neither Democratic nor Republican, was that after the president gave out his announcement, reporters in the Black Hills came upon a broken-down Model T with a hand-lettered sign on its fender, "I do not choose to run in 1927."[1]

After the initial shock, the question arose as to what Coolidge really meant. Here it was possible to be etymological, in terms of Coolidge's roots. Colonel Starling wrote in his memoirs that undoubtedly Coolidge was saying no, that such a remark was completely understood in such states as Kentucky, where life was akin to the simplicities of Vermont. In Kentucky language, the phrase meant, "I ain't gonna do it and I don't give a dern what you think." Sen. Alben W. Barkley, nearly a decade after his Kentucky countryman remarked this point, said the same thing. Barkley related that when he was a boy and they had company for dinner, it was considered polite, when his mother passed the vegetables or meat or preserves for the third or fourth time, for the guest to say, "No, I do not choose any more." He allowed as to how Secretary of Commerce Hoover in 1927–28 snatched away the jam in a hurry after Coolidge politely said, "I do not choose." Nonetheless, he said, in Kentucky the phrase was well known.[2]

Privately, the president lent support to this interpretation. In 1924, he had already written to his father that "I hope this is the last time I shall ever have to be a candidate for office." He told Starling, privately, of course, that his time in office was coming to an end. After he left the White House, he wrote a postscript to a letter to his secretary, Sanders, in regard to a woman who had not taken his withdrawal seriously: "The lady would never understand that anyone did not desire to be renominated."[3]

One important and almost never mentioned reason for the president's decision could have been his concern for Mrs. Coolidge's well-being, which was in a bad state that summer of 1927. The president understood, first of all, that his wife had had enough of the White House. She was a charming hostess, the best the mansion had possessed since at least the time of Frances Cleveland, perhaps even that of Dolley Madison. Many of the first ladies were awkward in their social roles. Even Edith Roosevelt, who performed as if to the mansion born, was a bit on the imperious side. Grace Coolidge possessed no side at all. But it was a strain to meet one group of visitors after another, and perhaps also to carry on conversations that her husband should have undertaken but for whom they were impossible. She had done this for several years, and it was wearing. Moreover, although she held her head high and hid her grief, the death of her younger son had devastated her. In 1927, she was also worried about her mother's illness, which the physicians feared was caused by a cancerous growth. She was also in physical trouble herself, although the Coolidges did not then know the reason. She had little energy and was losing weight.

Mrs. Coolidge had made known her sentiments about another term in an indirect way, as she was forbidden to show any interest in politics. Characteristically, she crocheted a bed coverlet that she gave to the White House, and even before the declaration in the Black Hills, she embroidered in the coverlet the dates 1923–1929 for the Coolidge administration.

But ambiguity is what reporters like to deal with, and many of them, as well as political leaders, claimed that Coolidge's statement in the Black Hills was in fact a maneuver to get the nomination. Dr. Boone believed that Coolidge meant it to be ambiguous, that he was receptive to being nominated but would have liked having the nomination served to him. He believed that the president privately took the position that he should have the opportunity of accepting or declining. Representative Martin of Massachusetts, who knew Coolidge well and understood reluctance and ambiguity in his state's politics, wrote long after Coolidge had passed on that he believed that Coolidge would have accepted renomination if offered. "But I do not believe," he added, "that he hoped for it or that he was disappointed when he did not get it." The head usher of the White House, Ike Hoover, was sure that the president wanted another four years.[4]

It was possible that Coolidge hoped to use his "do not choose" announcement to control the members of his party throughout the final lame-duck months of his presidency, at least until the convention. Although it is difficult to understand how he might have done that, the possibility was there. The spell he had cast upon his party after he took control at the end of Teapot Dome and the other so-called scandals had been nothing less than remarkable. His power was beyond question. At any point down to the convention, he might have changed his mind and taken the nomination if he wanted it. Senator Smoot thought so, even after Hoover secured a majority of the delegates: "No other candidate has a chance against Hoover." On 7 June Smoot wrote in his diary, "It will be Hoover or Coolidge as things stand tonight." Months before, he had told Coolidge privately that if the president would confide his intentions, he, the senator, would take his confidence and hold it sacred. Coolidge refused. "He thought it unwise to say one word about it." On another occasion when the two were talking, the senator asked whether Coolidge would accept if the convention nominated him. The presidential riddle for this occasion was, "I have made my statement."[5]

A tongue-in-cheek attempt to clarify the situation took place in the Senate, where Robert M. La Follette, Jr., successor to his illustrious father, introduced a resolution to the effect that failure to observe the Washingtonian tradition of two terms would be unwise and unpatriotic. The resolution closed with praise to Coolidge for following the tradition. A Republican senator, Simeon D. Fess of Ohio, proposed to omit the praise of Coolidge; Fess favored another term. Senator Norris, an enemy of Coolidge, suggested that deletion of the complimentary clause would be a slap at the president. The resolution passed without the praise.[6]

Coolidge could have hoped to use his wording of declination to try to control the Senate until the convention in 1928 nominated Hoover, so as to prevent the senators from putting up one of their own. But the president obviously did not like Hoover, who was too ardently seeking the presidency while holding his cabinet post. Coolidge also must have felt that a man who had held a prominent appointment in the Wilson administration, attended the Paris Peace Conference as one of the Democratic president's trusted advisers, and was uncertain of his party affiliation until 1920 was not entitled to the nomination on the Republican ticket eight years later.

It is possible that he spoke as he did to preserve his party influence long enough to choose someone other than Hoover, but he had nowhere to go; Hoover was the only strong Republican candidate. Charles Evans Hughes had run and lost a dozen years before. In 1928, Hughes refused to lift a finger for the nomination, which would have been necessary, for despite his brilliance and obvious competence, he possessed no personal attraction. If Vice President Dawes had played his political cards more carefully, he might have made it. To be sure, ever since his speech in the Senate on 4 March 1925, he was persona non grata to every single senator, and he foreclosed Coolidge's support by championing McNary-Haugenism. He could have remained aloof, spoken in general terms about the farmers' plight, spoken so generally that Coolidge might have backed him. But the general's flamboyant ways were not those of the president, and it is entirely possible that even if Dawes had been as quiet as a church mouse, saying nary a word about McNary-Haugenism, he could not have gained Coolidge's approval. In Kansas City, Governor Lowden, the perennial candidate, remained aloof from the Hoover enthusiasm; he stayed off the Hoover bandwagon until a proposed McNary-Haugen plank in the platform failed in the resolutions committee. Lowden then announced his withdrawal as a candidate so quickly that Dawes, who observers presumed was waiting in the wings to gather Lowden's followers, did not have time to gather them—they all rushed to get on the Hoover bandwagon.

Hoover's enemies could do little to stop him. Secretary Mellon went to the White House to see if Coolidge would change his mind, and the president almost snarled his reply. According to Mellon's diary, "He speaks of his position and cannot change. Is in accord with me on Hoover." Secretary of Agriculture Jardine advocated a farm bill that would get the farm problem off center stage prior to the convention, for with the Republicans assembling in the midst of the agricultural Midwest, the farm issue needed a temporary solution. Coolidge refused to help Hoover in this way and told Jardine, "That man has offered me unsolicited advice for six years, all of it bad!"[7] But that was all the president could do—refuse to help and tell cabinet members how he disliked Hoover.

Until the last minute, Coolidge seems to have been willing to keep Hoover nervous, and he managed to do that. The Hoover forces put one of their men up to talking to Coolidge, to smoke him out. Hoover's close confederate Edgar Rickard recorded the result in his diary:

Arrive 2300 [Hoover's house was at 2300 S Street, Washington] before family up but asked to sit by while Chief shaved and dressed; appears he wanted to talk about his candidacy with someone he could trust. Appears arrangement made for seeing [E. Bertram] Mott worked out as planned, but Mott had not returned to see H.H. after lunch with President and H.H. very anxious to have me find out from Mott if Pres. expressed any views on his [Coolidge's] candidacy. Appears that no one has been able to get anything concrete and the very trying situation as "Draft Coolidge" delegations may start stampede for him and very hard to get Hoover delegates back when President declines. H.H. is apparently very much disturbed over President's attitude. H.H. hands me $5000 in cash which had been given him for campaign purposes and accompanies me to station to take 9:10 a.m. train. Have strenuous few hours in office; see [Ethan Theodore] Colton and phone Chief that President did not give any intimation of plans to Mott.[8]

Whatever the ultimate purpose of "I do not choose," Hoover triumphed. He received the nomination in Kansas City by an overwhelming majority, 837 votes. Lowden retained 74 votes. Senator Curtis of Kansas was third with 64. Dawes received 4. Coolidge had 13 from Illinois and 4 from Ohio.

The only interesting aspect of the convention was the manner in which the vice-presidential nominee was chosen. The Republican regulars decided on former governor Channing H. Cox of Massachusetts, to balance the ticket containing a Californian. But overnight, Senator Smoot decided that this would not be a good idea, and the next morning he told a group in Secretary Mellon's suite at the Muehlebach Hotel that the majority leader of the Senate, Curtis, was the man. He called Curtis, who consented, and then asked Senator Borah to nominate him. For several conventions, the Idaho senator had thought that lightning might strike him, by which he meant presidential lightning, but Hoover's frenzied activity ended that hope, and when Smoot asked him to say a few words about Curtis, Borah readily assented. That was that. The conferees at the Muehlebach did not bother to consult the presidential nominee until it was all over. Curtis was a first-vote McNary-Haugenite, and it was wise to put him on the ticket to counteract Hoover's poor reputation with America's farmers.[9]

The way in which the Hoover-Curtis ticket was put together was a bad omen from the outset. The group of delegates in Secretary Mellon's suite had foisted the bald, paunchy senator off on Hoover, without a word of objection from the latter; they clearly felt that they could do this. There followed another bad sign: Hoover told Curtis that he wanted to appoint Secretary of the Interior Work as chairman of the national committee. Curtis did not approve of the appointment but seems to have said nothing.[10] In not consulting Curtis about Work, Hoover again showed poor judgment, as Curtis was a seasoned politician who had been in Congress since the 1890s. Nor did Curtis cover himself with glory. He should have refused to go on the ticket until he had Hoover's blessing. And when Hoover mentioned the appointment of Work, Curtis should have objected, forthrightly. Curtis was to become one of the most invisible vice presidents in American history, even more so than Harding's vice president.

But Hoover and Curtis duly won the November 1928 election against their Democratic opponents, Governor Smith and Sen. Joseph T. Robinson of Arkansas, by a wide margin, 28 million votes to 15 million, with 58 percent of the vote—better than Coolidge's 54 percent in 1924.

For Coolidge, the final months in the presidency passed quietly and, for the most part, enjoyably. Just before the convention, in the early summer of 1928, there was a flap over getting out of Washington for a vacation in Wisconsin. As the date for travel approached, it appeared as if Mrs. Coolidge, whose malady had been diagnosed as a tumor on the kidney, might not be able to go. The president wanted to get out of Washington in the worst way, for he did not wish to be available when the convention opened in Kansas City. Coolidge fretted, in a state of nervousness. Secretaries Sanders and Clark told the physicians that they should "ease up on the traces," but they refused. Boone went out of the city and came back on 8 June to discover Mrs. Coolidge looking badly. He said to her, "Oh Washington, oh Washington!" She said, "Just that." The president too was incapacitated, hobbling around because of a sore heel. His wife was not altogether helpful, remarking that "the elephant must have stepped on it." At last the doctors gave assent and the president and his wife left Washington just before the convention.[11]

The summer vacation in Wisconsin might have been invented so that the occupants of the second floor of the White House could "get out of town" and out of touch, but the stay at Cedar Island Lodge on a small island in the Brule River near Superior refreshed both Coolidges. After a few rainy days, the sun came out, and the brisk nights and sharp days, the Wisconsin greenery, and the glorious fishing made a difference. The first lady felt better. The president always believed that if he could take the outside air, as when he had escaped Northampton to Plymouth Notch, it would do him good. For him, Wisconsin was a lifesaver. He wrote to Stearns in Swampscott the sort of letter that he occasionally sent to close friends, a letter that avoided the prosaic style that marked almost all his correspondence. "The life out here has been very beneficial both to Mrs. Coolidge and to me," he ventured. This, to be sure, was an enthusiasm he rarely offered about anything. He resorted to measurements, which was typical, but gave untypical details: "She has gained in weight and looks very much like her old self. I have not gained in weight, in fact I did not wish to, but in other respects I am very much improved." He spoke of "resiliency," which had hardly been displayed in the preceding weeks and months when contemplating his replacement by Hoover. "I find this morning especially that I have a resiliency I have not had for months. I did not realize how exhausted I was until I reached here." Then came a recommendation that he must have known Stearns would not take, for the dry-goods store owner was overweight, and Stearns's idea of a good time was to sit in a chair and smoke a cigar. "I stay all the time in the open air," the president wrote, "which has been the real source of the benefits I have received. I therefore should like to commend that source to you. If you could find something like fishing that would keep you out of doors, I hope you might receive a like benefit."[12]

Coolidge instructed his people at Cedar Island that he did not want any visitors, but it was necessary to see the candidate, and of course Hoover wanted to be seen with the president. Hoover was moving around on the hustings and made sure that he would be in the vicinity of Cedar Island. Coolidge could hardly avoid inviting him. The visit was not a personal success, however. When Hoover's train arrived, the president did him the courtesy of coming to the station, but he sat in his car and let Hoover approach it. Whatever the two men said to each other on the trip to the lodge is unrecorded and may have been unrecordable; Coolidge may not have said anything. Coolidge sat on the front porch with Hoover, both of them almost visibly squirming as the photographers took pictures. A cameraman asked the president to say something to Hoover. "Let him talk," said Coolidge sourly. "He's going to be president."[13]

In the fall, the Coolidges took a second vacation in Virginia. Just before Christmas and lasting into the new year, they went for a third to Sapelo Island off the Georgia coast. It seemed as if, with his presidency coming to an end, Coolidge wanted to anticipate his leisure.

In the last days, Mrs. Coolidge continued to make up for the social brusqueness of her husband. The *Mayflower* was docked at the Navy Yard, and the ship's officers invited her to lunch. To their delight, she came and brought a package. It contained an iron Scottie dog fashioned into a doorstop. She had penned a note on an attached cloth tag, containing a poem entitled "Within This Room":

> Hark, hark, the dogs do bark,
> The Hoovers are coming to town.
> The Coolidges depart
> With a pain in the heart
> And Congress looks on with a frown.

> The city is dressed in its beautiful best,
> The Avenue bristles with seats
> The "Mayflower" rocks
> At the Navy Yard docks
> While we laugh and partake of the eats.

It was signed " 'Only', a dog."[14]

Inauguration day, 4 March 1929, saw the Coolidges receiving the Hoovers at the White House, as was customary. The retiring president and the president-elect then rode in an open limousine, with the majority leaders of the Senate and the House in jump seats in front, down Pennsylvania Avenue and up to the Capitol for the ceremony. Grace Coolidge and Lou Henry Hoover followed in another automobile. After the swearing in, the new president delivered his address. Rain began to fall, and the audience took shelter under umbrellas. The great crowd spread over the grass in front of the inaugural platform listened quietly until Hoover reached the speech's end. Then, again as was customary, the Coolidges bade their successors good-bye and left for Union Station and Northampton.

On the morning of 5 March 1929, Calvin and Grace Coolidge arrived in the city they had known so well. It was a dull, drizzling day, and they expected little or no notice. Their own lives had taken a drastic new turn, but there seemed no reason why it should concern the people of their home city. To their surprise and gratification, there was not merely a big crowd at the station but a long line of Smith College girls standing in the rain and waving as their automobile passed on its way to 21 Massasoit Street.

In a fairly short time, the former president discovered that he could no longer hope to live quietly in the house that he and his wife had occupied since 1906. He was virtually driven out of Massasoit Street because of the tourists. When the former president sat on the front porch, the cars that slowly passed by, with intent faces peering out to see if there was any movement in or about the house, virtually stopped dead in the street, and the hum of voices rose to a roar of "There he is!" It was disconcerting, and within a year, the former first family moved to a much more suitable place that had been built by a professor of history at Smith. Known as "The Beeches," the house was a brown shingled affair with three floors; it was a rambling place with a hallway, a library, and other rooms downstairs and the bedrooms upstairs. The third floor was a huge attic, where the former president could store the many boxes and other items he had accumulated during the Washington years. As Grace Coolidge described it, "The house is a friendly little house. The newspapers make it very elegant with sixteen rooms and an electric elevator. We can count only eleven rooms, one of which the billiard room on the third floor we shall have for storage. The elevator is a dumb waiter affair for freight propelled by pulleys. There is a sun parlor off the living room and two sleeping porches. A heavenly place for grandchildren!"[15] The house had a fence and a big gate to keep out the tourists. Its grounds, eight acres, sloped down to the Connecticut River.

Routine, whether on Massasoit Street or at The Beeches, continued, for the Coolidges were that sort of people. The president, as people called him, reestablished himself in his old law office, from which he had never formally departed. His name remained on the door of "Coolidge and Hemenway." The firm was on the second floor of a building that was around the corner and down a side street from Northampton's main thoroughfare containing the churches and the Academy of Music, that is, the town theater. Coolidge told his partner of fourteen years, Ralph W. Hemenway, whom he addressed as "Mr. Hemenway," that he desired a single office, and Hemenway gave up his own to "Mr. Coolidge." There, in a small room, the former president spent part of each day, sitting at the big desk with his feet in a drawer, sometimes with his shoes off, dictating letters. Most of the letters were necessary, but he hated doing them. In many he turned down requests to appear and, especially, make speeches. When he came home he would often say, "I have spent the whole day answering letters which do nobody any good."[16]

The accommodations at Coolidge and Hemenway did not bother him, although one day in 1932 when a friend called, he complained about his office furniture—the rolltop desk and the shabby chairs—comparing the furniture to that in the White House. He also offered a comparison to his former status. "I have been ignored and forgotten," he said.[17]

Coolidge faced a much larger problem than furniture—the business of "finding work." His successors would also face this problem, some taking a more graceful exit from prominence than others. Some were tempted to lend their names. Coolidge played with the possibility of entering the oil business. "You remember the oil industry wanted what is I think a sort of Judge Landis," he wrote to Sanders. (Kennesaw Mountain Landis had become baseball commissioner to prevent reoccurrence of the scandals of 1919, when eight members of the Chicago team took bribes to throw the World Series.) The oil industry had had its ups and downs. The scandal of 1923–24 had shown that oilmen were none too dainty about getting their way. A "tsar" might well have been in order. Coolidge told Sanders, "I am going to confer with them at the Vanderbilt Saturday morning. I suppose I should be not in the industry . . . but over all in the business." He was not sure that oil was a good idea. "I wonder how it looks to you. I have come to think I would find it agreeable work. Of course there are problems or they would not need anyone. I cannot find any place, even writing, where there are not problems and criticism of what I am doing."[18]

The oil business did not work out, and Coolidge stayed away from business propositions, except for a directorship in one of the big New York insurance companies. He went on the train to the city each month and enjoyed the directors' discussions around the table. For this duty he was paid nominally, not much more than expenses.

In discussing the oil proposition with Sanders, he mentioned "writing," to which he had been attracted for many years, and it became his best course in retirement. In 1929, he brought out his autobiography, published by Cosmopolitan Book Company. He seems to have written it while in the presidency or shortly afterward. For his literary effort he was paid the astounding sum of $5 per word. Critics guffawed that he filled his descriptions with the articles "a" and "the." The critics were wrong, for the autobiography contained the same stylistic felicities found in his speeches over the years. Describing life in Plymouth Notch and its surroundings, he wrote, "It was a hard but wholesome life, under which the people suffered many privations and enjoyed many advantages, without any clear realization of the existence of either one of them." On the armistice of 1918: "What the end of the four years of carnage meant those who remember it will never forget and those who do not can never be told." Nor was the book bereft of humor. "At first," he wrote, describing his entrance into the vice presidency, "I intended to become a student of the Senate rules and I did learn much about them, but I soon found that the Senate had but one fixed rule, subject to exceptions of course, which was to the effect that the Senate would do anything it wanted to do whenever it wanted to do it." Or, concerning his nomination for the presidency in 1924: "There were some quarters in the opposing party where it was thought it would be good strategy to encourage my party to nominate me, thinking that it would be easy to accomplish my defeat. I do not know whether their judgment was wrong or whether they overdid the operation, so that when they stopped speaking in my praise they found they could not change the opinion of the people which they had helped to create."[19]

Critics proclaimed the autobiography a straight, dull account, so lean that it crackled. But it was lithe description of a life begun close to the soil, in circumstances not merely rural but near to penury, of a man who rose through education and work and political acumen to the momentary (as Coolidge would have said) ceremonial of the White House, and after doing his best, had gone back to where he had begun.

There was also Coolidge's daily newspaper column, which he carried on for a year in 1930–31. "Calvin Coolidge Says," sometimes entitled

"Thinking Things Over with Calvin Coolidge," was more prosaic than the autobiography, by a good deal. In the first column, dated 1 July, the former president related, typically, "We need more faith in ourselves." His explanation: "Our country, our people, our civil and religious institutions may not be perfect, but they are what we have made them. They are good enough so that it has been necessary to build a high exclusion law to prevent all the world from rushing to possess them." A later message included the admonition that "sound finance calls for payment of debt and making the revenues of each year meet the expenditures." Once in a while, he took a position: "It will do no harm to have a reminder that when Congress passes laws requiring the expenditure of money the people will have to pay for it." Or, again about Congress: "The management of Muscle Shoals demonstrates the utter hopelessness of having any considerable enterprise conducted by the Congress." The column tended to bring out its author's reluctance to say sharp or politically awkward things, so it often lacked an edge. Moreover, the times were out of joint; the depression was beginning to envelope not merely the economy but also personal hopes and desires. People were reducing their expectations of what they might obtain out of life, of what had been known as the American dream. Coolidge himself was feeling that way, and it was difficult to maintain the necessary optimism. More and more he was pleading for the maintenance of what he had known, and the depression did not constitute such a thing.

Finally, Coolidge began to find the mechanics of writing, the need to make a deadline, if not boring then at least time-consuming. It was a task that he did not wish to continue. The former president was paid well enough for his column—the record price of $3.25 per word. He averaged 198 words. This meant $643.50, five days a week. He had to employ an assistant, first Herman C. Beaty, a former Associated Press writer, then Harry Ross. Coolidge read the newspapers and government bulletins and studied economic data of the Department of Commerce. He wrote drafts at night and dictated finished versions the next morning. He was never late. At the end of the year, the column had earned $203,045, most of which went to Coolidge, but he had had enough and quit.

In retirement, he did not often leave Northampton. He and his wife once went to Florida, where he had the distinct sensation that he was creating a circus. People were everywhere, pointing and waving and trying to talk to him. The Coolidges journeyed on to New Orleans and then to California, where they visited the sets in Hollywood. They accepted the hospitality of newspaper and real estate multimillionaire William Randolph Hearst, and it was said that Coolidge not merely accepted a glass of wine (at that time banned by the Volstead Act) but enjoyed it sufficiently to ask for another. In 1931, he went to Marion, Ohio, to assist President

Hoover in dedicating the Harding Memorial. Otherwise, it was excursions to New York for the insurance company meetings or to Plymouth Notch when the weather was decent. He enjoyed the trips to his birthplace and arranged to build a new house next to his old home, equipped with modern plumbing and a library for some of his books.

Only once after retirement did he go to Washington, to attend a ceremony marking proclamation of the Kellogg-Briand Pact. The occasion in July 1929 proved to be less important than the fact that it was his single postpresidential visit. Present were representatives of all signatories and adherents to the pact, sixty-six people, and the White House luncheon was crowded. Afterward he mistakenly began his short remarks without the microphones at hand, for they had been cleared for the signing of the documents. More enjoyable to Coolidge was probably renewing acquaintances outside the White House, at the New Willard, where he stayed. He had written to Sanders and Ted Clark that "I hope you can spend some time with me. In fact, I am going to depend on you to sort of take care of me." He asked to see Work and Davis and Mellon, and "also say to Senator Smoot that I should be pleased if he would drop in on his way through the Capital."[20]

In Northampton, he kept up with Washington gossip through Clark, who sent detailed letters. Ted described such events as the appointment of newspaperman Theodore Joslin to handle President Hoover's press affairs. The appointment occurred in 1931, when the president's reputation as the Great Engineer was being destroyed by the depression. Clark thought that the appointment was a case of a rat joining a sinking ship. Coolidge must have chuckled. But in rejoinders to Clark, encouragements for more letters, he did not say much. Clark was an Amherst graduate, and one might have thought that the connection would have brought a certain openness, but the former secretary only learned that "it is always interesting to get a letter from you and I appreciate them."[21]

In such ways the remaining years of his life went by. People speculated that he had left the presidency when he could have remained because he had foreseen what was to come. During his last weeks in the White House, he may have talked about a national economic depression to his wife. The biographer White ascribed to his fellow biographer Fuess a story about how Mrs. Coolidge had said to guests, "Poppa says there's a depression coming." The "Poppa" part was authentic, for that was what his wife called him when among friends, but the rest sounded apocryphal. No one, least of all Coolidge, anticipated what came. It was the sort of remark that people liked to believe he said, as against the stolidity and thoughtlessness, they said, of his successor.[22]

In the misery of jobs lost and about to be lost, people wondered whether the rural background of Coolidge might have been safer than the growth of industry, the lure of city life, and the assumptions that followed, such as that tomorrow could take care of itself. All this had been counter to what Coolidge stood for. As William Allen White described him, he had been a Puritan in Babylon.

Coolidge felt not merely that his time had passed but that in some manner he had failed. He felt out of place. "I no longer fit in with these times," he told newspaperman Henry Stoddard. The retired president added, "We are in a new era to which I do not belong, and it would not be possible for me to adjust myself to it."[23]

His health worsened in indefinable ways. He felt weak. The biographer Fuess said in 1962 in a tape-recorded oral history that Coolidge had had a heart attack during his presidency and knew that his days were numbered.[24] In Coolidge's time, heart attacks were becoming fairly well known; physicians by the end of the 1920s had begun to understand them as being different from strokes. It was well before the time of blood pressure pills, not to mention heart pumps and heart surgery, and in those days, the signs of cardiovascular trouble were signs of imminent death. In Coolidge's case, apart from the possible attack, there seem to have been no signs of the end, save tiredness and trouble breathing, which he credited to the catch-all illness of the time, asthma. It could have been cardiac asthma—heart disease with failing circulation.

The thirtieth president of the United States died on 5 January 1933, alone in his bedroom at The Beeches, while his wife was on a shopping trip downtown. She found him on the floor where he had fallen. He was buried three days later, after a service in the Edwards Church. Burial was in the Notch cemetery, alongside generations of Coolidges. Twenty cars from Northampton followed the hearse along the roads north to Brattleboro and Bellows Falls, through Ludlow, to Plymouth Union and up the Notch road. There was a short graveside service. The minister from Northampton closed his remarks with poetry, unsuitable words for the president whose years, as Alfred Dennis remembered, had not been filled with poetry.

What manner of president was Calvin Coolidge? One thing is clear, and that is that the caricatures to which his reputation has been mortgaged are not true. Because he was a New England president, he automatically acquired the supposed attributes of his region, traits that went back to the eighteenth century rather than to the nineteenth, not to mention the twentieth. He was supposed to have been a throwback to the virtuous (he was that), penurious (he was that), laconic (similarly) people who lived off the soil of a cold, windy, inhospitable part of the country. As Coolidge's star rose politically, he contributed to this interpretation, partly because as a

Massachusetts politician he needed to stress his local background, and partly because he was proud of his origin in the Vermont hill country and saw no reason to disguise it. But from the outset, it should have been evident that he was the son not of a farmer but of a storekeeper, the son of a man who served in the Vermont legislature and acquired the title of colonel for his political labors; he was no simple farmer or farmer's son. Coolidge attended one of the principal institutions of higher learning in Massachusetts and, by his own admission, let his hair grow long in the college way. He did not hesitate to remove himself from Plymouth Notch, because the opportunities for advancement, first in the law and then in politics, simply were not there. From the beginning of his adult years, he was a city man, not a country bumpkin or even a country philosopher.

There was a remarkable simplicity about Coolidge that is still attractive, and it helped him in his moves upward politically. He had the ability to peel off the layers of confusion and complexity that seem to attach to almost all questions not merely of politics but of life. He could have taken this quality from his rural beginnings or learned more about it from Morse and Garman at Amherst. There was an elemental quality about him that enabled him to analyze. It helped him to choose his courses and pursue them. There was little wasted motion. In the presidency, it allowed him to keep his head in heady situations. Consider the way in which he came into the presidency. He must have known that Harding's health was parlous; when his Boston friend called at the New Willard, shortly before Harding's death and raised the issue, Coolidge carefully did not say anything—a sure sign. He waited out the situation, as he had to. He then watched with care as the Teapot Dome and Veterans' Bureau and Daugherty issues rose and fell, and he dealt with those troubles based on the same advice he gave Hoover a few years later—if ten troubles are coming down the road straight at you, the best thing to do is wait most of them out. After almost national speculation about his inabilities as president, he eliminated his rivals or they eliminated themselves, and he became president in his own right. In retrospect, his simplicity in approaching problems and, when the time came, resolving them stands out against the frenzied actions of his rivals.

In estimating his personal qualities, it is necessary to remark the shyness and his willingness to work so hard that his rather fragile physique was almost convulsed, although he refused to give evidence of that. The result was the temper that his wife attributed to his growing up without a mother, under the care of his grandmother. But the tightness and private awkwardness that Calvin Coolidge displayed is nothing extraordinary. Many people are that way, tightly controlled and managed in public, irritable and sometimes nasty in private, for whatever reason. Coolidge had also shown himself bright enough to choose the most attractive girl in

Northampton, and the choice allowed him to "blow off" in private and continue upward in what otherwise might have been an impossible political career.

The public man needs judgment in these pages, and here the question must be how much a political leader can go against the spirit and factual necessities of his time. How far can he move the country if he is president and sees it going in the wrong direction? Like all his predecessors and successors in his high office, Coolidge needed to give the impression that he was in control, which was true enough in terms of the executive branch of the government. But even here he was prevented by the sheer impossibility of the physical task from dominating an executive that comprised half a million people. He did his best, appointing cabinet members or continuing those from the Harding administration who could do their jobs. The Coolidge cabinet during its five and a half years was by and large a competent group. Through these men, he managed a small government mechanism that did what cabinet departments traditionally were supposed to do. Secretary Mellon faithfully reduced the national debt by one-third during his tenure at the Department of the Treasury. If times had continued the same and if the Republican party had been permitted a similar treasury secretary and another dozen years in the presidency, the debt would have gone down to its March 1917 proportion—$1 billion—and by Coolidge's measurement, all would have been well.

In looking at the Coolidge presidency, two areas of activity (the president's critics would have said inactivity) stand out. One was the conduct of foreign relations during the 1920s. In the three geographical regions of presidential and national concern, there admittedly was far less interest than in later years. Foreign relations did not fascinate the nation, and Coolidge, like his countrymen, gave them less than his full attention. He passed the details to his two able secretaries of state. In retrospect, one would have hoped that Hughes and Kellogg, with complete backing from Coolidge, would have acted differently. In Latin America, they should have followed the full programs of Morrow and McCoy, undertaken a reorganization of Mexico's financial obligations, and reorganized the government of Nicaragua in the way that McCoy desired. In the Far East, there should have been far more interest in the internal confusion in China and Japan, and watchfulness for what that confusion might mean for the security of the United States. And in Europe, the possibility of a resurgent Germany should have brought the Coolidge administration and the American people around quickly to doing everything possible to preserve German democracy against the forces of nihilism that already, in the 1920s, were stirring. Based on what happened in the 1930s and 1940s, and what those happenings nearly succeeded in doing to the very foundation of Western civilization, the Coolidge administration should have done everything possible to prevent the several holocausts of our time. But to ask for judgments and action that presumed foresight of those events is unhistorical; it is too much to ask. History cannot be written that way.

The other aspect of the Coolidge administration is more troubling—that is, the manner in which the administration failed to face up to the stock market speculation of the time. The statistics of what was happening were at hand. The market speculation was clearly under way, but just as clearly, Coolidge did not understand it. He was not a speculative man, even though he was willing to participate in the opportunities of the moment by purchasing Standard Brands from the preferred list. By and large, the economy was something he did not understand. What he did was pass responsibility for its understanding to the third richest man in the United States, who was so financially secure that no market confusion could touch him. Thereafter, the president looked in other directions, doing the day's work and letting the economy move along by itself. He might have thought, in passing, that Secretary Hoover could poach as much on Mellon's preserve as he wished, and thereby the two experts, both rich men, could handle economic problems.

The economy was the greatest problem of the moment, and Coolidge understood it less than some of his contemporaries. If he failed in the presidency, this was his major failure. It could be argued that few if any individuals of the time beheld the dangers of underconsumption, but some of them did see the essential chicanery of holding companies and investment trusts. William Ripley was worth more of the president's time than Coolidge gave him. Somehow, one wishes that during the last presidential year or two, the bright, hardworking, slightly cynical, simple (in the right sense of that adjective) man in the White House had fixed his mind on the nation's fragile economy. One wishes that he had gathered the best minds, to use Harding's phrase for the cabinet members he hoped to appoint. He could have brought in Ripley, Morrow, Young, Gilbert, Strong, Harrison, and even that extrovert Dawes and asked them what to do, and then, although the task would have been difficult, sought to do it.

A failure to remedy something that might have involved going beyond the possibilities of his time may not be a proper measure for the presidency of Coolidge. Somehow, the student of Coolidge's era must confront that failure, as well as the much less resolvable failure to bring America's foreign relations into a more secure arrangement.

NOTES

CHAPTER 1
A NEW ENGLAND PRESIDENT

1. Ernest S. Kavanaugh, "Coolidge's Boyhood," *The Real Calvin Coolidge,* no. 4 (1986): 8–9.

2. Hendrik Booraem V, *The Provincial: Calvin Coolidge and His World, 1885–1895* (Lewisburg, Pa.: Bucknell University Press, 1994), p. 65.

3. Calvin Coolidge, *Autobiography* (New York: Cosmopolitan, 1929), p. 48.

4. Letter of 8 March 1892, in Edward Connery Lathem, ed., *Meet Calvin Coolidge: The Man Behind the Myth* (Brattleboro, Vt.: Stephen Greene, 1960), p. 32.

5. "The Place of the Party in the Political System," *Annals of the American Academy* 2 (1891–92): 300, 306.

6. Coolidge, *Autobiography,* p. 63.

7. John Almon Waterhouse, *Calvin Coolidge Meets Charles Edward Garman* (Rutland, Vt.: Academy, 1984), p. 11.

8. Quoted in Julius Seelye Bixler, "Charles E. Garman—Amherst's Scholar-Teacher," *American Scholar* 1 (1932): 100.

9. Booraem, *Provincial,* p. 179.

10. "Correspondence," *American Journal of Psychology* 9 (1898): 600–606.

11. Claude M. Fuess, *Calvin Coolidge: The Man from Vermont* (Boston: Little, Brown, 1940), p. 62.

12. Letter of 26 August 1897, in Lathem, *Meet Calvin Coolidge,* p. 83.

13. Alfred P. Dennis, *Gods and Little Fishes* (Indianapolis: Bobbs-Merrill, 1931), pp. 126–28.

14. William Allen White, *Calvin Coolidge: The Man Who Is President* (New York: Macmillan, 1925), p. 51.

15. Horace Green, *The Life of Calvin Coolidge* (New York: Duffield, 1924), p. 67.

16. William Allen White, *A Puritan in Babylon: The Story of Calvin Coolidge* (New York: Macmillan, 1938), p. 78; Mark Sullivan diary, 9 August 1923, Herbert Hoover Library, West Branch, Iowa (hereafter cited as HHL).

17. Joel T. Boone autobiography, chap. 21, pp. 7–8, box 46, Boone papers, Library of Congress, Washington, D.C. (hereafter cited as LC).

18. Stearns to Edward T. Clark, 5 February 1927, "Stearns, Frank W.," box 18, Clark papers, LC.

19. Fuess, *Calvin Coolidge*, p. 323.

20. Ibid., p. 153.

21. Donald R. McCoy, *Calvin Coolidge: The Quiet President* (New York: Macmillan, 1967), pp. 83–94.

22. Curtis D. Wilbur, "The Real Calvin Coolidge," *Good Housekeeping* 100 (April 1935).

23. Over the years, Stearns gave away 65,465 copies; 7,486 were sold. Fuess, *Calvin Coolidge*, p. 236.

24. For the following account of Coolidge's vice-presidential nomination, see Joe Martin, *My First Fifty Years in Politics* (New York: McGraw-Hill, 1960), pp. 143–44; Herbert F. Margulies, *Senator Lenroot of Wisconsin: A Political Biography, 1900–1929* (Columbia: University of Missouri Press, 1977), pp. 229–31; McCoy, *Calvin Coolidge*, p. 24.

25. Rand to Coolidge, 14 November 1924, Coolidge to Rand, 20 November, president's personal files no. 933, roll 10, Coolidge private papers, microfilm, Forbes Library, Northampton, Mass. (hereafter cited as FL).

26. White, *Puritan in Babylon*, p. 221.

27. White, *Calvin Coolidge*, p. 114.

28. Green, *Life of Calvin Coolidge*, pp. 177–78. See also Robert A. Woods, *The Preparation of Calvin Coolidge* (Boston: Houghton Mifflin, 1924), p. 215.

29. George Wharton Pepper, *Philadelphia Lawyer: An Autobiography* (Philadelphia: Lippincott, 1944), p. 202.

30. McCoy, *Calvin Coolidge*, p. 139.

31. Sullivan diary, 9 August 1923, HHL.

32. Coolidge, *Autobiography*, p. 164.

33. Ibid., p. 201; McCoy, *Calvin Coolidge*, pp. 287–88; Fuess, *Calvin Coolidge*, p. 327.

34. President's personal files no. 467, roll 9, Coolidge private papers, FL; Robert H. Ferrell, *Peace in Their Time: The Origins of the Kellogg-Briand Pact* (New Haven, Conn.: Yale University Press, 1952), p. 45.

35. Irwin H. Hoover, *Forty-two Years in the White House* (Boston: Houghton Mifflin, 1934), p. 127. The salary issue is in Joel T. Boone diary, 8 May 1927, box 40, Boone papers, LC.

36. Dennis, *Gods and Little Fishes*, pp. 128–29.

37. Lathem, *Meet Calvin Coolidge*, p. 216.

38. Fuess, *Calvin Coolidge*, p. 367.

39. Boone autobiography, chap. 21, pp. 104–5, 183–84, 326, 343–44, 544, 567, 569, 606–8, 621, 668, box 46, Boone papers, LC.

40. Ibid., chap. 21, pp. 48–51, 303.

41. To Grace Medinus, 5 October 1932, box 3, Medinus papers, FL.

42. Boone autobiography, chap. 21, p. 110.

43. Sullivan diary, 21 December 1923, HHL.

44. Hiram W. Johnson to Archibald M. and Hiram W. Johnson, Jr., 13 November 1926, in Robert E. Burke, ed., *The Diary Letters of Hiram Johnson: 1917–1945*, 7 vols. (New York: Garland, 1983), 4: n.p.; Coolidge to Stearns, 2 November 1924, president's personal files no. 58, roll 4, Coolidge private papers, FL; McCoy, *Calvin Coolidge*, p. 155.

CHAPTER 2
STATE OF THE UNION

1. The principal source for the following pages is *Historical Statistics of the United States: Colonial Times to 1970*, 2 vols. (Washington, D.C.: U.S. Government Printing Office, 1975).

2. In speaking with Sen. Charles Curtis of Kansas, Harding in 1923 referred to Coolidge as "that little fellow." *New York Times*, 9 February 1936.

3. William R. Castle, Jr., to Joseph C. Grew, 10 March 1924, "Switzerland 1922–1925," box 13, Castle papers, HHL.

4. Donald R. McCoy, *Calvin Coolidge: The Quiet President* (New York: Macmillan, 1967), p. 261; Merlo J. Pusey, *Charles Evans Hughes*, 2 vols. (New York: Macmillan, 1951), 2:613.

5. Robert H. Ferrell, *Frank B. Kellogg and Henry L. Stimson* (New York: Cooper Square, 1963), p. 7.

6. Diary, 12 January 1925, personal possession of Jan Shipps, Bloomington, Ind. (hereafter cited as S). See also Hiram W. Johnson to Archibald M. and Hiram W. Johnson, Jr., 13 January 1925, in Robert E. Burke, ed., *The Diary Letters of Hiram Johnson: 1917–1945*, 7 vols. (New York: Garland, 1983), 4:n.p.

7. Arthur M. Schlesinger, Jr., *The Crisis of the Old Order: 1919–1933* (Boston: Houghton Mifflin, 1957), p. 56.

8. Robert K. Murray, in Ellis W. Hawley, ed., *Herbert Hoover as Secretary of Commerce: Studies in New Era Thought and Practice* (Iowa City: University of Iowa Press, 1981), p. 32.

9. Bascom N. Timmons, *Portrait of an American: Charles G. Dawes* (New York: Holt, 1953), p. 247.

10. Frederick Lewis Allen, *Only Yesterday: An Informal History of the Nineteen-Twenties* (New York: Harper, 1931), p. 79.

11. Glenn A. Johnson, "Secretary of Commerce Herbert C. Hoover: The First Regulator of American Broadcasting, 1921–1928," dissertation, University of Iowa, 1970, p. 151.

12. Herbert Hoover, *Memoirs: The Cabinet and the Presidency, 1920–1933* (New York: Macmillan, 1951), p. 142.

13. Lizabeth Cohen, "Encountering Mass Culture at the Grassroots: The Experience of Chicago Workers in the 1920s," in Ronald Edsforth and Larry Bennett, eds.,

Popular Culture and Political Change in Modern America (Albany: State University of New York Press, 1991), p. 87.

14. Preston W. Slosson, *The Great Crusade and After: 1914–1928* (New York: Macmillan, 1930), pp. 365–71.

15. Ibid., p. 363; Jules Abels, *In the Time of Silent Cal* (New York: Putnam's, 1969), p. 203.

16. *Baltimore Sun*, 18 October 1920, in Malcolm Moos, ed., *A Carnival of Buncombe* (Baltimore: Johns Hopkins University Press, 1956), p. 15.

17. Slosson, *Great Crusade and After*, p. 428.

CHAPTER 3
I THOUGHT I COULD SWING IT

1. Claude M. Fuess, *Calvin Coolidge: The Man from Vermont* (Boston: Little, Brown, 1940), p. 311.

2. *Biography of an Idea: Memoirs of Public Relations Counsel Edward L. Bernays* (New York: Simon and Schuster, 1965), pp. 637–38.

3. LeRoy Ashby, *The Spearless Leader: Senator Borah and the Progressive Movement in the 1920s* (Urbana: University of Illinois Press, 1972), p. 206.

4. Sullivan diary, 10 December 1923, HHL.

5. Solomon Bulkley Griffin, *People and Politics: Observed by a Massachusetts Editor* (Boston: Little, Brown, 1923), p. 435.

6. Horace Green, *The Life of Calvin Coolidge* (New York: Duffield, 1924), pp. 191–92.

7. For these issues, see chapters 6–8.

8. Donald R. McCoy, *Calvin Coolidge: The Quiet President* (New York: Macmillan, 1967), p. 214.

9. Burl Noggle, *Teapot Dome: Oil and Politics in the 1920s* (Baton Rouge: Louisiana State University Press, 1962), p. 53.

10. Ibid., pp. 116–17.

11. James N. Giglio, *H. M. Daugherty and the Politics of Expediency* (Kent, Ohio: Kent State University Press, 1978); Robert H. Ferrell, *The Strange Deaths of President Harding* (Columbia: University of Missouri Press, 1996), pp. 121–30.

12. Boone autobiography, chap. 21, p. 145, box 46, Boone papers, LC.

13. McCoy, *Calvin Coolidge*, pp. 212–13.

14. Mary Randolph, *Presidents and First Ladies* (New York: Appleton-Century, 1936), p. 65.

15. Sullivan diary, 8 March 1924, HHL.

16. Boone autobiography, chap. 21, p. 502, box 46, Boone papers, LC.

17. Ibid., pp. 144–45.

18. Ibid., p. 1, 222, box 47; Daugherty to Boone, 5 October 1939, enclosing copy of letter to Coolidge, 17 February 1929, "Daugherty," box 29, Boone papers, LC.

19. John Hays Hammond, *Autobiography*, 2 vols. (New York: Farrar and Rinehart, 1935), 2:684–85; M. Nelson McGeary, *Gifford Pinchot: Forester-Politician* (Princeton, N.J.: Princeton University Press, 1960), pp. 306–10.

20. For Muscle Shoals, see chapters 4 and 5.

21. Preston J. Hubbard, *Origins of the TVA: The Muscle Shoals Controversy, 1920–1932* (Nashville: Vanderbilt University Press, 1961), p. 37.

22. Joe Martin, *My First Fifty Years in Politics* (New York: McGraw-Hill, 1960), p. 145.

23. Sullivan diary, 14 November 1923, HHL.

24. Ashby, *Spearless Leader,* p. 155.

25. Sullivan diary, 15 June 1924, HHL.

26. The following account is from Boone autobiography, chap. 21, pp. 177–78, box 46, Boone papers, LC.

27. Conversation of April 1925, Boone autobiography, ibid., p. 368.

28. Sullivan diary, 25 November 1923, HHL.

29. Paul R. Leach, *That Man Dawes* (Chicago: Reilly and Lee, 1930), pp. 230, 233–34.

30. Letter of 29 September 1924, president's personal files no. 33, roll 4, Coolidge private papers, FL.

CHAPTER 4
INDUSTRY AND LABOR

1. Press conference of 19 October 1926, in Howard H. Quint and Robert H. Ferrell, eds., *The Talkative President: The Off-the-Record Press Conferences of Calvin Coolidge* (Amherst: University of Massachusetts Press, 1964), p. 134.

2. David Burner, *Herbert Hoover: A Public Life* (New York: Knopf, 1979), p. 152; Sullivan diary, 16 April 1922, HHL.

3. Robert K. Murray, in Ellis W. Hawley, ed., *Herbert Hoover as Secretary of Commerce: Studies in New Era Thought and Practice* (Iowa City: University of Iowa Press, 1981), p. 21.

4. *Recent Social Trends in the United States: Report of the President's Research Committee on Social Trends,* 2 vols. (New York: McGraw-Hill, 1933), 2:882.

5. Sullivan diary, 13 April 1922, HHL.

6. Burner, *Herbert Hoover,* p. 147.

7. Murray, in Hawley, *Herbert Hoover as Secretary of Commerce,* p. 32.

8. Donald L. Winters, *Henry Cantwell Wallace as Secretary of Agriculture: 1921–1924* (Urbana: University of Illinois Press, 1970), p. 287; Homer E. Socolofsky, *Arthur Capper: Publisher, Politician, and Philanthropist* (Lawrence: University of Kansas Press, 1962), p. 154.

9. William R. Castle, Jr., to Alanson B. Houghton, 7 January 1926, "England Jan.–March 1926," box 3, Castle papers, HHL.

10. Louis Galambos, *The Public Image of Big Business in America, 1880–1940: A Quantitative Study in Social Change* (Baltimore: Johns Hopkins University Press, 1975), p. 12.

11. Ari Hoogenboom and Olive Hoogenboom, *A History of the ICC: From Panacea to Palliative* (New York: Norton, 1976), p. x.

12. Ian S. Haberman, *The Van Sweringens of Cleveland* (Cleveland: Western Reserve Historical Society, 1979), p. 153.

13. G. Cullom Davis, "The Transformation of the Federal Trade Commission," *Mississippi Valley Historical Review* 49 (December 1962): 449.

14. *Annual Report* for 1927, quoted in Thomas C. Blaisdell, Jr., *The Federal Trade Commission: An Experiment in the Control of Business* (New York: Columbia University Press, 1932), p. 93.

15. Robert K. Murray, *The 103rd Ballot: Democrats and the Disaster in Madison Square Garden* (New York: Harper and Row, 1976), p. 262.

16. Harry Barnard, *Independent Man: The Life of Senator James Couzens* (New York: Scribner, 1958), p. 178.

17. John Hays Hammond, *Autobiography,* 2 vols. (New York: Farrar and Rinehart, 1935), 2:683–84.

18. Robert H. Zieger, *Republicans and Labor: 1919–1929* (Lexington: University of Kentucky Press, 1969), p. 232.

19. Ibid., pp. 244–47.

20. Zieger, in Hawley, *Herbert Hoover as Secretary of Commerce,* pp. 83, 100.

21. Zieger, *Republicans and Labor,* p. 196.

22. Irving Bernstein, *The Lean Years: A History of the American Worker, 1920–1933* (Boston: Houghton Mifflin, 1960), pp. 195, 200–201.

23. Alpheus T. Mason, *William Howard Taft: Chief Justice* (New York: Simon and Schuster, 1965), p. 267; Bernstein, *Lean Years,* p. 191.

24. Mason, *William Howard Taft,* p. 187.

25. Bernstein, *Lean Years,* pp. 193–94.

CHAPTER 5
AGRICULTURE

1. James J. Flink, *The Car Culture* (Cambridge, Mass.: MIT Press, 1975), pp. 95–96.

2. Donald R. McCoy, *Coming of Age: The United States During the 1920s and 1930s* (Baltimore: Penguin, 1973), p. 139.

3. Gilbert C. Fite, in John Braeman, Robert H. Bremner, and David Brody, eds., *Change and Continuity in Twentieth-Century America: The 1920s* (Columbus: Ohio State University Press, 1968), pp. 81–82.

4. Donald L. Winters, *Henry Cantwell Wallace as Secretary of Agriculture: 1921–1924* (Urbana: University of Illinois Press, 1970), p. 271.

5. Press conference of 13 January, in Howard H. Quint and Robert H. Ferrell, eds., *The Talkative President: The Off-the-Record Press Conferences of Calvin Coolidge* (Amherst: University of Massachusetts Press, 1964), p. 124.

6. Joan Hoff Wilson, in Ellis W. Hawley, ed., *Herbert Hoover as Secretary of Commerce: Studies in New Era Thought and Practice* (Iowa City: University of Iowa Press, 1981), p. 120.

7. Donald R. McCoy, *Calvin Coolidge: The Quiet President* (New York: Macmillan, 1967), p. 234; Cooper to William Allen White, September 1936, in William Allen White, *A Puritan in Babylon: The Story of Calvin Coolidge* (New York: Macmillan, 1938), p. 344.

8. Hoff Wilson, in Hawley, *Herbert Hoover as Secretary of Commerce,* p. 133.

9. Gilbert C. Fite, *George N. Peek and the Fight for Farm Parity* (Norman: University of Oklahoma Press, 1954), p. 159.

10. Ibid., pp. 134–35.

11. George Soule, *Prosperity Decade: From War to Depression, 1917–1929* (New York: Rinehart, 1947), p. 250.

12. John Kennedy Ohl, *Hugh S. Johnson and the New Deal* (De Kalb: Northern Illinois University Press, 1985), p. 60.

13. Fite, *George N. Peek*, pp. 55, 101.

14. Fite, in Braeman et al., *Change and Continuity in Twentieth-Century America*, p. 92.

15. Ibid., p. 95.

16. Gilbert C. Fite, *Peter Norbeck: Prairie Statesman*, University of Missouri Studies, vol. 22, no. 2 (1948), p. 105.

17. Fite, *George N. Peek*, p. 51.

18. Ibid., pp. 83, 199.

19. Ibid., p. 175.

20. Ibid., p. 164.

21. Ibid., p. 179.

22. Peter T. Harstad and Bonnie Lindemann, *Gilbert N. Haugen: Norwegian-American Farm Politician* (Iowa City and Des Moines: State Historical Society of Iowa, 1992), p. 176.

CHAPTER 6
SOCIETY

1. Jules Abels, *In the Time of Silent Cal* (New York: Putnam's, 1969), p. 105.

2. John B. Rae, *The Road and the Car in American Life* (Cambridge, Mass.: MIT Press, 1971), p. 43.

3. James J. Flink, *The Car Culture* (Cambridge, Mass.: MIT Press, 1975), pp. 165–66.

4. Ibid., p. 162.

5. Charles N. Glaab, in John Braeman, Robert H. Bremner, and David Brody, eds., *Change and Continuity in Twentieth-Century America: The 1920s* (Columbus: Ohio State University Press, 1968), p. 404.

6. Undated letter, in Robert H. Ferrell, ed., *Dear Bess: The Letters from Harry to Bess Truman, 1910–1959* (New York: Norton, 1983), pp. 183–84.

7. John C. Burnham, "The Gasoline Tax and the Automobile Revolution," *Mississippi Valley Historical Review* 48 (December 1961): 447.

8. Ibid., 446.

9. Ronald Edsforth, *Class Conflict and Cultural Consensus: The Making of a Mass Consumer Society in Flint, Michigan* (New Brunswick, N.J.: Rutgers University Press, 1987), p. 13.

10. Mabel Walker Willebrandt, *The Inside of Prohibition* (Indianapolis: Bobbs-Merrill, 1929), p. 31.

11. Ibid., p. 135.

12. Norman H. Clark, *Deliver Us from Evil: An Interpretation of American Prohibition* (New York: Norton, 1976), p. 159.

13. Selig Adler, *The Isolationist Impulse: Its Twentieth-Century Reaction* (New York: Abelard-Schuman, 1957), p. 48.

14. A spokesman for the Federal Council of Churches suggested that "not more than one-quarter of this is sacramental—the rest is sacrilegious." Clark, *Deliver Us from Evil*, p. 159.

15. Alice Roosevelt Longworth, *Crowded Hours: Reminiscences* (New York: Scribner's, 1933), p. 324.

16. Frank O. Salisbury, *Portrait and Pageant* (London: Murray, 1944), p. 91.

17. Boone autobiography, chap. 21, p. 868, box 46, Boone papers, LC.

18. David Bryn-Jones, *Frank B. Kellogg: A Biography* (New York: Putnam's, 1937), pp. 125–26.

19. Boone oral history, 1967, by Raymond Henle, pp. 369–70, HHL.

20. William R. Castle, Jr., diary, 7 July 1926, Houghton Library, Harvard University, Cambridge, Mass. (hereafter cited as HL).

21. Sullivan diary, 7 May 1926, HHL.

22. Walter Evans Edge, *A Jerseyman's Journal: Fifty Years of American Business and Politics* (Princeton, N.J.: Princeton University Press, 1948), pp. 136–37, 142.

23. Joe Martin, *My First Fifty Years in Politics* (New York: McGraw-Hill, 1960), pp. 51–52.

24. Clark, *Deliver Us from Evil*, p. 146.

25. *Recent Social Trends in the United States: Report of the President's Research Committee on Social Trends*, 2 vols. (New York: McGraw-Hill, 1933), 1:561.

26. George Wharton Pepper, *Philadelphia Lawyer: An Autobiography* (Philadelphia: Lippincott, 1944), p. 146.

27. Martin, *My First Fifty Years in Politics*, p. 52.

28. LeRoy Ashby, *The Spearless Leader: Senator Borah and the Progressive Movement in the 1920s* (Urbana: University of Illinois Press, 1972), pp. 238, 243, 249–50.

29. Theodore Roosevelt, Jr., diary, 6 October 1923, Theodore Roosevelt, Jr., papers, LC.

30. Walter White, *A Man Called White* (New York: Viking, 1948), pp. 99–101.

31. Charles G. Dawes, *Notes as Vice President: 1928–1929* (Boston: Little, Brown, 1935), p. 23; Paul R. Leach, *That Man Dawes* (Chicago: Reilly and Lee, 1930), p. 226.

32. Paul L. Murphy, *The Constitution in Crisis Times: 1918–1969* (New York: Harper and Row, 1972), pp. 87–88.

33. Howard Zinn, *LaGuardia in Congress* (Ithaca, N.Y.: Cornell University Press, 1958), p. 90.

34. LeRoy Ashby, *William Jennings Bryan: Champion of Democracy* (Boston: Twayne, 1987), pp. 180–81.

35. Zinn, *LaGuardia in Congress*, pp. 89–90.

36. *Recent Social Trends*, 1:561; Robert A. Divine, *American Immigration Policy: 1924–1952* (New Haven, Conn.: Yale University Press, 1957), p. 52.

37. *Recent Social Trends*, 1:xx.

38. Telegram forwarded to C. Bascom Slemp, 17 July 1924, "President Coolidge 1924 May–July," box 477, commerce papers, Hoover papers, HHL.

39. Merlo J. Pusey, *Charles Evans Hughes*, 2 vols. (New York: Macmillan, 1951), 2:516.

40. Castle diary, 31 May 1924 and 25 February 1930, HL.

41. David J. Danelski and Joseph S. Tulchin, eds., *The Autobiographical Notes of Charles Evans Hughes* (Cambridge, Mass.: Harvard University Press, 1973), pp. 251–52.

42. Sidney DeVere Brown, "Shidehara Kijuro: The Diplomacy of the Yen," in Richard Dean Burns and Edward M. Bennett, eds., *Diplomats in Crisis: United States-Chinese-Japanese Relations, 1919–1941* (Santa Barbara, Calif.: ABC-CLIO, 1974), p. 204.

43. Dooman oral history, 1962, by Beate Gordon, pp. 18–19, Oral History Collection, Oral History Research Office, Butler Library, Columbia University, New York.

44. Abels, *In the Time of Silent Cal*, pp. 70–71.

45. Preston J. Hubbard, *Origins of the TVA: The Muscle Shoals Controversy, 1920–1932*, (Nashville, Tenn.: Vanderbilt University Press, 1961), p. 209.

CHAPTER 7

LATIN AMERICA

1. Joe Martin, *My First Fifty Years in Politics* (New York: McGraw-Hill, 1960), p. 49.

2. Robert H. Ferrell, *Frank B. Kellogg and Henry L. Stimson* (New York: Cooper Square, 1963), p. 292; Lorenzo Meyer, *Mexico and the United States in the Oil Controversy: 1917–1942* (Austin: University of Texas Press, 1972), p. 10.

3. Donald R. McCoy, *Calvin Coolidge: The Quiet President* (New York: Macmillan, 1967), p. 179.

4. Letter of 31 August 1923, president's personal files no. 55, roll 4, Coolidge private papers, FL.

5. Smoot diary, 11 June 1925, S.

6. Letter of 13 April 1925, president's personal files no. 613, roll 10, Coolidge private papers, FL.

7. Ferrell, *Kellogg and Stimson*, p. 31.

8. Coolidge to Sheffield, 21 April 1925, president's personal files no. 613, roll 10, Coolidge private papers, FL; Ferrell, *Kellogg and Stimson*, p. 32.

9. Richard V. Salisbury, "Mexico, the United States, and the 1926–1927 Nicaraguan Crisis," *Hispanic American Historical Review* 66 (1986): 444.

10. Ferrell, *Kellogg and Stimson*, p. 33.

11. Robert Freeman Smith, *The United States and Revolutionary Nationalism in Mexico: 1916–1932* (Chicago: University of Chicago Press, 1972), p. 238.

12. Marian C. McKenna, *Borah* (Ann Arbor: University of Michigan Press, 1961), p. 282; John Milton Cooper, "William E. Borah, Political Thespian," *Pacific Northwest Quarterly* 56 (1965): 145–58; LeRoy Ashby, *The Spearless Leader: Senator Borah and the Progressive Movement in the 1920s* (Urbana: University of Illinois Press, 1972), p. 212.

13. Ferrell, *Kellogg and Stimson*, p. 292; Castle diary, 24 March 1925, HL; Robert James Maddox, *William E. Borah and American Foreign Policy* (Baton Rouge: Louisiana State University Press, 1969), p. 176n; David Bryn-Jones, *Frank B. Kellogg: A Biography* (New York: Putnam's, 1937), p. 183.

14. Harold Nicolson, *Dwight Morrow* (New York: Harcourt, Brace, 1935), p. 310.

15. Ferrell, *Kellogg and Stimson*, pp. 38–39.

16. John Braeman, "The New Left and American Foreign Policy During the Age of Normalcy: A Re-examination," *Business History Review* 57 (spring 1983): 96–97.

17. Nicolson, *Dwight Morrow*, pp. 382–88; Ferrell, *Kellogg and Stimson*, pp. 42–43; Smith, *United States and Revolutionary Nationalism in Mexico*, pp. 260–64.

18. The leading account is William Kamman, *A Search for Stability: United States Diplomacy Toward Nicaragua, 1925–1933* (Notre Dame, Ind.: University of Notre Dame Press, 1968).

19. Dana Munro, *The United States and the Caribbean Republics: 1921–1933* (Princeton, N.J.: Princeton University Press, 1974), pp. 161, 171–72.

20. Ferrell, *Kellogg and Stimson*, pp. 48–49.

21. See Benjamin T. Harrison, *Dollar Diplomat: Chandler Anderson and American Diplomacy in Mexico and Nicaragua, 1913–1928* (Pullman: Washington State University Press, 1986).

22. Ferrell, *Kellogg and Stimson*, pp. 50–51.

23. Dispatch of 6 January 1927, 817.00/4510, Department of State records, National Archives, Washington, D.C.

24. Claude M. Fuess, "Calvin Coolidge—Twenty Years After," *Proceedings of the American Antiquarian Society* 63 (April–October, 1953): 362–63.

25. Harold Norman Denny, *Dollars for Bullets: The Story of American Rule in Nicaragua* (New York: Dial, 1929), p. 295.

26. On McCoy, see Andrew J. Bacevich, *Diplomat in Khaki: Major General Frank Ross McCoy and American Foreign Policy, 1898–1949* (Lawrence: University Press of Kansas, 1989).

27. Denny, *Dollars for Bullets*, p. 367.

28. Bacevich, *Diplomat in Khaki*, pp. 125–26.

29. Denny, *Dollars for Bullets*, p. 357.

30. Munro, *United States and the Caribbean Republics*, pp. 247–48.

31. Bacevich, *Diplomat in Khaki*, p. 130.

32. Ibid., pp. 127–30.

33. Ferrell, *Kellogg and Stimson*, p. 56.

34. Bacevich, *Diplomat in Khaki*, pp. 130–31.

35. Merlo J. Pusey, *Charles Evans Hughes*, 2 vols. (New York: Macmillan, 1951), 2:558–59.

36. Robert H. Ferrell, "Repudiation of a Repudiation," *Journal of American History* 51 (1965): 669–73; Munro, *United States and the Caribbean Republics*, p. 378.

CHAPTER 8
EUROPE AND THE FAR EAST

1. Letter of 30 November 1923, president's personal files no. 203, roll 7, Coolidge private papers, FL: Boone autobiography, chap. 21, p. 867, box 46, Boone papers, LC; B. J. C. McKercher, *Esme Howard: A Diplomatic Biography* (Cambridge, England: Cambridge University Press, 1989), p. 277.

2. William R. Castle, Jr., diary, 11 December 1923, HL.

3. Donald R. McCoy, *Calvin Coolidge: The Quiet President* (New York: Macmillan, 1967), p. 192; David Bryn-Jones, *Frank B. Kellogg: A Biography* (New York: Putnam's, 1937), pp. 154–55.

4. William C. McNeil, *American Money and the Weimar Republic: Economics and Politics on the Eve of the Great Depression* (New York: Columbia University Press, 1986), pp. 32–33.

5. Ibid., pp. 99–101.

6. Herbert Feis, *Diplomacy of the Dollar: First Era, 1919–1932* (Baltimore: Johns Hopkins University Press, 1950), pp. 11–12; McNeil, *American Money and the Weimar Republic*, pp. 45–46. See also John M. Carroll, "Owen D. Young and German Reparations: The Diplomacy of an Enlightened Businessman," in Kenneth Paul Jones, ed., *U.S. Diplomats in Europe: 1919–1941* (Santa Barbara, Calif.: ABC-CLIO, 1981), p. 51.

7. Castle diary, 20 April 1925, HL; McNeil, *American Money and the Weimar Republic*, p. 40.

8. *New York Times*, 6 January 1995.

9. Coolidge to Edward T. Clark, 14 February 1931, "Coolidge, Calvin," box 3, Clark papers, LC; Theodore Roosevelt, Jr., diary, 5 October 1923, Theodore Roosevelt, Jr., papers, LC; Milton F. Heller, Jr., ed., "When 'Silent Cal' Used Cocaine," *The Real Calvin Coolidge*, no. 6 (1988): 26–28.

10. Boone diary, 18 April 1927, box 40, Boone papers, LC.

11. See Harding to Henry P. Fletcher, "Special Corres.—Warren G. Harding 1922–1923," box 1, Fletcher papers, LC.

12. Sullivan diary, 3 August 1922, HHL.

13. Memorandum on the World Court dictated 9, 11 August 1923, Theodore Roosevelt, Jr., diary, Theodore Roosevelt, Jr., papers, LC.

14. William R. Castle, Jr., diary, 25 September 1923, HL.

15. Theodore Roosevelt, Jr., diary, 6 August, 2 October 1923, Theodore Roosevelt, Jr., papers, LC.

16. Ibid., 29 November.

17. George Wharton Pepper, *Philadelphia Lawyer: An Autobiography* (Philadelphia: Lippincott, 1944), pp. 175–76.

18. Merlo J. Pusey, *Charles Evans Hughes*, 2 vols. (New York: Macmillan, 1951), 2:602–3.

19. Press conference of 3 September 1926, in Howard H. Quint and Robert H. Ferrell, eds., *The Talkative President: The Off-the-Record Press Conferences of Calvin Coolidge* (Amherst: University of Massachusetts Press, 1964), p. 211.

20. See Robert H. Ferrell, *Peace in Their Time: The Origins of the Kellogg-Brand Pact* (New Haven, Conn.: Yale University Press, 1952), and other titles in the bibliographical essay.

21. Warren I. Cohen, *Empire Without Tears: America's Foreign Relations, 1921–1933* (Philadelphia: Temple University Press, 1987), p. 32; Warren I. Cohen, *The Chinese Connection: Roger S. Greene, Thomas W. Lamont, George E. Sokolsky and American-East Asian Relations* (New York: Columbia University Press, 1978), pp. 97–98.

22. Bernard D. Cole, *Gunboats and Marines: The United States Navy in China, 1925–1928* (Newark: University of Delaware Press, 1983), p. 113.

23. Thomas H. Buckley, "John Van Antwerp MacMurray: The Diplomacy of an American Mandarin," in Richard Dean Burns and Edward M. Bennett, eds., *Diplomats in Crisis: United States–Chinese–Japanese Relations, 1919–1941* (Santa Barbara, Calif.: ABC-CLIO, 1974), p. 30; Russell D. Buhite, *Nelson T. Johnson and American Policy Toward China: 1925–1941* (East Lansing: Michigan State University Press, 1968).

24. Kellogg to Alanson Houghton, 2 May 1927, Kellogg papers, Minnesota State Historical Society, St. Paul.

25. Sidney DeVere Brown, "Shidehara Kijuro: The Diplomacy of the Yen," in Burns and Bennett, *Diplomats in Crisis*, p. 207.

CHAPTER 9
COOLIDGE PROSPERITY

1. Press conference of 4 October 1927, in Howard H. Quint and Robert H. Ferrell, eds., *The Talkative President: The Off-the-Record Press Conferences of Calvin Coolidge* (Amherst: University of Massachusetts Press, 1964), p. 108.

2. 19 November 1926, ibid., p. 107.

3. Ellis W. Hawley, in Ellis W. Hawley, ed., *Herbert Hoover as Secretary of Commerce: Studies in New Era Thought and Practice* (Iowa City: University of Iowa Press, 1981), p. 20.

4. George Wharton Pepper, *Philadelphia Lawyer: An Autobiography* (Philadelphia: Lippincott, 1944), p. 196.

5. Sullivan diary, undated [March 1924], HHL.

6. Quoted in Benjamin G. Rader, "Federal Taxation in the 1920s: A Reexamination," *Historian* 33 (1971): 433.

7. Howard Zinn, *LaGuardia in Congress* (Ithaca, N.Y.: Cornell University Press, 1958), pp. 153–54.

8. Ibid., pp. 156–57, 161.

9. For the following account, see Harry Barnard, *Independent Man: The Life of Senator James Couzens* (New York: Scribner, 1958), pp. 162–67.

10. Thomas B. Silver, *Coolidge and the Historians* (Durham, N.C.: Carolina Academic Press, 1982), pp. 112–19.

11. Jules Abels, *In the Time of Silent Cal* (New York: Putnam's 1969), pp. 217, 219; Edgar Rickard diary, 26 March 1925, HHL.

12. Elizabeth Kimball MacLean, *Joseph E. Davies: Envoy to the Soviets* (Westport, Conn.: Praeger, 1992), p. 16.

13. James Grant, *Money of the Mind: Borrowing and Lending in America from the Civil War to Michael Milken* (New York: Farrar Straus Giraux, 1992), pp. 184–85.

14. Elmus R. Wicker, *Federal Reserve Monetary Policy: 1917–1933* (New York: Random House, 1966), p. 47.

15. Grant, *Money of the Mind*, p. 192.

16. "Confidential Memoranda," box 1, Goldenweiser papers, LC.

17. Lester V. Chandler, *American Monetary Policy: 1928–1941* (New York: Harper and Row, 1971), p. 47.

18. *New York Times*, 7 February 1929.

19. Memorandum by Harrison, 11 February 1929, "Young, Roy A. 1929," box 3, Federal Reserve Bank of New York papers, HHL.

20. Robert Sobel, *The Great Bull Market: Wall Street in the 1920s* (New York: Norton, 1968), p. 118.

21. "Confidential Memoranda," box 1, Goldenweiser papers, LC.

22. Abels, *In the Time of Silent Cal*, p. 262; Sullivan diary, 2 August 1923, HHL.

23. James J. Flink, *The Car Culture* (Cambridge, Mass.: MIT Press, 1975), p. 171.

24. Grant, *Money of the Mind*, p. 162.

25. Press conference of 12 January 1926, in Quint and Ferrell, *Talkative President*, pp. 128–29.

26. Sullivan diary, 24 September, 2 December 1923, HHL.

27. *Recent Economic Changes in the United States*, 2 vols. (New York: McGraw-Hill, 1929), 1:xxi; *Recent Social Trends in the United States: Report of the President's Research Committee on Social Trends*, 2 vols. (New York: McGraw-Hill, 1933), 1:xiii.

28. Grant, *Money of the Mind*, pp. 163, 167.

29. Hugh Bullock, *The Story of Investment Companies* (New York: Columbia University Press, 1959), p. 27.

30. *Recent Social Trends*, 1:247.

31. William Z. Ripley, "From Main Street to Wall Street," *Atlantic Monthly* 137 (January–June 1926): 105-6.

32. Quint and Ferrell, *Talkative President*, pp. 130–34.

33. John Kenneth Galbraith, *The Great Crash: 1929* (Boston: Houghton Mifflin, 1955), p. 52.

34. Sobel, *Great Bull Market*, pp. 64, 86, 116–17, 135, 152.

35. Donald R. McCoy, *Calvin Coolidge: The Quiet President* (New York: Macmillan, 1967), pp. 319–21; Claude M. Fuess, *Calvin Coolidge: The Man from Vermont* (Boston: Little, Brown, 1940), pp. 433–34.

36. Quint and Ferrell, *Talkative President*, pp. 137–38.

CHAPTER 10
RETIREMENT

1. Donald R. McCoy, *Calvin Coolidge: The Quiet President* (New York: Macmillan, 1967), p. 384; Richard Norton Smith, "Calvin Coolidge: The Twilight Years," *The Real Calvin Coolidge*, no. 4 (1986): 20.

2. Edmund W. Starling and Thomas Sugrue, *Starling of the White House* (New York: Simon and Schuster, 1946), p. 259; Alben W. Barkley, *That Reminds Me* (Garden City, N.Y.: Doubleday, 1954), p. 133.

3. Edward Connery Lathem, ed., *Your Son, Calvin Coolidge: A Selection of Letters from Calvin Coolidge to His Father* (Montpelier: Vermont Historical Society, 1968), pp. 194–95. The letter is dated 23 October, and the president's son had died not long before. Starling and Sugrue, *Starling of the White House*, pp. 248–49; Coolidge to Sanders, 6 May 1929, "Calvin Coolidge," box 1, Sanders papers, LC.

4. Boone autobiography, chap. 21, p. 1057c, box 46, Boone papers, LC; Joe Martin, *My First Fifty Years in Politics* (New York: McGraw-Hill, 1960), p. 146; Irwin H. Hoover, *Forty-two Years in the White House* (Boston: Houghton Mifflin, 1934), pp. 167–75.

5. Smoot diary, 23 April, 20 October 1927, 31 May, 7 June 1928, S.

6. Walter Evans Edge, *A Jerseyman's Journal: Fifty Years of American Business and Politics* (Princeton, N.J.: Princeton University Press, 1948), pp. 143–44.

7. Robert J. Rusnak, "Andrew W. Mellon: Reluctant Kingmaker," *Presidential Studies Quarterly* 13 (1983): 275; William Allen White, *A Puritan in Babylon: The Story of Calvin Coolidge* (New York; Macmillan, 1938), p. 400.

8. Rickard diary, 7 June 1928, HHL; see also 9 June 1928, 14 April 1929.

9. Smoot diary, 15 June 1928, S.

10. Ibid., 20 June 1928.

11. Boone oral history, by Raymond Henle, pp. 113–14, HHL; Boone autobiography, chap. 21, pp. 999ff, box 46, Boone papers, LC.

12. Letter of 24 July 1928, president's personal files no. 58, roll 4, Coolidge private papers, FL.

13. Starling and Sugrue, *Starling of the White House*, pp. 268–69.

14. Boone oral history, by Raymond Henle, p. 143, HHL.

15. To Grace Medinus, 21 April 1930, box 2, Medinus papers, FL.

16. Ralph W. Hemenway and Grace Coolidge, in "The Real Calvin Coolidge," *Good Housekeeping* 100 (April 1935).

17. Claude M. Fuess, *Calvin Coolidge: The Man from Vermont* (Boston: Little, Brown, 1940), p. 457n.

18. Coolidge to Sanders, 28 November 1929, "Calvin Coolidge," box 1, Sanders papers, LC.

19. Calvin Coolidge, *Autobiography* (New York: Cosmpolitan, 1929), pp. 6, 124, 162, 187.

20. Coolidge to Sanders, 20, 22 July 1929, "Calvin Coolidge," box 1, Sanders papers, LC; he wrote similarly to Clark.

21. Coolidge to Edward T. Clark, 25 January 1932, "Coolidge, Calvin," box 3, Clark papers, LC.

22. White, *Puritan in Babylon*, p. 366; White attributed the story to Fuess, but Fuess did not use it in his book published two years later.

23. Stoddard, in Edward Connery Lathem, ed., *Meet Calvin Coolidge: The Man Behind the Myth* (Brattleboro, Vt.: Stephen Greene, 1960), pp. 213–14.

24. McCoy, *Calvin Coolidge*, p. 453.

BIBLIOGRAPHICAL ESSAY

Sources for the era of President Calvin Coolidge are extraordinarily rich. The period of Coolidge's presidency may have seemed a quiet time following World War I and the vicissitudes of conversion to peacetime concerns. It marked a few economic ups and downs but contained nothing equal to the sharp recession, virtually a depression, in 1920–21. Economically, the country encountered boom times, production rising by 25 percent. That rise was itself a markedly interesting story, about which many books and articles have been written. Socially, it was the "golden twenties," which again inspired a large literature. And in government, the principal concern of the present volume, Coolidge and his assistants may have seemed low-key participants in political problems, but they were complicated individuals, many of them skilled political leaders, and their lives and activities have attracted writers of books and articles.

For the Coolidge era in the American presidency, the raw materials are concentrated in the Library of Congress in Washington, the Herbert Hoover Library in West Branch, Iowa, and the new annex to the National Archives known as Archives II in College Park, Maryland. The Coolidge presidential papers in the manuscript division of the Library of Congress are available on microfilm in large public or university libraries. See John E. Haynes, "The Calvin Coolidge Papers at the Library of Congress," *The Real Calvin Coolidge,* no. 8 (1990): 17–26. Coolidge's presidential letters are, for the most part, uninteresting; the president was accustomed to giving directions to secretaries by annotating his mail, after which the secretaries filled out the letters. A better collection of presidential letters is in Forbes Library, the public library of Northampton, Massachusetts. This is his more private correspondence, sequestered at the end of Coolidge's administration and sent to the ancestral house in Plymouth Notch, where for many years the letters were stored in the attic and some of them nibbled by mice. The president's son, John Coolidge, gave them to the library in 1983–84, and they are available on microfilm; see Lawrence E. Wikander, ed., *A Guide to the Personal Files of President Calvin Coolidge* (Northampton, Mass.: Forbes Library, 1986). The library has prepresidential letters, including those of Coolidge's governorship, listed in Kerry W. Buckley, comp., *Guide to the Microfilm Edition of the Calvin Coolidge Papers Contained in the Coolidge Collection of the Forbes Library, Northampton, Massachusetts* (Northampton, Mass.: Forbes Library, 1993).

The Herbert Hoover Library has collected manuscript material relating to Hoover's years as secretary of commerce; see Dale C. Mayer and Dwight M. Miller, comps., *Historical Materials in the Herbert Hoover Presidential Library* (West Branch, Iowa: Herbert Hoover Presidential Library, 1996). Papers of cabinet departments and independent agencies are in Archives II; see *Guide to Federal Records in the National Archives of the United States,* 3 vols. (Washington, D.C.: National Archives and Records Administration, 1995). The Department of State has published many of its documents in *Foreign Relations of the United States* (Washington, D.C.: U.S. Government Printing Office, 1861–); unlike more recent volumes in the series, those for the 1920s do not include documents from other cabinet departments or independent agencies.

There is no published collection of Coolidge's public papers—messages, speeches, statements—akin to collections of presidents Hoover through William J. Clinton. Presidential messages appear in the *Congressional Record*. Speeches often appeared in the *New York Times;* reading copies are in the Coolidge Collection at Forbes Library. Presidential statements must be searched out in contemporary newspapers.

For its special subject, see *Historical Statistics of the United States: Colonial Times to 1970,* 2 vols. (Washington, D.C.: U.S. Government Printing Office, 1975).

The literature about Coolidge the man is large. The best place to start is the president's *Autobiography* (New York: Cosmopolitan, 1929), an eloquent little book that is poignant about the president's early years, and on the diplomatic side for the presidency. It has few if any peers as a presidential autobiography—despite contemporary criticism that its author obtained $5 per word and filled the book with "a's" and "the's." For Coolidge's youth, see Hendrik Booraem V, *The Provincial: Calvin Coolidge and His World, 1885–1895* (Lewisburg, Pa.: Bucknell University Press, 1994). A notable collection is Edward Connery Lathem, *Your Son, Calvin Coolidge: A Selection of Letters from Calvin Coolidge to His Father* (Montpelier: Vermont Historical Society, 1968). John L. Blair has covered "The Governorship of Calvin Coolidge: 1919–1921," dissertation, University of Chicago, 1971. The two best biographies are Claude M. Fuess, *Calvin Coolidge: The Man from Vermont* (Boston: Little, Brown, 1940), supplemented by Fuess's "Calvin Coolidge—Twenty Years After," *Proceedings of the American Antiquarian Society* 63 (April–October 1963): 351–69; and Donald R. McCoy, *Calvin Coolidge: The Quiet President* (New York: Macmillan, 1967; reprinted, with new preface, Lawrence: University Press of Kansas, 1988). Fuess's volume is reliable and nicely written. The McCoy book contains scholarship since the appearance of the Fuess book, especially on the presidency. The book by William Allen White, *A Puritan in Babylon: The Story of Calvin Coolidge* (New York: Macmillan, 1938), is not very good, despite the attention it received. White was slapdash and emotional, and considering the real nature of the 1920s, his drawing of the country as Babylonian constituted a wild overstatement; nor, for that matter, was Coolidge any sort of Puritan. It was, of course, impossible for any of these biographers to use the remarkable Joel T. Boone papers, opened in the Library of Congress in 1994. Assistant physician to the president and his wife and sons, Boone knew the family; his unpublished autobiography, deposited with his papers, contains one thousand typescript pages on the Coolidge years alone.

For an understanding of President Coolidge, see also Edmund W. Starling and Thomas Sugrue, *Starling of the White House* (New York: Simon and Schuster, 1946), by the chief of the secret service's presidential detail. Newspaperman Mark Sullivan kept a diary during the early 1920s; the original is in the Hoover Institution in Stanford, California, and a copy is in the Herbert Hoover Library. It contains interesting information about Coolidge's early presidency, when Sullivan and other reporters, knowing almost nothing about the former vice president of the United States, were scrambling to learn what they could. Retrospective appraisals by administration officials and friends, introduced by Grace Coolidge, appear in "The Real Calvin Coolidge," five articles in *Good Housekeeping* 100 (February–June 1935). A selection of articles is in Edward Connery Lathem, ed., *Meet Calvin Coolidge: The Man Behind the Myth* (Brattleboro, Vt.: Stephen Greene, 1960). Articles and documents are in booklets entitled *The Real Calvin Coolidge* (Plymouth Notch, Vt.: Calvin Coolidge Memorial Foundation, 1983–); twelve have appeared as of the present writing (1998). See also Edward Connery Lathem, ed., *Calvin Coolidge: Cartoons of His Presidential Years* (Plymouth Notch, Vt.: Calvin Coolidge Memorial Foundation, 1973).

For Grace Coolidge, see Mary Randolph, *Presidents and First Ladies* (New York: Appleton-Century, 1936); Ishbel Ross, *Grace Coolidge and Her Era* (New York: Dodd, Mead, 1962); and Lawrence E. Wikander and Robert H. Ferrell, eds., *Grace Coolidge: An Autobiography* (Worland, Wyo.: High Plains, 1992).

General accounts of the 1920s are Arthur M. Schlesinger, Jr., *The Crisis of the Old Order: 1919–1933* (Boston: Houghton Mifflin, 1957); William E. Leuchtenburg, *The Perils of Prosperity: 1914–32* (Chicago: University of Chicago Press, 1958); John D. Hicks, *Republican Ascendancy: 1921–1933* (New York: Harper, 1960); Jules Abels, *In the Time of Silent Cal* (New York: Putnam's, 1969); and Donald R. McCoy, *Coming of Age: The United States During the 1920s and 1930s* (Baltimore: Penguin, 1973). Most of the general accounts are critical of Coolidge, and a feisty defense is Thomas B. Silver, *Coolidge and the Historians* (Durham, N.C.: Carolina Academic Press, 1982).

On the issue of progressive politics, lively during the Coolidge era, there are many books and articles, but see Kenneth Campbell MacKay, *The Progressive Movement of 1924* (New York: Columbia University Press, 1947); Arthur S. Link, "What Happened to the Progressive Movement in the 1920's," *American Historical Review* 64 (1959): 833–51; Stuart I. Rochester, *American Liberal Disillusionment in the Wake of World War I* (University Park: Pennsylvania State University Press, 1977); Eugene M. Tobin, *Organize or Perish: America's Independent Progressives, 1913–1933* (New York: Greenwood, 1986); Neil V. Salzman, *Reform and Revolution: The Life and Times of Raymond Robins* (Kent, Ohio: Kent State University Press, 1991).

For presidential elections, see David Burner, *The Politics of Provincialism: The Democratic Party in Transition, 1918–1932* (New York: Knopf, 1968); Robert K. Murray, *The 103rd Ballot: Democrats and the Disaster in Madison Square Garden* (New York:

Harper and Row, 1976); J. Leonard Bates, "The Teapot Dome Scandal and the Election of 1924," *American Historical Review* 60 (1954–55): 303–22; William H. Harbaugh, *Lawyer's Lawyer: The Life of John W. Davis* (New York: Oxford University Press, 1973); Edmund A. Moore, *A Catholic Runs for President: The Campaign of 1928* (New York: Ronald, 1956); Allen J. Lichtman, *Prejudice and the Old Politics: The Presidential Election of 1928* (Chapel Hill: University of North Carolina Press, 1979); Donn C. Neal, *The World Beyond the Hudson: Alfred E. Smith and National Politics, 1918–1928* (New York: Garland, 1983).

The rule of Coolidge press conferences was that reporters never attributed presidential commentaries to their source but to "the White House spokesman." Coolidge kept a stenographer in the room who took down verbatim accounts, and in 1929, a wooden box of transcriptions went to Forbes Library. In 1951, librarian Lawrence Wikander brought the box down from the library attic and opened it for me. See Howard H. Quint and Robert H. Ferrell, eds., *The Talkative President: The Off-the-record Press Conferences of Calvin Coolidge* (Amherst: University of Massachusetts Press, 1964). Ira R. T. Smith, *"Dear Mr. President . . ." The Story of Fifty Years in the White House Mail Room* (New York: Messner, 1949) has interesting material on the Coolidge years by the man whose initials caused Coolidge to describe him as "Rapid Transit" Smith.

Prominent among officials of the Coolidge administration was Charles G. Dawes, vice president in 1925–29; see his *Notes as Vice President: 1928–1929* (Boston: Little, Brown, 1935). There is no good biography of the colorful Chicagoan. For the Department of State, see Merlo J. Pusey, *Charles Evans Hughes,* 2 vols. (New York: Macmillan, 1951); Dexter Perkins, *Charles Evans Hughes and American Democratic Statesmanship* (Boston: Little, Brown, 1956); David J. Danelski and Joseph S. Tulchin, eds., *The Autobiographical Notes of Charles Evans Hughes* (Cambridge, Mass.: Harvard University Press, 1973); L. Ethan Ellis, *Frank B. Kellogg and American Foreign Relations: 1925–1929* (New Brunswick, N.J.: Rutgers University Press, 1961); Robert H. Ferrell, *Frank B. Kellogg and Henry L. Stimson* (New York: Cooper Square, 1963). Agriculture appears in Donald L. Winters, *Henry Cantwell Wallace as Secretary of Agriculture: 1921–1924* (Urbana: University of Illinois Press, 1970). Commerce is in Herbert Hoover, *Memoirs: The Cabinet and the Presidency, 1920–1933* (New York: Macmillan, 1951); Joan Hoff Wilson, *Herbert Hoover: Forgotten Progressive* (Boston: Little, Brown, 1975); David Burner, *Herbert Hoover: A Public Life* (New York: Knopf, 1979). Papers of Coolidge cabinet members are available in various depositories. Those of Secretary Mellon are presumably still held by the family. Robert J. Rusnak, "Andrew W. Mellon: Reluctant Kingmaker," *Presidential Studies Quarterly* 13 (1983): 269–78, used Mellon papers obtained by the biographer Burton J. Hendrick, including a diary; the article is about the Republican convention in Kansas City, Missouri, in 1928.

Congress in the 1920s offers an embarrassment of riches, especially for the Senate. The leading senator was Borah, for whom see Robert James Maddox, *William E. Borah and American Foreign Policy* (Baton Rouge: Louisiana State University Press, 1969); Marian McKenna, *Borah* (Ann Arbor: University of Michigan Press, 1961); John Milton Cooper, "William E. Borah, Political Thespian," *Pacific Northwest Quarterly* 56 (1965): 145–58; LeRoy Ashby, *The Spearless Leader: Senator Borah and the Pro-*

gressive Movement in the 1920s (Urbana: University of Illinois Press, 1972). Coolidge's first majority leader was Henry Cabot Lodge, for whom see John A. Garraty, *Henry Cabot Lodge: A Biography* (New York: Knopf, 1953). Upon Lodge's death in 1924, the post went to Charles Curtis, who left very few papers; see James C. Malin, "Charles Curtis," *Dictionary of American Biography, Supplement 2* (New York: Scribner's, 1958), pp. 136–37. For other senators, see George F. Sparks, ed., *A Many-Colored Toga: The Diary of Henry Fountain Ashurst* (Tucson: University of Arizona Press, 1962); Alben W. Barkley, *That Reminds Me* (Garden City, N.Y.: Doubleday, 1954); George W. McDaniel, *Smith Wildman Brookhart: Iowa's Renegade Republican* (Ames: Iowa State University Press, 1995); Homer E. Socolofsky, *Arthur Capper: Publisher, Politician, and Philanthropist* (Lawrence: University Press of Kansas, 1962); Harry Barnard, *Independent Man: The Life of Senator James Couzens* (New York: Scribner, 1958); Richard L. Lowitt, *Bronson M. Cutting: Progressive Politician* (Albuquerque: University of New Mexico Press, 1992); Clarence C. Dill, *Where Water Falls* (Spokane: privately printed, 1970); Walter Evans Edge, *A Jerseyman's Journal: Fifty Years of American Business and Politics* (Princeton, N.J.: Princeton University Press, 1948); Robert E. Burke, ed., *The Diary Letters of Hiram Johnson: 1917–1945*, 7 vols. (New York: Garland, 1983); Richard Coke Lower, *A Bloc of One: The Political Career of Hiram W. Johnson* (Stanford, Calif.: Stanford University Press, 1993); Frances Parkinson Keyes, *All Flags Flying* (New York: McGraw-Hill, 1972), by the wife of Henry W. Keyes of New Hampshire; Fola La Follette and Belle C. La Follette, *Robert M. La Follette* (New York: Macmillan, 1953); Patrick J. Maney, *"Young Bob" La Follette: A Biography of Robert M. La Follette, Jr., 1895–1952* (Columbia: University of Missouri Press, 1978); Herbert F. Margulies, *Senator Lenroot of Wisconsin: A Political Biography, 1900–1929* (Columbia: University of Missouri Press, 1977); Steve Neal, *McNary of Oregon: A Political Biography* (Portland: Oregon Historical Society, 1985); Gilbert C. Fite, *Peter Norbeck: Prairie Statesman*, vol. 22 (1948), University of Missouri Studies; Richard L. Lowitt, *George W. Norris: The Persistence of a Progressive, 1913–1933* (Urbana: University of Illinois Press, 1971); George Wharton Pepper, *In the Senate* (Philadelphia: University of Pennsylvania Press, 1930), and the same author's *Philadelphia Lawyer: An Autobiography* (Philadelphia: Lippincott, 1944); Fred L. Israel, *Nevada's Key Pittman* (Lincoln: University of Nebraska Press, 1963); Betty Glad, *Key Pittman: The Tragedy of a Senate Insider* (New York: Columbia University Press, 1986); Milton R. Merrill, *Reed Smoot: Apostle in Politics* (Logan: Utah State University Press, 1990), an unrevised Columbia University dissertation of 1950 that needs supplementing with the Smoot diary, in possession of Jan Shipps, Bloomington, Indiana; James E. Watson, *As I Knew Them* (Indianapolis: Bobbs-Merrill, 1936); Burton K. Wheeler, *Yankee from the West* (Garden City, N.Y.: Doubleday, 1962).

Members of the House appear in Sol Bloom, *Autobiography* (New York: Putnam's, 1948); Vera Bloom, *There's No Place Like Washington* (New York: Putnam's, 1944), by the representative's daughter; Cyrenus Cole, *I Remember, I Remember: A Book of Recollections* (Iowa City: State Historical Society, 1936); Robert Paul Browder and Thomas G. Smith, *Independent: A Biography of Lewis W. Douglas* (New York: Knopf, 1986); Peter T. Harstad and Bonnie Lindemann, *Gilbert N. Haugen: Norwegian-American Farm Politician* (Iowa City and Des Moines: State Historical Society of Iowa,

1992); Cordell Hull, *Memoirs*, 2 vols. (New York: Macmillan, 1948); Howard Zinn, *LaGuardia in Congress* (Ithaca, N.Y.: Cornell University Press, 1958); Thomas Kessner, *Fiorello H. LaGuardia and the Making of Modern New York* (New York: McGraw-Hill, 1989); Alice Roosevelt Longworth, *Crowded Hours: Reminiscences* (New York: Scribner's, 1933), wife of Speaker Nicholas Longworth; Joe Martin, *My First Fifty Years in Politics* (New York: McGraw-Hill, 1960); Robert A. Waller, *Rainey of Illinois: A Political Biography, 1903–34* (Urbana: University of Illinois Press, 1977).

The Supreme Court appears in the general volume by Paul L. Murphy, *The Constitution in Crisis Times: 1918–1969* (New York: Harper and Row, 1972). Individual justices are in Melvin I. Urofsky, *Louis D. Brandeis and the Progressive Tradition* (Boston: Little, Brown, 1981); Philippa Strum, *Louis D. Brandeis: Justice for the People* (Cambridge, Mass.: Harvard University Press, 1984); Liva Baker, *The Justice from Beacon Hill: The Life and Times of Oliver Wendell Holmes* (New York: HarperCollins, 1991); G. Edward White, *Justice Oliver Wendell Holmes: Law and the Inner Self* (New York: Oxford University Press, 1993); Alpheus T. Mason, *Harlan Fiske Stone: Pillar of the Law* (New York: Viking, 1956); Henry F. Pringle, *The Life and Times of William Howard Taft*, 2 vols. (New York: Farrar and Rinehart, 1939); Alpheus T. Mason, *William Howard Taft: Chief Justice* (New York: Simon and Schuster, 1965).

The centerpiece of concern by the Coolidge administration was the economy, and the best place to begin is *Recent Economic Changes in the United States*, 2 vols. (New York: McGraw-Hill, 1929), a government-sponsored study. Later scholarship appears in George Soule, *Prosperity Decade: From War to Depression, 1917–1929* (New York: Rinehart, 1947). See also Louis Galambos, *The Public Image of Big Business in America, 1880–1940: A Quantitative Study in Social Change* (Baltimore: Johns Hopkins University Press, 1975); and the volume by the same author and Joseph Pratt, *The Rise of the Corporate Commonwealth: U.S. Business and Public Policy in the Twentieth Century* (New York: Basic Books, 1988). For the Coolidge era, in which Secretary of Commerce Hoover often spoke of a more human, cooperative, and social economy, see Ellis W. Hawley, *The Great War and the Search for a Modern Order: A History of the American People and Their Institutions* (New York: St. Martin's Press, 1979); and his edited volume, *Herbert Hoover as Secretary of Commerce: Studies in New Era Thought and Practice* (Iowa City: University of Iowa Press, 1981). An earlier study, before the Herbert Hoover Library opened, was Joseph Brandes, *Herbert Hoover and Economic Diplomacy: Department of Commerce Policy, 1921–1928* (Pittsburgh, Pa.: University of Pittsburgh Press, 1962). See also Peri Ethan Arnold, "Herbert Hoover and the Department of Commerce: A Study of Ideology and Policy," dissertation, University of Chicago, 1972; William J. Barber, *From New Era to New Deal: Herbert Hoover, the Economists, and American Economic Policy, 1921–1933* (New York: Cambridge University Press, 1976).

Regulatory agencies are in Ari Hoogenboom and Olive Hoogenboom, *A History of the ICC: From Panacea to Palliative* (New York: Norton, 1976); Alfred E. Eckes, Jr., *Opening of America's Market; U.S. Foreign Trade Policy Since 1776* (Chapel Hill: University of North Carolina Press, 1995); Fred Greenbaum, *Fighting Progressive: A Biography of Edward P. Costigan* (Washington, D.C.: Public Affairs Press, 1971); J. Richard Snyder, *William S. Culbertson: In Search of a Rendezvous* (Washington, D.C.: University Press of America, 1980); Thomas C. Blaisdell, Jr., *The Federal Trade Commission: An Experiment in the Control of Business* (New York: Columbia University Press, 1932); G. Cullom Davis, "The Transformation of the Federal Trade Commission, 1914–1929," *Mississippi Valley Historical Review* 49 (December 1962): 437–55. Radio appears in Glenn A. Johnson, "Secretary of Commerce Herbert C. Hoover: The First Regulator of American Broadcasting, 1921–1928," dissertation, University of Iowa, 1970.

For labor issues, see Irving Bernstein, *The Lean Years: A History of the American Worker, 1920–1933* (Boston: Houghton Mifflin, 1960); Robert H. Zieger, *Republicans and Labor: 1919–1929* (Lexington: University of Kentucky Press, 1969), and the same author's *John L. Lewis: Labor Leader* (Boston: Twayne, 1986).

Agriculture is in Theodore Saloutos and John D. Hicks, *Agricultural Discontent in the Middle West: 1900–1939* (Madison: University of Wisconsin Press, 1951); Don S. Kirschner, *City and Country: Rural Responses to Urbanization in the 1920s* (Westport, Conn.: Greenwood, 1970); Gilbert C. Fite, *George N. Peek and the Fight for Farm Parity* (Norman: University of Oklahoma Press, 1954); John Kennedy Ohl, *Hugh S. Johnson and the New Deal* (De Kalb: Northern Illinois University Press, 1985); Gary H. Koerselman, "Herbert Hoover and the Farm Crisis of the Twenties: A Study of the Commerce Department's Efforts to Solve the Agricultural Depression, 1921–1928," dissertation, Northern Illinois University, 1971.

The federal government's interest in social problems is in *Recent Social Trends in the United States: Report of the President's Research Committee on Social Trends*, 2 vols. (New York: McGraw-Hill, 1933), sponsored by Secretary Hoover. See also John Braeman, Robert H. Bremner, and David Brody, eds., *Change and Continuity in Twentieth-Century America: The 1920s* (Columbus: Ohio State University Press, 1968); Paul A. Carter, *The Twenties in America* (New York: Crowell, 1968), the same author's *Another Part of the Twenties* (New York: Columbia University Press, 1977), and his edited *The Uncertain World of Normalcy: The 1920s* (New York: Pitman, 1971); Robert S. Lynd and Helen M. Lynd, *Middletown: A Study in Contemporary American Culture* (New York: Harcourt, Brace, 1929); Ronald Edsforth, *Class Conflict and Cultural Consensus: The Making of a Mass Consumer Society in Flint, Michigan* (New Brunswick, N.J.: Rutgers University Press, 1987); *Report of the American Committee on Highway Transport* (Washington, D.C.: National Chamber of Commerce, 1925); Frederick L. Paxson, "The American Highway Movement, 1916–1935," *American Historical Review* 51 (1945–46): 236–53; John C. Burnham, "The Gasoline Tax and the Automobile Revolution," *Mississippi Valley Historical Review* 48 (December, 1961): 435–59; John B. Rae, *The Road and the Car in American Life* (Cambridge, Mass.: MIT Press, 1971); James J. Flink, *The Car Culture* (Cambridge, Mass.: MIT Press, 1975), the same author's *The Automobile Age* (Cambridge, Mass.: MIT Press, 1988); Mabel Walker Willebrandt, *The Inside of Prohibition* (Indianapolis: Bobbs-Merrill, 1929); Norman H. Clark, *Deliver Us from Evil: An Interpretation of American Prohibition* (New York: Norton, 1976); Walter White, *A Man Called White* (New York: Viking, 1948); Robert A. Divine, *American Immigration Policy: 1924–1952* (New Haven, Conn.: Yale University Press, 1957); Preston J. Hubbard, *Origins of the TVA: The Muscle Shoals Controversy, 1920–1932* (Nashville, Tenn.: Vanderbilt University Press, 1961); Bruce Alan Lohof, "Hoover and the Mississippi Valley Flood of 1927: A Case Study of the Political Thought of Herbert Hoover," dissertation, Syracuse University, 1968; John M.

Barry, *The Great Mississippi Flood of 1927 and How It Changed America* (New York: Simon and Schuster, 1997).

Foreign policy during the Coolidge years is in Allan Nevins, *The United States in a Chaotic World: 1918–1933* (New Haven, Conn.: Yale University Press, 1950); L. Ethan Ellis, *Republican Foreign Policy: 1921–1933* (New Brunswick, N.J.: Rutgers University Press, 1968); Selig Adler, *The Uncertain Giant: 1921–1941* (New York: Macmillan, 1985); Warren I. Cohen, *Empire Without Tears: America's Foreign Relations, 1921–1933* (Philadelphia: Temple University Press, 1987); Alexander DeConde, ed., *Isolation and Security* (Durham, N.C.: Duke University Press, 1957); Selig Adler, *The Isolationist Impulse: Its Twentieth-Century Reaction* (New York: Abelard-Schuman, 1957); Roland N. Stromberg, *Collective Security and American Foreign Policy: From the League of Nations to NATO* (New York: Praeger, 1963); Thomas N. Guinsburg, *The Pursuit of Isolationism in the United States Senate from Versailles to Pearl Harbor* (New York: Garland, 1982); John K. Nelson, *The Peace Prophets: American Pacifist Thought, 1919–1941* (Chapel Hill: University of North Carolina Press, 1967); Charles Chatfield, *For Peace and Justice: Pacifism in America, 1914–1941* (Knoxville: University of Tennessee Press, 1971); Charles De Benedetti, *Origins of the Modern American Peace Movement: 1915–1929* (Millwood, N.Y.: KTO Press, 1978); George Peter Marabell, *Frederick Libby and the American Peace Movement, 1921–1941* (New York: Arno, 1982); Robert David Johnson, *The Peace Progressives and American Foreign Relations* (Cambridge, Mass.: Harvard University Press, 1995); William Appleman Williams, "The Legend of Isolationsim in the 1920's," *Science and Society* 18 (1954): 1–20; Robert J. Maddox, "Another Look at the Legend of Isolationism in the 1920's," *Mid-America* 53 (January 1971): 35–43; John Braeman, "Power and Diplomacy: The 1920's Reappraised," *Review of Politics* 44 (1982): 342–69, the same author's "The New Left and American Foreign Policy During the Age of Normalcy: A Re-examination," *Business History Review* 57 (spring 1983): 73–104; Herbert Feis, *Diplomacy of the Dollar: First Era, 1919–1932* (Baltimore: Johns Hopkins University Press, 1950); Melvyn P. Leffler, "1921–1932: Expansionist Impulses and Domestic Constraints," in William H. Becker and Samuel F. Wells, eds., *Economics and World Power: An Assessment of American Diplomacy Since 1789* (New York: Columbia University Press, 1984), pp. 225–75.

For Latin America, see Harold Nicolson, *Dwight Morrow* (New York: Harcourt, Brace, 1935); John W. F. Dulles, *Yesterday in Mexico: A Chronicle of the Revolution, 1919–1936* (Austin: University of Texas Press, 1961); Lorenzo Meyer, *Mexico and the United States in the Oil Controversy, 1917–1942* (Austin: University of Texas Press, 1972); Robert Freeman Smith, *The United States and Revolutionary Nationalism in Mexico: 1916–1932* (Chicago: University of Chicago Press, 1972); Robert E. Quirk, *The Mexican Revolution and the Catholic Church: 1910–1929* (Bloomington: Indiana University Press, 1973); Benjamin T. Harrison, *Dollar Diplomat: Chandler Anderson and American Diplomacy in Mexico and Nicaragua, 1913–1928* (Pullman: Washington State University Press, 1988); William Kamman, *A Search for Stability: United States Diplomacy Toward Nicaragua, 1925–1933* (Notre Dame, Ind.: University of Notre Dame Press, 1968); Richard N. Current, *Secretary Stimson: A Study in Statecraft* (New Brunswick, N.J.: Rutgers University Press, 1954); Elting E. Morison, *Turmoil and Tradition: A Study of the Life and Times of Henry L. Stimson* (Boston: Houghton Mifflin,

1960); Neill Macaulay, *The Sandino Affair*, 2d ed. (Durham, N.C.: Duke University Press, 1985); Andrew J. Bacevich, *Diplomat in Khaki: Major General Frank Ross McCoy and American Foreign Policy, 1898–1949* (Lawrence: University Press of Kansas, 1989); Dana G. Munro, *The United States and the Caribbean Republics, 1921–1933* (Princeton, N.J.: Princeton University Press, 1974); Robert H. Ferrell, "Repudiation of a Repudiation," *Journal of American History* 51 (1965): 669–73.

For Europe, there is Kenneth Paul Jones, ed., *U.S. Diplomats in Europe, 1919–1941* (Santa Barbara, Calif.: ABC-CLIO, 1981); Peter H. Buckingham, *International Normalcy: The Open Door Peace with the Former Central Powers, 1921–29* (Wilmington, Del.: Scholarly Resources, 1983); Joan Hoff Wilson, *American Business and Foreign Policy: 1920–1933* (Lexington: University of Kentucky Press, 1971); Michael J. Hogan, *Informal Entente: The Private Structure of Cooperation in Anglo-American Economic Diplomacy, 1918–1928* (Columbia: University of Missouri Press, 1977); Brian McKercher, "Wealth, Power, and the New International Order: Britain and the American Challenge in the 1920s," *Diplomatic History* 12 (1988): 411–41, the same author's *The Second Baldwin Government and the United States, 1924–1929: Attitudes and Diplomacy* (Cambridge, England: Cambridge University Press, 1984), and an edited volume, *Anglo-American Relations in the 1920s: The Struggle for Supremacy* (Edmonton: University of Alberta Press, 1990); Charles S. Maier, *Recasting Bourgeois Europe: Stabilization in France, Germany, and Italy in the Decade After World War I* (Princeton, N.J.: Princeton University Press, 1975); Stephen A. Schuker, *The End of French Predominance in Europe: The Financial Crisis of 1924 and the Adoption of the Dawes Plan* (Chapel Hill: University of North Carolina Press, 1976); Walter A. McDougall, *France's Rhineland Diplomacy, 1914–1924: The Last Bid for a Balance of Power in Europe* (Princeton, N.J.: Princeton University Press, 1978); Melvyn P. Leffler, *The Elusive Quest: America's Pursuit of European Stability and French Security, 1919–1933* (Chapel Hill: University of North Carolina Press, 1979); William C. McNeil, *American Money and the Weimar Republic: Economics and Politics on the Eve of the Great Depression* (New York: Columbia University Press, 1986); Stephen A. Schuker, *American "Reparations" to Germany, 1919–33: Implications for the Third-World Debt Crisis* (Princeton, N.J.: Princeton University, 1988).

Naval arms limitation appears in Gerald E. Wheeler, *Prelude to Pearl Harbor: The United States Navy and the Far East, 1921–1931* (Columbia: University of Missouri Press, 1963); Thaddeus V. Tuleja, *Statesmen and Admirals: Quest for a Far Eastern Naval Policy* (New York: Norton, 1963); Robert G. Kaufmann, *Arms Control in the Pre-Nuclear Era: The United States and Naval Limitation Between the Two World Wars* (New York: Columbia University Press, 1990); Emily O. Goldman, *Sunken Treaties: Naval Arms Control Between the Wars* (University Park: Pennsylvania State University Press, 1994); Richard W. Fanning, *Peace and Disarmament: Naval Rivalry and Arms Control, 1922–1933* (Lexington: University Press of Kentucky, 1995).

The uproar over air power has coverage in Alfred F. Hurley, *Billy Mitchell: Crusader for Air Power*, rev. ed. (Bloomington: Indiana University Press, 1975).

Relations with Russia are in Joan Hoff Wilson, *Ideology and Economics: U.S. Relations with the Soviet Union, 1918–1933* (Columbia: University of Missouri Press, 1974); Benjamin D. Rhodes, *James P. Goodrich, Indiana's "Governor Strangelove": A*

Republican's Infatuation with Soviet Russia (Selinsgrove, Pa.: Susquehanna University Press, 1996).

For the Far East, see Richard Dean Burns and Edward M. Bennett, eds., *Diplomats in Crisis: United States–Chinese–Japanese Relations, 1919–1941* (Santa Barbara, Calif.: ABC-CLIO, 1974); Akira Iriye, *After Imperialism: The Search for a New Order in the Far East, 1921–1931* (Cambridge, Mass.: Harvard University Press, 1965); Dorothy Borg, *American Policy and the Chinese Revolution: 1925–1928* (New York: Macmillan, 1947); Wesley R. Fishel, *The End of Extraterritoriality in China* (Berkeley and Los Angeles: University of California Press, 1952); Russell D. Buhite, *Nelson T. Johnson and American Policy Toward China: 1925–1941* (East Lansing: Michigan State University Press, 1968); Warren I. Cohen, *The Chinese Connection: Roger S. Greene, Thomas W. Lamont, George E. Sokolsky and American-East Asian Relations* (New York: Columbia University Press, 1978); Bernard D. Cole, *Gunboats and Marines: The United States Navy in China, 1925–1928* (Newark: University of Delaware Press, 1983).

Peaceful settlement is in Michael Dunne, *The United States and the World Court: 1920–1935* (New York: St. Martin's Press, 1988); Richard W. Leopold, *Elihu Root and the Conservative Tradition* (Boston: Little, Brown, 1954); Robert H. Ferrell, *Peace in Their Time: The Origins of the Kellogg-Briand Pact* (New Haven, Conn.: Yale University Press, 1952); John E. Stoner, *S. O. Levinson and the Pact of Paris: A Study in the Techniques of Influence* (Chicago: University of Chicago Press, 1942); John C. Vinson, *William E. Borah and the Outlawry of War* (Athens: University of Georgia Press, 1957).

Coolidge prosperity began with the Mellon tax reforms, for which see Benjamin G. Rader, "Federal Taxation in the 1920s: A Reexamination," *Historian* 33 (1971): 415–35; Burton W. Folsom, Jr., "Cutting Taxes to Raise Revenue: Andrew Mellon and the 1920s," in the same author's *The Myth of the Robber Barons* (Herndon, Va.: Young America's Foundation, 1991). Financial and fiscal practices are in James W. Prothro, *The Dollar Decade* (Baton Rouge: Louisiana State University Press, 1954); James Grant, *Money of the Mind: Borrowing and Lending in America from the Civil War to Michael Milken* (New York: Farrar Straus Giroux, 1992); Lester V. Chandler, *Benjamin Strong: Central Banker* (Washington, D.C.: Brookings Institution, 1958); Elmus R. Wicker, *Federal Reserve Monetary Policy: 1917–1933* (New York: Random House, 1966); Stephen V. D. Clarke, *Central Bank Cooperation: 1924–1931* (New York: Federal Reserve Bank of New York, 1967); Silvano Alfons Wueschner, "Herbert Hoover, Benjamin Strong, and American Monetary Policy, 1917–1928," dissertation, University of Iowa, 1993.

Boom times appear in William Z. Ripley, "From Main Street to Wall Street," *Atlantic Monthly* 137 (January–June 1926): 94–108; Frederick Lewis Allen, *The Lords of Creation* (New York: Harper, 1935); Giulio Pontecorvo, "Investment Banking and Security Speculation in the Late 1920's," *Business History Review* 32 (1958): 166–91; Forrest McDonald, *Insull* (Chicago: University of Chicago Press, 1962); Ian S. Haberman, *The Van Sweringens of Cleveland* (Cleveland, Ohio: Western Reserve Historical Society, 1979); Robert Sobel, *The Great Bull Market: Wall Street in the 1920s* (New York: Norton, 1968); John Kenneth Galbraith, *The Great Crash: 1929* (Boston: Houghton Mifflin, 1955).

Coolidge's retirement is in John L. Blair, "I Do Not Choose to Run for President in

Nineteen Twenty Eight," *Vermont History* 30 (1962): 177–95; Edward Connery Lathem, ed., *Calvin Coolidge Says* (Plymouth Notch, Vt.: Calvin Coolidge Memorial Foundation, 1972), newspaper columns; Herman Beaty, "The Calvin Coolidge Nobody Knew," *Hearst's International-Cosmopolitan* 94 (April, 1953): 16–17, 86, 88, 90; Clarence Day, *In the Green Mountain Country* (New Haven, Conn.: Yale University Press, 1934).

INDEX